Middle Leadership in Schools

W/D
21/6/21

Leadership skills in education management

Other titles in this series

The Head Teacher in the 21st Century
Being a successful school leader
by Frank Green

Mastering Deputy Headship
Acquiring the skills for future leadership
by Trevor Kerry

The Special Educational Needs Coordinator
Maximising your potential
by Vic Shuttleworth

Effective Classroom Teacher
Developing the skills you need in today's classroom
by Trevor Kerry and Mandy Wilding

Performance Management in Schools
Unlocking your team potential
by Susan Tranter and Adrian Percival

Teaching and Managing in Schools
The next step
by Susan Tranter

Middle Leadership in Schools

Harmonising Leadership and Learning

Second edition

Sonia Blandford

PEARSON
Education

Harlow, England • London • New York • Boston • San Francisco • Toronto
Sydney • Tokyo • Singapore • Hong Kong • Seoul • Taipei • New Delhi
Cape Town • Madrid • Mexico City • Amsterdam • Munich • Paris • Milan

PEARSON EDUCATION LIMITED
Edinburgh Gate
Harlow CM20 2JE
Tel: +44 (0)1279 623623
Fax: +44 (0)1279 431059
Website: www.pearsoned.co.uk

First published as *Middle Management in Schools* in 1997
Second edition published in Great Britain in 2006

© Pearson Education Limited 1997, 2006

The right of Sonia Blandford to be identified as Author
of this Work has been asserted by her in accordance
with the Copyright, Designs and Patents Act, 1988.

ISBN–13: 978-1-4058-2371-2
ISBN–10: 1-4058-2371-2

British Library Cataloguing in Publication Data
A catalogue record for this book is available from the British Library

Library of Congress Cataloging in Publication Data
Blandford, Sonia
    Middle leadership in schools : harmonising leadership and learning / Sonia Blandford.
       p. cm. -- (Leadership skills in education management)
    ISBN-13: 978-1-4058-2371-5 (alk. : alk. paper)
    ISBN-10: 1-4058-2371-2
    1. School management and organization. 2. Educational leadership. 3. Middle
managers. I. Title. II. Leadership skills in education management series.

LB2805.B5636 2006
371.2--dc22

2006044489

All rights reserved; no part of this publication may be reproduced, stored
in a retrieval system, or transmitted in any form or by any means, electronic,
mechanical, photocopying, recording, or otherwise without either the prior
written permission of the Publishers or a licence permitting restricted copying
in the United Kingdom issued by the Copyright Licensing Agency Ltd,
90 Tottenham Court Road, London W1T 4LP. This book may not be lent,
resold, hired out or otherwise disposed of by way of trade in any form
of binding or cover other than that in which it is published, without the
prior consent of the Publishers.

10 9 8 7 6 5 4 3 2 1
10 09 08 07 06

Typeset by Pantek Arts Ltd, Maidstone, Kent.
Printed and bound in Great Britain by Bell & Bain Ltd, Glasgow

The Publisher's policy is to use paper manufactured from sustainable forests

PROFESSOR SONIA BLANDFORD is Pro-Vice Chancellor (Dean of Education) at Canterbury Christ Church University, which is among the largest providers of initial teacher training and professional development in the United Kingdom. Following a successful career as a teacher and senior leader in primary and secondary schools, Sonia moved to higher education in 1995. Sonia has acted as consultant to the European Commission, Department for Education and Skills, Training and Development Agency and to ministries of education in Eastern Europe, South America and South Africa. Sonia has also worked as an advisor to LAs, EAZs and leads the Teach First initiative.

As an author of a range of education leadership and management texts, Sonia has a reputation for her straightforward approach to difficult issues. She writes in an accessible style, communicating ideas in a pragmatic manner as illustrated in her weekly *Education Guardian* column 'Master Class'.

To my team: Charlie, Bethany and Mia

Contents

Preface   xii
Foreword   xvii
Author's acknowledgements   xviii
Publisher's acknowledgements   xix
List of figures   xx
List of tables   xxii
List of acronyms   xxiii

Section 1: Role   1

1   Middle leadership   3
    Leadership for learning   4
    Middle leadership defined   4
    Leading learning from the middle: the player manager   6
    What is leadership?   8
    Leadership styles   10
    Framework for practice   11
    Whole school context   14
    Leadership structure   15
    Middle leadership in practice   18
    Teams   22
    Participation and delegation   23
    Leadership behaviour   25
    Management accountability   27
    Summary   34

2   The learning community   36
    Schools as community   37
    School ethos   41
    The school environment   42
    School, home and the community   43
    Remodelling   45

Partnership – a code for practice 46
Managing extended schools 48
Community schools 49
Building with the community 51
Sports centres 53
Summary 55

Section 2: Planning 57

3 School organisation: vision, mission and aims 59

Effective schools 60
Organisational structure and culture 60
Collaborative framework 62
Cultures – the theory 64
Defining vision and mission 70
Aims 75
Summary 76

4 Strategic plans: policy creation and
implementation 78

Strategic planning 79
Operational planning 80
The planning process 81
The school improvement plan (SIP) 83
Implementing the SIP 91
Developing a policy: professional development 92
From theory to practice 97
Creating and implementing an inclusion policy 98
Monitor, review and evaluate 100
Summary 101

5 Planning 103

What is planning? 104
Strategic and operational planning 106
The department improvement plan (DIP) 107
Decision-making 109
Curriculum planning 110
Timetabling 112
Summary 119

Section 3: Tasks   121

   6 Leading teams   123

       Effective teamwork   124
       Developing team leadership skills   126
       The team   128
       Motivation   130
       Middle leadership in practice   131
       Middle leadership responsibilities   133
       Summary   137

   7 Management of change   139

       Why change?   140
       Middle leaders and change   143
       Change management teams   144
       Analysis of change   145
       Resistance to change   147
       Choosing a change strategy   148
       Implementing change   149
       National Remodelling Team approach to change   151
       Evaluating change   152
       Summary   155

   8 Learning organisations: inclusion, individualised learning and collaboration   157

       The inclusive practitioner   158
       An inclusive approach to learning and teaching 158
       Creating inclusive classrooms   160
       Individual learning plans   161
       Collaboration   162
       Working in partnership with local authorities   163
       LAs and children's trusts   164
       Challenges and opportunities   167
       A common assessment framework   167
       Summary   169

   9 Administration and communication   171

       Efficient and effective practice   172
       Managing the timetable   175
       Assessment   175

Reporting 179
Inspection 182
Effective communication 186
Verbal and non-verbal communication 190
Information technology 195
Summary 201

10 Monitoring and evaluation 204
Context 205
Monitoring 205
Evaluation 209
Summary 212

Section 4: Resources 213

11 Financial management 215
Government funding 216
Standards Fund/Schools Development Grant 217
Value for money 218
Leadership and management 219
Local authorities 220
Budget format and functions 222
Building and managing a budget 222
Budget construction 223
Draft budget 225
Implementing the budget 225
Accountability 226
Summary 230

12 Workforce reform 232
Background 233
Partnership: national structure for remodelling 237
Leadership implications 238
Implications for teachers 238
Leadership responsibility 246
Workload planning 246
Summary 250

13 Recruitment, selection and induction 252
Employment 253

Recruitment   253
Selection   257
Work–life balance   260
Induction   261
Mentoring   264
Summary   265

14 Performance management and professional   268
   development
   Professional development   269
   Performance, management and review   269
   Leaders' role in professional development   273
   Teacher Training Agency/Training and Development
   Agency   276
   The General Teaching Council for England   279
   National College for School Leadership   280
   Sector Skills Council   280
   Accreditation   282
   Summary   282

CODA

                                                   285

15 Self-development: where next?   287
   Self-evaluation   288
   Self-management   293
   Stress   297
   National Professional Qualification for Head teachers 301
   Promotion   302
   Summary   306

Useful contacts   309
References and further reading   311
Index   327

Preface

The purpose of the first edition of this book was to provide advice to practitioners in schools: aspiring middle managers (leaders), senior managers, teacher educators, governors and inspectors. At the time middle management in schools was compared with being on a roller-coaster, travelling at speed through many hoops, having to participate in many teaching and management activities from the 'top-down' and 'bottom-up'. During the journey a middle manager assimilates the view from every perspective: pupil, teacher, parent and governor. As with the first edition, this edition attempts to take the reader through the middle management journey progressing forward, presenting ideas, and providing the opportunity to reflect and revise. Based on empirical, documentary and literature research each edition is the product of rich evidence of research and practice.

Empirical evidence has been gathered by a team of researchers through interviews (telephone and face-to-face), questionnaires and focus groups. Documentary evidence from policy (local and national) and school prospectuses served either to introduce or support empirical evidence. An intensive literature search, broader than middle leadership itself, further illuminated the evidence-base. The culmination of all this is a book providing an original source of knowledge and understanding of middle leadership in schools.

Since the publication of the first edition in 1997 there have been significant events in middle management.

The National College for School Leadership established in Nottingham in 2000 created a 'Leading from the Middle' programme for the training and guidance of middle leaders (further advice can be found on the NCSL website www.ncsl.org.uk). Over the years the focus and use of terminology has moved from management to leadership. This will not be debated within the context of this book, now renamed *Middle Leadership in Schools*. Much of the first edition captured both leadership and management in the introduction of the player manager role for middle leaders: this continues in the second edition.

The context in which middle leaders work has changed. In 2000, government negotiations with a range of agencies led to workforce reform; a remodelling of practice in schools which would provide teachers with time to focus on raising standards in schools. The changes that followed emanated from the good practice that was already evident in many schools. The 'one size fits all' model of the 1988 Education Reform Act (ERA) was to be revisited. The remodelling process is predicated on change which is a feature that will remain with schools for the foreseeable future. This future holds many challenges and opportunities for the wider workforce who are tasked with the planning and delivery of workforce reform, extended schools and the five outcomes of *Every Child Matters* (DfES, 2003b).

In 2003, the National Remodelling Team (NRT) was established by DfES and hosted by the National College of School Leadership (NCSL) to promote and progress the school workforce remodelling agenda. The NRT was tasked with working in partnership with LEAs (now LAs) to release the capacity for change which exists in schools and to create and manage their own self-directed and supported change process (NCSL, 2003). As from 1 April 2005, it has been hosted by the Teacher Training Agency (TTA) which became the Training and Development Agency (TDA) for Schools in September 2005. From April 2006 the NRT is redesignated to focus on developing policies for extended schools within the TDA. The Workforce Agreement Monitoring Group (WAMG) representing teaching unions and other partners within the *National Agreement for Raising Standards and Tackling Workload* (WAMG, 2003) supported the launch of the NRT. Dame Pat Collarbone, the NRT National Director, stated that 'as we collect more and more evidence of a revolution beginning to take place in our schools, the realisation is beginning to dawn, not only that remodelling is achievable, but that it represents perhaps the most powerful tool we have for changing the education landscape' (NRT, 2003).

Initiatives are rarely entirely new; remodelling emanated from existing good practice demonstrated in a number of schools and therefore the notion that remodelling of schools is an initiative created by government policy is inaccurate. Many of the central tenets of a remodelled school (employment of support staff in classrooms, schools as learning environments managed by teachers, extended hours, and multi-agency provision in partnership with children and youth agencies) are not new. There are elements of such practice evident in many primary and secondary community schools in England and Wales since the introduction of compulsory education. It should also be noted that the majority of state schools have been well-led and efficiently managed organisations with committed staff who inspire children to learn.

Prior to the Education Reform Act (ERA) schools had been able to approach learning and teaching in response to local and individual needs. The ERA introduced a common curriculum with statutory assessment at 7, 11, 14 and 16. In addition to a national curriculum and common assessment framework, parents were able to select the school their child attended, and schools were to be responsible for budgets and marketing. In the context of control and change, teachers were increasingly required to deliver a curriculum created by government committees. At this time, teachers felt disempowered and under pressure; many left the profession.

Those that remain contrive to be highly committed professionals working in partnership with other agencies, delivering a curriculum and assessing children within a common framework. As demonstrated by local leagues and concerts, many schools continue to provide sports and performing arts activities that extend the curriculum beyond the school day. For example, the National Festival of Music for Youth celebrates the ever-increasing number of school ensembles and reflects the high standards of performance in schools and local communities. Schools also continue to support children with special educational and social needs at a basic level, they serve free school meals and some have already extended provision with the introduction of breakfast clubs.

In 2004, the Office for Standards in Education (Ofsted) acknowledged the significant improvements that have taken place in schools. These achievements are evidenced by the year-on-year increase in the number of students gaining qualifications at 16 and 18 (DfES, 2005d). The introduction of the national teaching awards has also been a public recognition of the skill and commitment of those dedicated to raising standards in schools.

As the second edition is published the global phenomenon of poor recruitment and retention of skilled and informed professionals has been further evidenced by the OECD. Many agencies have recognised that schools are not static organisations. Set within the context of the 21st century knowledge society, the shared view is that graduates from all disciplines might find teaching a more attractive profession. A significant factor within the remodelling process is the focus on supporting teachers, who for many years have worked 'above and beyond' contracted hours, by reducing the number of administrative tasks encountered each day.

Schools are central to the government's aim to develop a world-class children's workforce that is competent and confident, one which people aspire to be part of and want to remain in, where they one develop their skills and build satisfying and rewarding careers so that parents, carers, children and young children trust and respect them (DfES, 2004b).

Remodelling the workforce underpins the government's drive to improve outcomes for all children and young people so that they are healthy, stay safe, enjoy and achieve, make a positive contribution and achieve economic well-being as detailed in *Every Child Matters* (DfES, 2003b). All teachers now have teaching and learning responsibilities (TLRs), in effect making them all middle leaders.

The 'new professionalism' espoused by government ministers and the TDA is based on developments within and beyond education. The wider workforce embraces a number of professions concerned with the well-being of children and young people. The TDA when drafting standards for teachers stated:

The work of practising teachers should be informed by an awareness, appropriate to their level of experience and responsibility, of legislation concerning the well-being of children and young people expressed in the Disability Discrimination Act (2005) and the Special Educational Needs and Disability Act (SENDA) 2001 and its associated codes of practice, the Race Relations Act 1976 as amended by the Race Relations (Amendment) Act (RR(A)A) 2000, and the Department for Education and Skills (DfES) guidance Safeguarding Children in Education. Item 2.7 in Professional Knowledge and Understanding should be interpreted in the light of the requirements of these documents.

(TDA, 2006)

As illustrated in Figure (i) the second edition is presented in four sections. Section 1 focuses on the **role** of middle leaders; section 2 defines the framework for practice, **planning**; section three describes the **tasks** of middle leadership; section 4 indicates the financial and human **resources** available to the middle leader. The book concludes with a chapter on self-evaluation as middle leaders may wish to consider, where next?

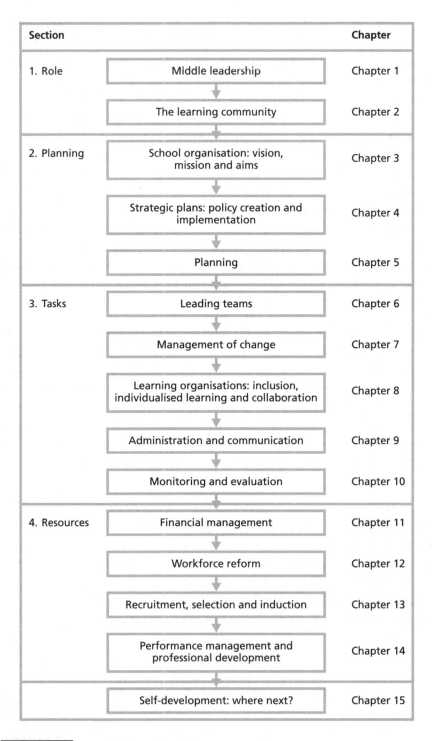

Section		Chapter
1. Role	Middle leadership	Chapter 1
	The learning community	Chapter 2
2. Planning	School organisation: vision, mission and aims	Chapter 3
	Strategic plans: policy creation and implementation	Chapter 4
	Planning	Chapter 5
3. Tasks	Leading teams	Chapter 6
	Management of change	Chapter 7
	Learning organisations: inclusion, individualised learning and collaboration	Chapter 8
	Administration and communication	Chapter 9
	Monitoring and evaluation	Chapter 10
4. Resources	Financial management	Chapter 11
	Workforce reform	Chapter 12
	Recruitment, selection and induction	Chapter 13
	Performance management and professional development	Chapter 14
	Self-development: where next?	Chapter 15

FIG. (i)   Structure of the book

Foreword

Effective and successful middle leadership is fundamental to school improvement, raising standards and the implementation of *Every Child Matters*. Middle leaders are pivotal in the process of translating broad principles and strategies into the actual concrete experiences of every learner. The movement from 'middle management' to 'middle leadership' is symbolic of the increasing recognition of this significant and fundamental change in attitude. This is reflected in this very welcome second edition of Sonia Blandford's book.

Middle leaders are central to two of the most important developments in our understanding of leadership in schools – learning-centred leadership and distributed or shared leadership. Taken together these two initiatives provide the basis for rethinking roles, structures and relationships in schools and are essential to building leadership capacity and securing sustainability.

Sonia Blandford has produced a detailed, comprehensive and systematic book that will prove to be an invaluable resource for those aspiring to middle leadership; middle leaders wishing to develop their own effectiveness and those responsible for the development of middle leadership in schools.

In this authoritative study Sonia Blandford offers a clear and accessible route into the knowledge, skills and qualities that are the basis of successful middle leadership. However, the book will also be a useful resource for those holding senior leadership positions and for those studying for qualifications in educational leadership.

One of the central precepts of leadership, at whichever level and in any context, is that leaders are models of effective learning. This resource is a valuable contribution to realising that aspiration.

John West-Burnham

Author's acknowledgements

The first edition of this book would not have been possible without the generous help and support of friends and colleagues. A large number of primary and secondary middle leaders (managers) provided the empirical evidence and advisory material found throughout the book.

My thanks to the 'team' who contributed to the process of creating the final copy: in particular, Rachel Soper and Charlie Eldridge who word-processed each draft with speed and accuracy; Dawn Newstead, Clive Cambers, Patricia Sage, Linet Arthur, Dr Nicki McCormack, Michael Ormston, Dr Paul Trembling and Jean McPhee for their professional advice and support; and Professor John Wood and Gill Fox for proof-reading and valuable comments. My thanks also to John West-Burnham and Professor Brent Davies for their support.

The approach to the writing of the second edition was to gather a team of interested and valued practitioners; it would not have been written without their expertise, encouragement and time. I wish to express my thanks to Marissa Newton, Kent County Council, Dr Viv Wilson, Kit Field and Simon Hughes, Canterbury Christ Church University; and the schools who participated in the empirical research.

Particular thanks to Catherine Knowles, Dr Lynne Graham-Matheson and Linda Herivel who assisted with research, editing and processing.

I am grateful to Paula Parish and Pearson colleagues who continue to provide support and guidance during the development and publication of my books and manuals.

Publisher's acknowledgements

We are grateful to the following for permission to reproduce copyright material:

Figure 3.4 from p.37, *The Self-Managing School*, Caldwell, B.J. and Spinks, J.M., Falmer Press (1988); Table 4.1 from *The Continuing Professional Development of Teachers* (1993) General Teaching Council for England and Wales: London; Figure 4.3 from West-Burnham, J. (1994) 'Strategy, policy and planning.' In: Bush, T. and West-Burnham, J. (eds.) *The Principles of Educational Management*. Harlow: Longman; Table 6.2 from 'Leading Teams' from Middle Management in Primary Schools © Neville West, 1995. Reproduced by permission of David Fulton Publishers. www.fultonpublishers.co.uk; Table 7.2 from Westhuizen, P.C. van der (1996) *Resistance to change in educational organisations*, British Education Management and Administration Society (BEMAS) Conference (Cambridge), March 22–27, 1996; Table 9.3 first published in Hughes S. (2004), *Subject Leadership: Resource Management*, Optimus Publishing; Figure 10.1 from Hargreaves, D.H. (1995) Self-managing schools and development planning – chaos or control? *School Organisation*, 15(3), pp.215–17. Reproduced by permission of Taylor & Francis (http://www.tandf.co.uk/journals); Figure 12.1 from National Remodelling Team (NRT), 2004, *Times for Standards: Planning, Preparation and Assessment Resource Pack*, Birmingham: National Governors' Council Ref: NRT/0025/2004; Figure 15.1 from Manchester LEA (1986) Model for Self-evaluation, Manchester: Manchester LEA.

In some instances we have been unable to trace the owners of copyright material, and we would appreciate any information that would enable us to do so.

List of figures

1.1	Middle leadership in context	5
1.2	The role of the player manager	7
1.3	School leadership – agencies	16
1.4	Model A: school organisational structure – nursery, primary and small secondary schools	16
1.5	Model B: school organisational structure – large primary or secondary schools	17
1.6	The role of the middle leader	19
1.7	Maslow's Hierarchy of Needs (Maslow, 1943)	27
1.8	The learning community – behaviour management	30
1.9	Behaviour management plan	32
2.1	Community schools	50
2.2	Community support	51
3.1	School leadership – interlinking model	61
3.2	School leadership – tall model	61
3.3	School leadership – flat model	62
3.4	Collaborative framework	63
3.5	The power culture	66
3.6	The role culture	67
3.7	The task culture	68
3.8	The person culture	69
3.9	School vision and mission statements	72
3.10	Vision to objectives	76
4.1	Strategic plan	79
4.2	The management cycle	81
4.3	Strategic planning in context	82
4.4	The planning process	84
4.5	Effectiveness: school improvement plan	87
4.6	Professional development policy	93
4.7	Model for professional development within the context of school	96

4.8 Implementation: school and professional development
    policies and plans   98
5.1 The planning cycle   106
5.2 Position of DIP in SIP   107
5.3 Curriculum plan – process of development and
    implementation   111
6.1 School leadership teams   124
10.1 Development planning feedback loop   205
11.1 Funding responsibilities   216
11.2 Remodelling: resource management   219
12.1 Implementation of PPA   241
13.1 Areas of support for newly appointed staff   262
13.2 Stages of mentoring   265
14.1 The review process   271
14.2 TDA teaching standards   278
15.1 A model of self-evaluation   292
15.2 Stress levels   298
15.3 A model of stress levels   298

List of tables

1.1	The changing culture of schools	15
3:1	A mission statement	73
3.2	Mission statements from a variety of schools	74
3.3	Further examples of mission statements	74
3.4	Example of school aims	75
4.1	Staff development policy	95
5.1	Planning stages	105
5.2	Timetable changes – music department	114
6.1	Membership of leadership teams	125
6.2	Leading teams	127
6.3	A middle leader's additional responsibilities	133
7.1	Key developments and policy documents	141
7.2	Factors influencing change	146
7.3	Remodelling barriers to change	147
8.1	Pupil support	165
9.1	Documentation action plan	174
9.2	Communication channels	188
9.3	Technical specification for ICT	197
10.1	Monitoring remodelling	207
10.2	Geography DIP monitoring activities 2006–07	207
11.1	Budget activity and action	226
12.1	Allocation of workload hours	247
13.1	Selection rating form	259
14.1	Setting targets	272
15.1	Personal audit	303

List of acronyms

AAR	Assessment, Recording and Reporting
ACA	Area Cost Adjustment
ACAS	Advisory Conciliation and Arbitration Service
AEN	Additional Educational Needs
AMT	Asset Management Plan
ARR	Assessment, Recording and Reporting
ASB	Aggregated Schools Budget
AST	Advanced Skills Teacher
AT	Attainment Target
ATL	Association of Teachers and Lecturers
AWPU	Age Weighted Pupil Unit
BSF	Building Schools for the Future
CAF	Common Assessment Framework
C&AG	Comptroller and Auditor General
CFR	Consistent Financial Reporting
CMC	Community Music Centre
CMT	Change Management Team
CoP	Code of Practice
CPD	Continuing Professional Development
CRB	Criminal Records Bureau
CV	*Curriculum Vitae*
CWDC	Children's Workforce Development Council
DES	Department of Education and Science
DfEE	Department for Education and Employment
DfES	Department for Education and Skills
DIP	Department Improvement Plan
DT	Department Team
EAZ	Educational Action Zones
EBD	Emotional and Behavioural Difficulties
EBP	Education Business Partnership
EdD	Doctor of Education

EDP	Educational Development Plan
EFSS	Education Formula Spending Shares
EiC	Excellence in Cities
ERA	Education Reform Act
ESRA	Extended Schools Remodelling Advisory
ESS	Education Standard Spending
ESSA	Education Standard Spending Assessment
FAS	Funding Agency for Schools
FFS	Formula Funding Share
FMS	Funding Management for Schools
FMSR	Financing of Maintained Schools Regulations
FSS	Formula Spending Shares
GCSE	General Certificate of Education
GDP	Gross Domestic Product
GEST	Grants for Education Support and Training
GM	Grant Maintained
GNVQ	General National Vocational Qualification
GSB	General Schools Budget
GTC(E)	General Teaching Council (England)
HCP	High Cost Pupils
HEADLAMP	Headteacher Leadership and Management Programme
HEI	Higher Education Institution
HIP	Headteacher Induction Programme
HLTA	Higher Level Teaching Assistant
HMCI	Her Majesty's Chief Inspector
HMI	Her Majesty's Inspector
HMG	Her Majesty's Government
HRM	Human Resource Management
ICT	Information and Communication Technology
IIP	Investors In People
ILP	Individual Learning Plan
IMC	International Music Centre
INSET	In-Service Education and Training
IRU	Implementation Review Unit
IRU	Internal Review Unit
ISB	Individual Schools Budget
ISCG	Independent Institution for School and College Governors
ITT	Initial Teacher Training

KS	Key Stage
LA	Local Authority
LFM	Local Financial Management
LMS	Local Management of Schools
LPSH	Leadership Programme for Serving Headteachers
LSA	Learning Support Assistants
LSB	Local Schools Budget
LSC	Learning and Skills Council
MIS	Management Information Systems
MPG	Main Pay Grade
NAGM	National Association of Governors and Managers
NAHT	National Association of Headteachers
NASUWT	National Association of Schoolmasters' Union of women Teachers
NC	National Curriculum
NCE	National commission on Education
NCSL	National College for School Leadership
NEOST	National Employers' Organisation for School Teachers
NGC	National Governors' Council
NJC	National Joint Council
NPBEA	National Policy Board for Education Administration
NPQH	National Professional Qualification for Headteachers
NQT	Newly Qualified Teachers
NRA	National Record of Achievement
NRT	National Remodelling Team
ODPM	Office of the Deputy Prime Minister
OECD	Organisation for Economic and Co-operation Development
Ofsted	Office for Standards in Education
PANDA	Performance and Assessment
PAT	Professional Association of Teachers
PE	Physical Education
PERT	Programme Evaluation and Review Technique
PES	Public Expenditure Survey
PFI	Private Finance Initiative
PhD	Doctor of Philosophy
PPA	Planning Preparation and Assessment
PPBS	Programme Planning Budgeting System
PPP	Public Private Partnership

PRU	Pupil Referral Unit
PSHE	Personal, Social and Health Education
PTR	Pupil Teacher Ratio
PVI	Private, Voluntary and Independent
PWP	Personal Workload Planning
QCA	Qualifications and Curriculum Authority
QTS	Qualified Teacher Status
RE	Religious Education
RSG	Revenue Support Grant
SCDP	Sports College Development Plan
SDP	School Development Plan
SEF	Self-Evaluation Form
SEN	Special Educational Needs
SENCO	Special Educational Needs Co-ordinator
SENDA	Special Educational Needs Disability Act
SF	Schools Forum
SFSS	Schools Funding Spending Share
SHA	Secondary Heads Association
SIP	School Improvement Plan
SLT	Senior Leadership Team
SMART	Specific, Measurable, Attainable, Relevant, Timed
SMT	School Management Team
SSA	Standard Spending Assessment
SSFA	Schools Standard Funding Assessment
STPCD	*School Teacher Pay and Conditions Document*
STRB	School Teachers' Review Body
SWOT	Strengths, Weaknesses, Opportunities, Threats
TA	Teacher Assistant
TCF	Targeted Capital Fund
TDA	Training and Development Agency
TGWU	Transport and General Workers' Union
TLR	Teaching and Learning Responsibilities
TTA	Teacher Training Agency (now the TDA)
VA	Voluntary Aided
VAC	Visual, Auditory, Kinaesthetic
VFM	Value for Money
VSU	Voluntary Service Unit
WAMG	Workforce Agreement Monitoring Group
YAG	Youth Action Group
ZZB	Zero-based Budgeting

ROLE

Chapter one: Middle leadership
This chapter develops the theoretical and policy framework of the book. Drawing on related research since 1960, citing key writers and leading practitioners, this chapter will provide an update on current thinking that underpins schools and colleges as learning communities.

Chapter two: The learning community
Set within the context of *Every Child Matters* this chapter will examine the role of the middle leader in a community that extends beyond the school.

chapter one

Middle leadership

Leadership for learning

Middle leadership defined

Leading learning from the middle: the player manager

What is leadership?

Leadership styles

Framework for practice

Whole school context

Leadership structure

Middle leadership in practice

Teams

Participation and delegation

Leadership behaviour

Management accountability

Summary

_____ Leadership for learning _____

Historically, school leaders were senior colleagues with expert teaching skills who led their team of teachers by example. Today this concept has ceased to exist – school leaders are responsible and accountable for establishing the climate, planning and resources. Everard (1986) defined a leader as someone who:

- _knows what he or she wants to happen and causes it to happen_
- _is responsible for controlling resources and ensuring that they are put to good use_
- _promotes effectiveness in work done, and a search for continual improvement_
- _is accountable for the performance of the unit he or she is managing, of which he or she is a part_
- _sets a climate or tone conducive to enabling people to give of their best._

Leadership in practice is achievement of objectives through people. Leaders, as managers are responsible for the work of others. Bush and West-Burnham (1994) provide a definition of the principles of leadership and management which encompass planning, resourcing, controlling, organising, leading and evaluating. In brief, these involve:

- _leadership_ – values, missions and vision
- _management_ – planning, organisation, execution and deployment
- _administration_ – operational details.

School leadership extends beyond the head teacher to the leadership team supported by a range of teams accountable to stakeholders including: central government, local authorities, governors, parents and pupils/students. The role of the head teacher is now compared to that of leader of learning. This chapter explores the concept of middle leaders, leading learning.

_____ Middle leadership defined _____

The process by which teachers become middle leaders is unclear, yet many teachers are now in the role. Teachers are leaders of learning in their classrooms, but priorities change when teachers become leaders of others.

It is axiomatic that learning is central to leading and teaching in schools. A teacher is responsible for the development of knowledge and understanding, and the skills and abilities of their pupils. A middle leader also develops the knowledge and understanding, skills and abilities of colleagues.

In both roles the teacher/leader is required to work with other people. This involves working with values and beliefs which are manifest in the ethos of the school. Middle leaders are therefore continuously creating, forming and applying practices and policies in order to achieve an environment for learning.

A middle leader is also led and therefore has a role within a team. Team membership and leadership are critical to the function of a school as a learning organisation. The middle leader has contrasting roles within management teams. Middle leadership requires individuals to identify with different tasks and different people, acting variously as teacher, leader, team member. This hybrid role within school leadership provides the framework for the daily practice of the middle leader. Figure 1.1 places the middle leader in context, as a teacher, leader and team member.

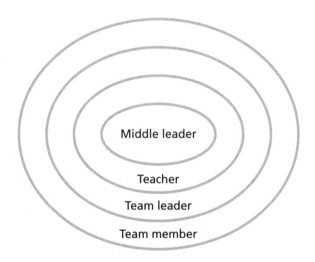

FIG. 1.1 Middle leadership in context

Player managers in schools focus on the needs of children, planning all activities to enable all children to achieve through:

- management of class sizes
- leading a good permanent team of teachers
- engaging staff in continuing professional development
- resource management

- extending links with the wider community (business and community leaders)

- collaboration with local schools.

Central to effective middle leadership is the ability of the middle leader to identify their role at any given moment in the school day. An effective leader would, in practice, differentiate between each role as required. It is therefore essential that a middle leader understands the nature of their job. In defining middle leaders, there are problems and ambiguities which exist in practice.

Leading learning from the middle: the player manager

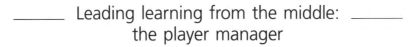

Middle leaders in schools are very much players, participating in the daily tasks of teaching while fulfilling the role of team leaders. At an interview for the post of deputy head teacher in a large (over 1000 pupils) rural 11–18 comprehensive a candidate was asked, 'What is the difference between a manager and a leader?' Her response:

If the task of the team was to climb a mountain, a leader would climb to the top, throw a rope down and ask the team to join them. In contrast, a manager would consult their team at every stage of the climb which they would then complete together!

This demonstrates how important it is for player managers to know their role as middle leaders in relation to both senior leaders and their own team. Busher (2000a, 105) suggests that *organisational hierarchical distinctions are not neatly delineated* in schools. *Many staff*, he suggests *are involved in a complex switching of roles and lines of accountability*. A school middle leader is guided by the senior leadership team and the governing body. Research within the field of organisational structures has highlighted the influence of middle leaders beyond the boundaries of their teams. Chatwin (2004, 13) citing Lincoln's (1982) social network theory, which employs the idea of *nodes and networked relationships* to examine influence within organisations, suggests that middle leaders exert influence beyond their team through a series of *interdependencies* based on work needs:

- *Their positioning within the communication networks which give access to information and the possibility of conveying (and interpreting it) to others*

- *Their degree of mastery of the techniques and approaches needed to exert upward influence*

- *The extent to which they are seen as competent by top management*
- *The degree of open or closed mindedness of senior management*
- *The extent to which they are trusted by senior management, this trust being related to time in post.*

There is status to being a leader, it is important to identify what this means. Equally there is a distinct status attached to team membership. For example, a position as head of year 8 may involve duties within the senior pastoral team. The role of player manager is illustrated in Figure 1.2.

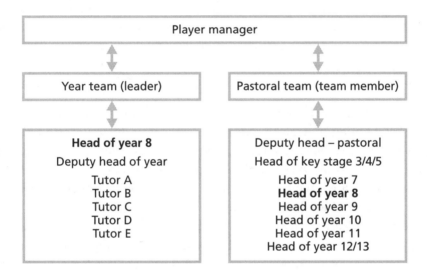

FIG. 1.2   The role of the player manager

It is therefore essential for each middle leader to:

- know their role
- know their team
- know their leaders.

A middle leader in school may experience dilemmas which generally arise out of a conflict between leading learning and leading people. Hall and Oldroyd (1990a, 38) in identifying role strain as a difficult area for middle leaders, highlighted the following sources:

- *role ambiguity* – when you are unclear about what is expected
- *role conflict* – when one of the roles you have is in conflict with another
- *role overload* – when more is expected of you in a role than you could manage
- *role underload* – when you feel under-utilised in your role.

In 1986 Handy and Aitken suggested a commonsense approach to reducing the strains imposed by role problems:

The more positive approach would be to reduce the ambiguity by agreeing with everyone what the job is all about [. . .] to reduce the conflict by dropping some roles or at least putting clear boundaries around each so that they interfere with each other as little as possible; [. . .] and to reduce the overload by thinking out the priorities properly instead of coping with the crises as they occur.

(1986, 60)

However, defining the job may only go part way to solving the problem, a job description may also produce its own set of dilemmas. As Holmes (1993) identified, *maintaining a healthy professional community while focusing on learning can create its own conflict.* As a solution Holmes suggested *trade-offs* when required, which would seem to be a more pragmatic approach to resolving conflict than defining roles.

Being in a learning team requires an understanding of personal needs and capabilities of the team whilst recognising the importance of relevant information for those who lead and those who are led.

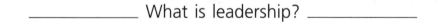

What is leadership?

Theories and practice

There are many definitions of leadership in educational and business literature. The backdrop to school leadership is school effectiveness. Educationalists have found that effective school leaders contribute to the development of effective schools. However as Holmes (1993, 9) stated:

If you followed all the advice from the available literature on school leadership you would become a very confused and ineffective leader.

More recently Fidler (2002, 32) commented:

Leadership is a complex area with many apparently contradictory requirements. Suggestions that particular approaches to leadership should be universal . . . should be resisted . . . . Leadership will need to exhibit many actions in different styles on different occasions.

John Harvey-Jones (2003, 20), former ICI chairman, compared leaders to conductors of symphony orchestras. A conductor is responsible for interpreting the work of others (composer) through a large body of people (the orchestra) who are divided into teams (instrumental sections) with their own team leaders (principal players). The conductor directs and guides the orchestra in order to achieve and communicate musical excellence to a diverse and critical audience.

Similarly a school leader is responsible for interpreting the work of others:

- local and national policies through a large body of people
- staff, parents and pupils who are divided into teams – according to task
- academic, pastoral, non-teaching and support
- their own team leaders – senior and middle in order to achieve and communicate excellence through learning to a diverse and informed audience – educationalists, parents, local and national government.

Although the analogy will not be referred to directly it permeates the definitions of leadership described in this book.

Middle leaders may wish to reflect on Bennis's (1959) theory of leadership. As an academic industrialist, Bennis's perceptions of leadership came from the context of administrative behaviour. He found (1959, 259–301):

Of all the hazy and confounding areas in social psychology, leadership theory undoubtedly contends for top nomination [. . . .] The lack of consensus in this whole area of leadership cannot be blamed on a reluctance by social scientists to engage in empirical research on projects related to these topics [. . . .] The problems involved in developing a coherent leadership theory are certainly not new [. . . .] As McGregor points out 'The eagerness with which new ideas in this field are received, and the extent to which many of them become fads, are indications of the dissatisfaction with the status quo in organizational theory.'

Bennis (Ibid.) placed the evolution of leadership theory in three phases:

PHASE 1   **Scientific Management and Bureaucracy**

Organisations without people including:

1. scientific management – Taylor (1947)

2. bureaucracy – Weber (1918)

PHASE II   **The Human Relations approach**

People without organisations focusing on:

1. wide participation in decision-making

2. the face-to-face group rather than the individuals as the basic unit of organisation

3. mutual confidence rather than authority as the integrative force in organisation

4. the supervisor as the communication agent

5. growth of members of the organisation to greater responsibility [. . . .]

PHASE III   **The Revisionist**

During the *revisionist* phase, a number of theorists attempted to reconcile Phases I and II which led to a new definition of leadership (Bennis, 1959, 296):

Leadership [. . .] involves three major components: (a) an agent who is typically called a leader; (b) a process of induction or the ability to manipulate rewards that will be termed power; and (c) the induced behaviour, which will be referred to here as influence.

In essence, theorists define leaders as those with power and influence. How this applies to middle leaders in practice is described as follows.

Leadership styles

Middle leaders will decide on their own leadership style; some will appear charismatic, others less so. This is unimportant. Each individual's qualities will be identified according to their ability to get the job done. In their book *In Search of Excellence: Lessons from America's Best-Run Companies*, Tom Peters and Robert Waterman (2004, 82) defined leadership as:

[. . .] being visible when things are going awry, and invisible when they are working well. It's building a loyal team at the top that speaks more or less with one voice. It's listening carefully much of the time [. . .]. It's being tough when necessary, and it's the occasional naked use of power – or the 'subtle accumulation of nuances, a hundred things done a little better' as Henry Kissinger once put it.

As stated, middle leaders do things, or manage others to do things. How this is achieved is dependent on the leadership style adopted. This will be influenced by:

- previous experience of other leaders
- previous experience of managing and leading
- personal qualities and characteristics
- the levels of influence from other agencies
- the function or task.

However, management styles will differ according to:

- **the leader** *his or her personality and preferred style.*
- **the led** *the needs, attitudes and skills of the subordinates or colleagues.*
- **the task** *the requirements and goals of the job to be done.*
- **the contact** *the school, its values and beliefs, visions and missions.*

(Tannenbaum and Schmidt, 1973)

Selection of the 'best or preferred' style is critical to the success of the leader and team. A leader should not adopt a style which is unsustainable. 'Sincere insincerity' is easily spotted, leaders need to be themselves and adapt as required. Remember that schools are learning institutions.

Framework for practice

If to lead is to get things done, school leaders get things done within a framework of practice determined by the school as a community. Harrison (1995, 8) commented that *managers live in a practical world.* As a community, each school is self-centred, self-reliant and culturally 'different' from any other school. As an organisation, each school can work within existing structures or create new structures, and as Greenfield and Ribbins (1993, 54) stated *the self cannot escape organisations.*

A school community will reflect its environment. In contrast, the structural organisation of most schools will be very similar. Pugh and

Hickson in *Writers on Organisations* (1989) collated a variety of definitions applied to the management of organisations described by management gurus since the mid-1800s. Each focuses on the need to place individuals in the workplace within an identifiable structure. This applies to schools irrespective of cultural, social or community differences. There are generic responsibilities which apply to all schools, from a small nursery, primary, secondary or special school to a large comprehensive school. It therefore follows that a framework for the organisation of schools can apply to all schools. Differentiation will occur in practice; in the 'real world' leaders will make choices as to how their schools will be organised. Each framework for practice can only function as a model interpreted by individuals, as illustrated in the following case studies.

CASE STUDY

The role of middle leaders

School A

School A is a 'selective' girls' grammar school where expectations are high and pupils are encouraged to aspire to excellence through good pupil–teacher relationships, founded on mutual respect and encouragement. This culture is also reflected by the middle leaders.

Head of year 11 sees the purpose of her job as *putting the girls in a position where they can learn*. She sees her role as *challenging, rewarding and different each day*, where the emphasis is on team work. She highlights the difficulty in prioritising tasks – *if a girl has a problem she needs you then, not in two days' time* – but underlines the excellent channels of communication which are a strength of the school. Although she sees the value of formal CPD for middle leaders, she is of the opinion that *training is no real substitute for experience*.

The head of economics, business and IT is also a member of the SLT, but sees no conflict of interests – *it works well in this school. The SLT make the big decisions and decide on rationale, whilst middle leaders are responsible for 'how' to implement the change.* His experience as a senior leader is also transferred to his role as middle leader. For example, *I put 'creativity' on the agenda for department meetings to exchange examples of good practice.* Although subject leaders work closely together and support each other, which he sees as a strength of the school, he highlights the competition between departments.

Head of technology sees the main role of the job as being that of *motivating and supporting staff*, whilst *managing both sides. The middle leader's responsibility is to keep the head informed* she says. She sees her teaching responsibilities as being crucial to her role as middle leader – *you're doing the same job as your team and they respect it.* She cites the importance of experience and learning on the job for her role as middle leader – *with experience you improve people skills, learn from situations and how to handle people differently.*

School B

School B, a boys' school with 'specialist' status, has 1000 pupils on its roll. Although it has a relatively high proportion of pupils with SEN, a recent Ofsted inspection described it as a 'successful school'. The head teacher says *middle leaders are valued. They know their expertise is needed to move forward.*

Head of whole school teaching and learning, who is also a member of the SLT, values the *culture of autonomy* which exists within the school, where middle leaders are *encouraged to develop.* Although there is a perceived conflict of interests (between his two roles), he thinks the tall model organisational structure of the school (see Figure 1.5 later) demands greater clarity of roles. However, he underlines the benefits as a middle leader of the *no blame culture* of the school and *supportive atmosphere.*

Head of ICT, and also an AST, highlights the *culture of openness* and team approach promoted by the school as being crucial to his success as a middle leader. Although the additional responsibility of being an AST puts added pressure on his time management, he underlines the benefits of the open communication channels fostered by the school.

The SENCO, also a member of the SLT, sees *talking in the staff room* as a very important part of the role. She feels, as a member of the SLT, she is able to show *leadership* and consequently has greater *influence at the whole school level* in her role as a middle leader.

Former head of PE, now an AST sees his role as that of *capacity building – looking for opportunities to develop teaching staff, fill gaps and build strength. Career development*, he says is an important part of the *school's ethos.* There is a supportive environment, where teaching staff are encouraged to be *innovative* and achievement is *recognised.* As a middle leader, he feels keeping people focused is important, where delegation of tasks contributes to the *capacity building* of others.

School C

School C is a primary school with 250 pupils on roll. In addition to the head, deputy head and appointed head of infants, all staff are given responsibility for one or in certain cases two subject areas.

The deputy head teacher sees team work as being very important to her role. She finds the job satisfying – *being able to see the whole picture, the aims and being able to plan and work to achieve them*. The school provides a supportive environment for staff, where all staff are leaders, which gives people *status and ownership* and staff are encouraged to make decisions. She considers the provision made by the school for CPD to be excellent, where training courses are available for middle managers. She sees the new *phenomena of job shares* in primary schools as being difficult in practice.

The year six classroom teacher and numeracy and art co-ordinator considers the head teacher to be excellent, *allowing her time out of the classroom to organise* her extra work. *As a numeracy co-ordinator I observe teaching, make sure resources are centralised and kept up-to-date and make decisions about teaching and training targets. In addition, co-ordinators regularly review books, feedback to staff and keep the marks of all children to check that they are progressing.* She believes management responsibilities provide an opportunity to *utilise people's skills*. Although she does not like being out of the classroom, she says *it would be useful to have more non-teaching time. PPA time has made a real difference, but this only gives time for lesson planning and preparation* and not for management-related tasks.

Whole school context

Schools are places where change is a constant. Rapid changes to the context and curriculum and the devolution of responsibilities have led to a shift in focus. As illustrated in Table 1.1 (Knutton and Ireson, 1995, 61), a middle leader has to be adaptable; the emphasis is on flexibility, sharing, collaboration and empowerment. Middle leaders and their team are responsible for:

- Day-to-day delivery of teaching, learning and management of resources (staff and material). Collaboration on clearly defined tasks, monitoring and evaluation.
- Participation by representation in working groups set up by the senior leadership team to discuss specific tasks or directives from governing agencies or school policy groups.

TABLE 1.1   The changing culture of schools

From:	To:
Fixed roles	Flexible roles
Individual responsibility	Shared responsibility
Autocratic	Collaborative
Control	Release
Power	Empowerment

Divisions of responsibility within a school are determined by the needs of the learners within the school community, underpinned by government, LA and school policies at macro and micro levels which will include:

- assessment and reporting procedures
- staff development
- curriculum
- learning and teaching styles
- support
- equal opportunities
- pastoral care.

A middle leader will be required to have knowledge and understanding of whole school issues as determined by the government, local authorities, senior leadership team and governors. There will also be other agencies involved in the daily management of the school, e.g. support groups, social services, education welfare and educational psychologists, inspection teams and consultants. A middle leader should know who these agencies are and how frequently they visit, including those identified in Figure 1.3.

———————— Leadership structure ————————

Participant players in school leadership are placed within a school leadership structured as shown in Figures 1.4 and 1.5.

In Figure 1.4, pastoral and academic issues are integrated. Model A places full responsibility for academic and pastoral issues in the role of a key stage co-ordinator. The organisational structure shown in Model A may not require each position to be filled by one person. Teachers may have shared responsibilities or have more than one responsibility. The allocation of posts will be determined by local needs, staff availability and financial resources.

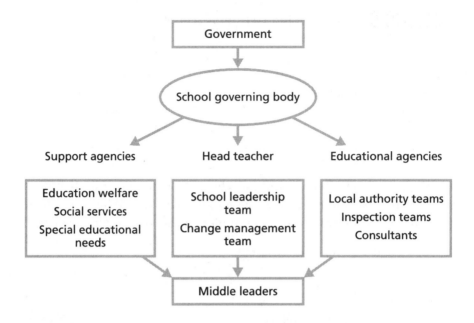

FIG. 1.3 School Leadership – agencies

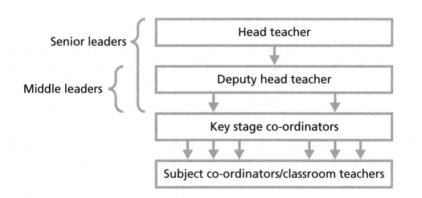

FIG. 1.4 Model A – school organisational structure – nursery, primary and small secondary schools

Model B shown in Figure 1.5 would require a significant number of middle leaders, which in practice may lead to dual responsibilities, e.g. head of year and head of academic team where head of year may lead those with academic team responsibilities. Inevitably there will be 'overlaps' within leadership teams. From experience, this requires an awareness of the parameters of each position. Clear lines of communication are required, as are good interpersonal skills. For example, a pastoral co-ordinator with head of year responsibilities and primary liaison duties in a large comprehensive might lead a team of class tutors and liaise with KS2 co-ordinators. The same teacher might be a member of a subject department, where the head of department is a member of the same pastoral team. Good working relationships are needed.

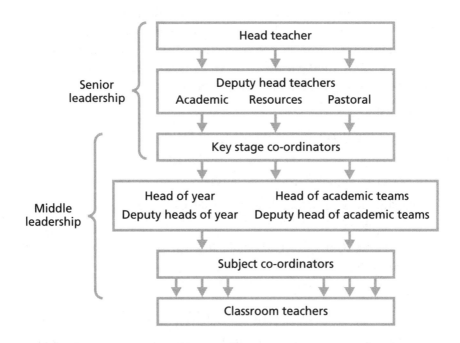

FIG. 1.5 Model B: school organisational structure – large primary or secondary schools

The size of the department or faculty accommodating each subject area will be determined by the size of the school. Formula funding determines the amount of income for each school and therefore the number of staff. Whilst it might be desirable to employ a drama specialist for example, this may not be affordable in all schools. For a middle leader responsible for a department or faculty, the number of staff within each academic team will reflect the number of pupils attending the school. The size of the academic team will also determine the financial incentive allocated to the post and the level of delegation possible.

In contrast, the tasks of each academic team will not differ according to size. At each key stage, teachers are required to deliver the national curriculum. Each pupil is to be assessed and reporting criteria are to be met. Curriculum support teams, special needs, language support and peripatetic music staff have to be co-ordinated. Communication, written or oral, is essential for the success of the team. A middle leader will be a disseminator and gatherer of information, acting as the 'gate-keeper' for the team. It is important to be aware of the team's needs and try not to make assumptions unsupported by evidence. In the majority of cases teachers will want to be informed of policies that affect their practice. They will also wish to be informed of staff development opportunities. Middle leaders should try not to be too protective of their staff: there will be a 'need to know'. A middle leader will be the central person for their team.

Leadership systems and structures should:

- be workable
- recognise the needs of the school
- be understood and acknowledged by all staff
- relate to the school's vision and mission
- allow middle and senior leaders to develop knowledge and understanding, skills and abilities
- allow middle leaders to participate in and contribute to professional development programmes.

Middle leadership in practice

If the school is to be effective, middle leaders need to adopt good practice. Harris (2000, 184) highlights the influence of effective middle leaders on the overall effectiveness of the school. The National Commission on Education (NCE) (1996, 366) stated that school effectiveness involves:

leadership, ethos, high expectations of pupils and staff, positive teaching and learning styles, sound assessment procedures, recognition of pupils' participation in learning, parental involvement in the life of the school and a programme of extra-curricular activities.

As middle leaders are player managers who both lead and teach (Figure 1.6) they will need to consider their teaching commitment within the context of their leadership role. This is not merely an issue of time management, but also the compatibility of the roles. If a practitioner's values and beliefs are transferable to management practice, teaching and middle leadership may co-exist quite successfully. However, if leaders adopt values and beliefs which differ from their values and beliefs as a practitioner, this will be problematic.

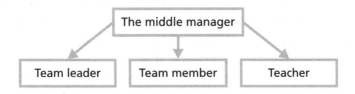

FIG. 1.6   The Role of the middle leader

To know how to lead is an ongoing process. The development of the knowledge and understanding, skills and abilities required to lead others takes time. A middle leader is a reflective practitioner; a professional leader who evaluates their role. This is a two-way process; leaders knowing themselves and their team members, and the team knowing their leader. However, being a middle leader does not mean being 'all things to all people'. Knowing what is required is the key in taking responsibility for:

- the implementation of school-wide strategies, policies and aims
- being role models for staff
- the passing on of good practices.

A middle leader, with responsibility for teams and non-teaching staff (TLRs) will always have problems and dilemmas. Choices will need to be made and difficult people confronted. In a context where the teaching profession is reluctant to recognise failure, identifying colleagues as 'difficult' can itself be problematic. It is important to resolve difficulties as they arise. Courage, in measured doses, is required to deal with situations in a non-confrontational manner. How middle leaders approach such situations often reflects their personal integrity. Northouse (2004, 20) underlines the centrality of personal integrity in effective leadership:

Leaders with integrity inspire confidence in others because they can be trusted to do what they say they are going to do. They are loyal, dependable, and not deceptive. Basically, integrity makes a leader believable and worthy of our trust.

Listening skills are critical in the management of others; leaders must listen and use information sensitively. Finally, persistence is a valuable tool. As a middle leader has many audiences in their role, it may be difficult to resolve dilemmas quickly. Persistence, without being over-bearing, will produce outcomes; changes which will benefit the middle leader and their team.

Effective team leadership will contribute much to the development of an effective team able to create an effective learning school. A middle leader will be concerned with the building blocks of teams.

West Sussex Advisory and Inspection Service (1994) provided a summary of the qualities required for effective leadership. These are based on a survey of middle leaders and their staff during 1994 and are equally pertinent today:

Personal qualities

- *Modelling professionalism, e.g. behaving with integrity, displaying consistency, being open and honest with colleagues, displaying firmness but fairness in their dealings with staff, hard working, committed, putting concern for students' well-being before personal advancement;*
- *Being well-organised and well-prepared;*
- *Being personable, approachable and accessible;*
- *Having a positive outlook and striving to act in a constructive manner, rather than being negative and overly critical;*
- *Manifesting confidence and calmness;*
- *Not standing on ceremony or taking advantage of their position; being prepared to help out or take their turn, if necessary;*

Managerial qualities

- *Formulating a vision for the future development of their school based on personal philosophy, beliefs and values;*
- *Displaying the capacity to think and plan strategically;*
- *Displaying a consultative style of management, with the aim of building consensus and at the same time empowering others. Typically, determining overall direction and strategy, following wide consultation, and then handing over to staff to implement what has been agreed. Effectively delegating responsibility to other people, though following through and requiring accountability;*
- *Ensuring that effective whole school structures are in place;*
- *Behaving forcefully yet not dictatorially. Having the ability to drive things along, yet at the same time displaying sensitivity to staff feelings, circumstances and well-being. Maintaining a good balance of pressure and support;*
- *Being prepared to embrace ultimate responsibility for the school and by manner and actions enabling staff to feel confident and secure;*

- *Displaying decisiveness when the situation demands;*

- *Paying attention to securing the support and commitment of colleagues and enjoying their trust. Actively shaping the ethos and culture of the school and fashioning a sense of community;*

- *Being adept at communicating, and being a good listener as well as keeping people informed;*

- *Being seen to act on information and views deriving from staff, so that consultation is seen as a meaningful exercise;*

- *Emphasising the central importance of quality in the school's operations and encouraging colleagues to aim high, discouraging complacency;*

- *Ensuring that they keep abreast of new initiatives, though taking care not to be seen to be 'jumping on bandwagons'. Taking steps to prepare staff for future developments, thereby avoiding ad hoc decision-making and crisis management – though being sensitive to the risk of overwhelming colleagues with new practices;*

- *Revealing by their statements and actions that they are in touch with the main events in the everyday life of the school, and that they have their finger on the pulse of the school;*

- *Being proficient at motivating staff e.g., by providing encouragement or active support, by acknowledging particular endeavour;*

- *Being able to convey to colleagues that they have their concerns and well-being at heart, and behaving in such a way as to demonstrate this e.g., facilitating their development as professionals;*

- *Protecting staff from political wrangling and backing them publicly in any dispute involving external agencies.*

The local authority team also gathered evidence that determined ineffective leaders:

Personal qualities

- *Lacking dynamism and failing to inspire;*

- *Being insufficiently forceful;*

- *Failing to be at ease with others and to enable them to feel at ease, particularly in difficult and demanding situations;*

- *Inability to accept any form of questioning or perceived criticism.*

Managerial qualities

- *Being insufficiently decisive. Although most teachers were adamant about the importance of consultation, there came a point where a firm decision needed to be taken;*

- *Either failing to delegate sufficiently or leaving staff too much to their concerns;*
- *Failing to unite the staff, and to build a sense of a community whose members were all pulling together;*
- *Failing to communicate effectively e.g., with respect to their vision, specific objectives or reasons for a particularly contentious decision;*
- *Lacking proficiency in managing fellow professionals e.g., being seen to carp at trivialities, behaving in a petty or patronising manner, treating colleagues as if they were children;*
- *Failing to display interest in and concern for staff, or to praise and celebrate their achievements;*
- *Being disorganised and insufficiently thorough, especially as regards administration.*

Earley and Evans (2003, 27), reporting on the DfES-funded school leadership project, highlighted characteristics common to head teachers of very effectively led schools:

- problem solvers, 'solution driven' and highly visible during the school day
- develop strong senior management or leadership teams
- clear and high expectations of staff and students
- regard middle leaders as 'the experts', who enjoy professional efficacy as a result
- Strong emphasis on CPD
- Effective mediators of change.

Teams

The process of managing a team is dependent on the task. The characteristics of effective teams are (Hall and Oldroyd, 1990c, 34–5):

- **Clear objectives and goals** – *according to task.*
- **Openness and confrontation** – *dependent on effective communication and interpersonal relationships.*
- **Support and trust** – *requiring active listening and understanding.*
- **Co-operation and conflict** – *working together, sharing and developing ideas in a democratic and creative manner.*
- **Sound procedures** – *enable everyone to contribute to decision-making.*
- **Appropriate leadership** – *knowing and understanding team members, their beliefs and values.*

- **Regular review** – *monitoring and evaluating in a rigorous manner.*
- **Individual development** – *enabling individuals to develop strengths, involving appraisal and staff development.*
- **Sound inter-group relations** – *a commitment to teaching pupils through openness and trust.*

Perhaps the most positive model of effective school teams is provided by Caldwell and Spinks (1988) as outlined in the introduction. Following research into the introduction of collaborative school management, Spinks (1990, 140–1) was able to identify its advantages. In brief:

- *information is readily available to all concerned*
- *policies and learning activities for students are clearly linked together*
- *it is easy for participants to see the relevance of their work to the overall process of providing an education to meet student needs*
- *participants gain satisfaction and develop commitment as they are able to participate in a way that is relevant to them*
- *most of the operations involved already exist in the school – policies, plans, budgets and evaluations*
- *provides a clear method for accountability*
- *openness of information is guaranteed*
- *teams co-operate to benefit each other rather than to compete for resources*
- *the overall process is clear and easily understood*
- *there is inbuilt flexibility within programmes to respond immediately to new or emerging student needs.*

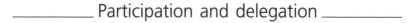 Participation and delegation _____

The opportunity to participate in decision-making teams which impact on school effectiveness is a relatively new phenomenon. In previous generations teachers were autonomous in their classrooms and, apart from crises, they were responsible for the management of their classroom and not much more. Middle leaders now have the freedom to participate in decision-making.

Caldwell and Spinks (1988, 8) described, a *self-managing school as an effective school*. Harris and Muijs (2005, 27), highlight the strong evidence from recent research which suggests that *distributed leadership* contributes to *school improvement* and enhances the *internal capacity for development*. The process is culturally different to previous practice as Knutton and Ireson (1995, 61) explained:

Leaders and senior managers relocate their 'power', and are then freed to guide new developments. Teachers are given ownership in some significant parts of their own working environment and are consequently empowered to act.

This involves participation by team members and delegation from leaders. For some middle leaders participation and delegation can be difficult to manage. Reliance and dependency on colleagues can be perceived as a weakness. If a team is effective, participation and delegation will be necessary parts of team management.

Participation

A confident, open middle leader encourages participation which has meaning and relevance to daily practice. Middle leaders should interpret participation in a genuine way, the process should not be mechanical. Participation can function in these forms:

- **Consultation** – team members are invited to suggest ideas; decision-making remains the responsibility of the middle leader.
- **Consent** – team members, as a group, can veto any decision made by the middle leader.
- **Consensus** – team members are consulted, followed by whole team involvement in decision-making through majority vote.

A middle leader should be able to identify which participatory style is applicable to any specific task or situation. Democracy is fine if applicable, equally autocracy is acceptable and can work in the right circumstances. A middle leader will need to decide which style to adopt.

In practice, decisions may be beyond the mandate of the middle leader and their team. Senior leadership may be responsible for the initiation of policies, therefore leaving middle leadership to implement decisions which have been made by others. In this situation, participation is at an operational rather than strategic level.

Delegation

Both being led and leading will involve the middle leader in the process of delegation. Leaders can save time by delegating tasks to colleagues or teams. There are several factors which need to be considered in the delegation process:

- **Quality of the result** – will the outcome be good enough?
- **The ability of the individual** – how capable is the individual of completing the task?
- **Relationship** – will the individual be coached or left to the task? Either could cause problems.
- **Time** – have your staff the time to complete the task?

In essence, delegation will enhance the quality of learning for the team and its pupils. It will demonstrate a move from an autocratic style to a democratic style of leadership. It is worth noting that reluctant and poor delegation is often worse than no delegation at all.

The Chartered Management Institute (2004) provides the following advice:

- *Delegators should have positive aims, for example CPD. Do not pass a job because it is unpleasant to do.*
- *The delegator should have a clear understanding of both the purpose and process of the task that is delegated*
- *Do not abdicate all responsibility for a delegated task, but maintain a fine balance between interest, support and motivation on the one hand and interference or neglect on the other.*
- *Letting go can be difficult. But success has much to do with trust and depends on working things out in a realistic way.*
- *Clear and open communication is essential for effective delegation.*

Leadership behaviour

In practice, the way leaders and their teams behave is dependent on numerous factors which influence individuals and affect the lives of the people they contact. Leadership activities involve contact with other people.

Motivation

Human motivation is central to both leadership of learning and leadership of staff. Middle leaders should have knowledge and understanding of how to provide staff with meaningful work. Middle leaders should have little difficulty in identifying the teaching and learning elements which colleagues find satisfying and rewarding. Identification of motivational factors beyond the classroom might be more challenging, involving managerial skills and abilities. In brief, several models exist which can be summarised as follows (from Pugh and Hickson, 1989):

The social model (Mayo, 1933):

- people are motivated by social needs, friendship and acceptance; their basic sense of identity is formed through relationships with other people
- people are responsive to peer group pressure
- people are responsive to management if management meets their needs (belonging, etc.).

The rational-economic model (Taylor, 1947):

- people act to maximise their financial and material rewards
- people will perform specialised tasks for high rewards.

Self-actualising model (Maslow, 1943):

- hierarchical needs
- people work to develop skills
- people are self-motivated and self-controlled
- people will integrate their goals with those of the organisation.

Whilst the advantages of each model can be debated, the leader's need to understand what motivates a team is both relevant and important.

Maslow's Hierarchy of Needs (1943) provides an introduction to the analysis of human behaviour. The model is also accessible to practitioners who can identify with the developmental approach. Maslow suggested that there are five levels of need that influence an individual's behaviour:

- *physiological needs* – food, drink and shelter
- *safety needs* – protection against danger, threat and deprivation
- *social needs* – to associate, have relationships, affection, belonging
- *ego needs* – self-esteem, reputation, status
- *self actualisation* – the need for realising one's own potential for continual self-development.

According to Maslow, the needs hierarchy means that the lower-order needs have to be satisfied before the other needs become paramount. In behavioural terms these determine the needs that motivate individuals (see Figure 1.7).

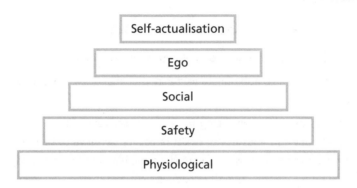

FIG. 1.7   Maslow's Hierarchy of Needs (Maslow, 1943)

Essentially teachers and leaders have needs, as Maslow (1943) stated:

A musician must make music, an artist must paint, a poet must write, if he is to be ultimately happy [....] This need we may call self-actualisation.

—————— Management accountability ——————

Education reflects society and as society becomes increasingly more complex, education leaders encounter many new (and challenging) values and expectations. As their environment changes, teachers and leaders of learning teams are increasingly accountable for their actions, as the following indicates:

- **Pupils** – lesson content, examination results and attendance
- **Parents** – reporting, consultation and pupil support
- **Colleagues** – teaching, management of staff and situations
- **Senior leadership teams** – participation and delegation, team effectiveness, teaching, results (league tables)
- **Governors** – results (league tables)
- **Government** – Ofsted (league tables).

Middle leadership should understand and use accountability in a positive manner. There is little to be gained from viewing the tools of accountability with fear and anxiety.

Good leadership

- As a middle leader recognise and act upon relevant information.
- A style of leadership appropriate to the individual and the task is essential for success.
- Effective leadership means being forceful not dictatorial, decisive when necessary, driving things along, whilst remaining sensitive to team members, keeping abreast of initiatives and preparing the team for future developments. In addition it means securing the commitment and trust of the team.
- Middle leaders will recognise those tasks which can be delegated.
- Motivate the team by identifying the areas which individuals find satisfying and rewarding. Provide individuals with meaningful work.

Behaviour management is often the cause of stress in schools. The following case study focuses on behaviour management issues.

Note: It is important to learn from others. Case studies provide the opportunity for you to reflect on your own context. The advice should be taken not as a template for practice, but as an exemplar of good practice.

CASE STUDY

Behaviour management

This case study is taken from a small inner-city co-educational secondary school. The pupils were from the local community, a socially disadvantaged area, where many were sent to the school as a last resort, having previously attended other local comprehensive schools in the area. The deputy head teacher had been in the post for five years and the majority of staff were reasonably accepting of the challenges with which they were confronted. The deputy head teacher, with the support of the LA and governors, worked with a colleague to develop and implement a behaviour management plan for the school.

The school had previously based the management of discipline on the principles of assertive discipline. The newly appointed behaviour co-ordinator considered assertive discipline, 'to be worse than no discipline at all'. He believed that many teachers could not deal with discipline issues effectively because assertive discipline had become known as a system based on management structures, rather than a philosophy to be shared by all. Inevitably, where systems and structures existed they could be leant on by some teachers who believed that they were no longer responsible for the behaviours in their classrooms. Further training and development was required to create a system based on shared expectations.

The lack of esteem in the community compounded the problem; pupils needed to be made aware that they were able to succeed. There needed to be a change in perceptions and attitudes in order to raise expectations and, consequently, standards. The behaviour co-ordinator decided to develop a code for success in consultation with all members of the school community. The code for success included expectations for behaviour and attitudes for the whole school community. The management team was also reviewing teaching and learning styles as pupils were low-achievers academically.

Pupil–teacher relationships were good. A positive feature of the school was its work as part of the local community. This had triggered funding for support mechanisms for pupils and teachers. The structure for a multi-agency approach to school-based initiative was in place. The extra funding available for additional needs and family support reduced pressure on staff enabling them to assist pupils and parents in these areas. In practice, however, there was a need to increase the level of communication and the effectiveness of support.

Many pupils lacked self-discipline, reflecting their lack of self-esteem in a learning environment. The consequence was disastrous; there were a high number of permanent exclusions. A behaviour management plan was considered, by all, as a significant means of resolving the problem of managing discipline.

Behaviour management plan

The aim of the behaviour management plan was to create and maintain the environment and expectations required for a learning community as defined in Figure 1.8. The diagram shows how a behaviour management plan should encompass all aspects of a pupil's experience in school. The plan relates the elements of teaching and learning to expectations.

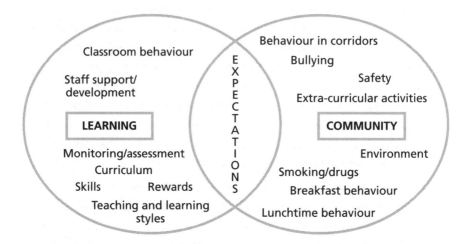

Classroom behaviour

Staff support/
development

LEARNING

Monitoring/assessment
Curriculum
Skills   Rewards
Teaching and learning
styles

EXPECTATIONS

Behaviour in corridors
Bullying
Safety
Extra-curricular activities

COMMUNITY

Environment
Smoking/drugs
Breakfast behaviour
Lunchtime behaviour

FIG. 1.8   The learning community – behaviour management

The behaviour management plan was shaped by three strands of activity within the school.

- **systems:** behaviour management plan, clear guidelines, constant review and evaluation, consultation (pupils, parents, governors and staff), clarity and simplification and agreed criteria

- **expectations:** code for success, assemblies, teaching expectations, parental contracts and meetings, staff discussions, clear guidelines and expectations for specific times of the day

- **support:** staff, development for class teachers, heads of faculty, tutors and new staff, directed support for difficult pupils.

Every pupil was given a pupil guide explaining how they should behave generally and a specific description of how they should behave in lessons. This was developed through the school council, a body that represented all members of the school.

Teachers and support staff were trained in behavioural management techniques based on case studies within the school. A key element was the support for staff to help them develop their own classroom management techniques. Class teachers took responsibility for the management of discipline in their lessons. The behaviour co-ordinator believed that, as an outcome of the consultation and training programmes, teachers were becoming more reflective.

Parking pupils

The behaviour management plan recognised that not all pupils were able to remain in class throughout the day. There would be those that would continue to disrupt lessons in an unacceptable manner. The behaviour co-ordinator had devised a scheme for 'parking' disruptive pupils in host lessons in order to avoid further disruption. The pupil is taken to a designated area in the host classroom; the principle being that when 'parked' they calm down and do not disrupt the lesson. In time, they will be ready to leave and rejoin their class. A pupil will be placed in 'parking' only after all agreed classroom strategies and sanctions have been applied and failed. There is an agreed system to follow up the original incident that draws on the further expectations from the expectation sheet; the aim being to reduce the likelihood of the incident happening again. Figure 1.9 illustrates the pattern of events leading to, and from, parking. Further documentation has been prepared to support the plan including:

- parent guidelines
- senior leadership team guidelines
- letters to parents
- rewards and sanctions
- procedures for placing a pupil in 'parking'.

Questions

1 Would this approach work in your school? Why? Why not?

2 What are the underlying values in this case study?

3 Is there a need to develop a similar system in your school?

4 What can you learn from this case study?

5 How do the three strands of activity – systems, expectations, support – relate to your school?

6 Do you have a behaviour management co-ordinator? Is this needed?

7 What positive aspects of middle leadership *are* demonstrated by the behaviour co-ordinator?

Having read the case study above, what can be done to improve behaviour management? Note your observations under the headings shown on the form.

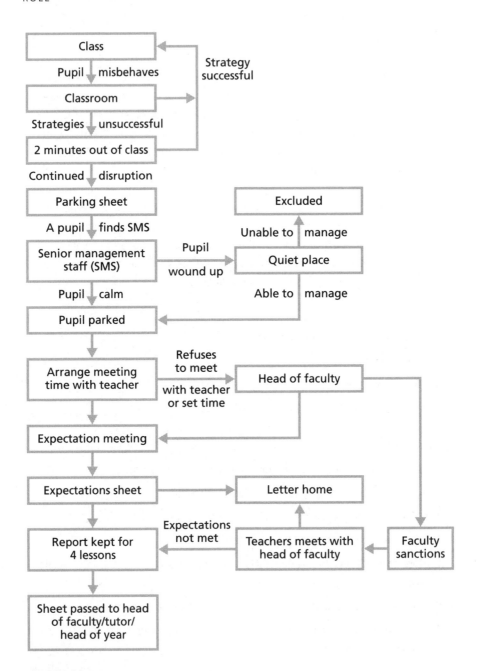

FIG. 1.9   Behaviour management plan

FOCUS: BEHAVIOUR

MIDDLE LEADER	TEAM
Develop leadership for learning role?	Developing a team approach
Developing a learning community	The team's contribution to the community
Developing a code of behaviour	How can the team embed a code of behaviour?
Increasing partnership with parents/carers	Engaging with parents/carers

Summary

Middle leaders are very much player managers participating in the daily tasks of teaching while fulfilling the role of team leader/managers. There is a distinctive status to being a leader, it is important to identify what this means early in your management career. It is essential to know your role, know your team and know your managers.

There are many definitions of leadership and theorists define leaders as those within an organisation with power and influence. How middle leaders do things, or get others to do things, will be dependent on their own leadership style. Leadership styles will differ according to *the leader, the led, the task and the context* (Tannenbaum and Schmidt, 1973).

The culture of schools is changing, and a middle leader has to be adaptable; the emphasis is on flexibility, sharing, collaboration and empowerment.

Effective team leadership produces effective teams. Middle leaders will develop personal and managerial qualities related to their position. Effective teams and leaders have clear objectives, and sound procedures. They exist in a climate of openness, support and trust. As a consequence there are sound inter-group relations.

Participation and delegation are made possible in such environments. Participation involves consultation in order to gain consent or a consensus. A middle leader will need to decide which participating style is applicable to their team: democracy or autocracy. Delegation will enhance the quality of your work and that of your teams. Should a member of staff have any problems with this process, they would be able to consult the relevant senior leader.

Human motivation is central to the leadership of staff. There are several theories which focus on analysis of needs. A middle leader should have an understanding of what motivates their team. Finally, middle leaders should understand and use accountability in a positive manner.

REVIEW QUESTIONS

1 Learning is central to leading and teaching in schools. What is the role of the teacher/middle leader?

2 An aspiring leader was asked at interview, 'What is the difference between a manager and a leader?' How would you respond?

3 What determines leadership style?

4 A middle leader requires knowledge of various aspects of the school. What should an effective middle leader know?

5 What managerial qualities delineate effective leadership?

6 'Delegating tasks is a waste of time; it only increases my workload.' Do you agree with this statement?

7 A member of your team is demotivated. What would you consider and/ or implement to enhance their motivation?

chapter two

The learning community

Schools as community

School ethos

The school environment

School, home and the community

Remodelling

Partnership – a code for practice

Managing extended schools

Community schools

Building with the community

Sports centres

Summary

_____ Schools as a community _____

Since the introduction of *Every Child Matters* (DfES, 2003b) the government has recognised that local leadership, dynamism and ownership are vital if change is to succeed. A shared programme is intended to lead to improved outcomes for all children and young people (DfES, 2005a). The analysis of local priorities, secured through more integrated front-line delivery, processes, strategy and governance, will ensure that everyone delivering services for children and young people will have an important role to play in working towards the five outcomes. This includes those working in childcare settings, schools, health services, social care, youth services, the police and criminal justice system and education, sports and play organisations.

This chapter examines government policy intending to develop schools in the context of 'wraparound' childcare. The government's vision is for integrated services and activities that extend beyond the school day.

It sets out its vision in its document *Extended Schools? Access to Opportunities and Services for All – A Prospectus* (DfES, 2005, 7):

Extended schools provide a range of services and activities... to help meet the needs of children, their families and the wider community... we want all schools and children and families to be able to access a core of extended services which are developed in partnership with others.

Extended schools are based on good classroom teaching and high standards of leadership and management but recognise that to achieve the highest standards and sustain improvement, the curriculum and other learning experiences of the child should be considered as a whole. Funding for extended schools is a core offer that makes it possible for all schools to develop as extended schools; this is an inclusive policy with no blueprints. Extended schools are a base for the delivery of integrated services for children and families. The Workforce Agreement Monitoring Group (WAMG) (2005) advise that the:

delivery of the Every Child Matters *agenda will involve widespread initiatives across a number of sectors to ensure coherence in children's services. Extended schools will be at the heart of this delivery. We are also confident that the principles of workforce remodelling, if appropriately applied, should enable schools to identify the appropriate skill set for those involved in the development and delivery of extended services.*

This concept introduces a new approach to community-based support, which has a child-centred, outcome-led vision that will provide integrated front-line delivery, integrated processes and strategy, and inter-agency governance.

37

For many, this is an ambitious initiative to further advance standards by promoting more 'connectedness'.

Extended schools embrace the five outcomes of *Every Child Matters* (DfES, 2003b) that every child will: be healthy; stay safe; enjoy and achieve; make a positive contribution; and achieve economic well-being. With an extended school, the balance of activities is shared amongst the school workforce leaders: teachers, support staff, administrators, technicians, external agents and the voluntary sector. Extended schools are to be learning communities that guide and support all members of the extended community.

As evidenced in community schools, there is a huge potential in cooperating with parents and local community organisations; this now extends to include professionals in health, youth justice and social care. Those involved also recognise the time needed to bring together these services, which require:

■ values shared by all

■ children placed at the centre of all activity

■ practice shared by all

■ a venue shared by all.

In practice, the core offer being funded by the government and to be directly provided by or made available through all schools includes (DfES, 2002; 2004):

■ study support which covers out of school hours activities such as sports, arts and drama, as well as more formal learning opportunities like homework clubs or Saturday schools

■ family support including family learning and parenting classes

■ childcare from 8 am to 6 pm throughout the year, provided on site or through other providers, including school holidays in primary schools and for children aged up to 14 in secondary schools

■ 'things to do and places to go' for young people in secondary schools

■ swift and easy referral to more specialised support services for children and young people when needed

■ widespread community use of school facilities.

It is easy to see that, through the core offer, extended schools can move beyond the classroom to encompass:

■ involvement of parents and families

■ childcare

- study support
- supporting families
- improving health
- opportunities for young people
- opportunities for community activities
- community renewal
- lifelong learning.

The notion of the extended school is described in the *Five Year Strategy for Children and Learners* (DfES, 2004d) which clearly indicates the government's intention to increase the number of schools that will provide a range of family and community services. However, it is important that there is a clear understanding within schools as to what is intended.

It is through the extended school initiative that the government appears to recognise that a child's environment and circumstances have a significant effect on their learning, attainment and future life chances and, that by engaging parents and carers with learning, may have a positive effect on children's achievement. Extended schools will provide the facilities and resources to develop and deliver a range of services that support and address the needs of individual children and their communities.

This chapter will examine the school as a community within a community and from this, how the school can involve others in the creation of an extended school.

Community – place and function

An extended school will need to determine its place and function as a community. Schools are a community within a community and as such reflect the social and educational needs of the community. Learning and teaching do not happen in a vacuum. Each activity can inform the relationships with parents and the broader community which are central to the effectiveness of an extended school.

Middle leaders have a responsibility to understand that their school is a community, within a community, which can be defined as multi-dimensional with its:

- location – where it is, the influence of the environment and systems of control

- structure – the administrative elements and guidance that determine equality of provision
- process – the management of people and development of a shared understanding of beliefs and values
- agencies – government, business, voluntary, sport and the arts.

All members of the school, as participants in the school and local community, need to be encouraged to have a shared commitment to the school as a learning community. Stoll *et al.* (2003, 132) highlight the centrality of the whole community in the shaping of the school:

Schools that are learning communities have a mindset that helps people understand how they can influence their own destiny and create knowledge they can use. In common with the learning organisation, members of the learning community understand that they create their own reality and can, therefore, shape it.

Schools need organisational structures, aims and guiding rules if they are to be effective. As active players in the daily life of the school, pupils, teachers, parents, governors and support agencies work in partnership, sharing an understanding of the goals and targets that are to be achieved in an effective school. The determination of these goals is:

- reflective, in that the school mirrors the local community, involving its key players in determining values and practices
- individual, as all members will have their own identity with personal goals and objectives
- collective, in that shared understanding of common beliefs and values will create a sense of community bound together by a recognisable identity and geographical location.

The principles on which community provision is built are based on certain assumptions that may also relate to the remodelling agenda and inclusion (Blandford and Gibson, 2005):

- education relates to other branches of social provision; it does not exist solely as an academic entity
- social provision is determined by the prevailing social and economic framework of society
- both social and educational provision have become more centrally controlled

- there has been a move towards devolution of power reflecting the need to provide community-type activities led by the community
- there is a greater emphasis on participation that contributes to the emancipation of the teacher.

Critically, education in schools should be concerned with education within and for communities, not of communities (Poster, 1982). Community education begins with and for the individual. However, as Stoll *et al.* (2003, 136) suggest:

everything people do on a daily basis, within the school and in relation to parents and the local community, is underpinned by a sense of belonging and collective commitment to each other's learning and ensuring that the school is moving.

School ethos

Schools, like other communities, have their own characteristics and personalities. Differences between schools may be explained in terms of organisational and social structures which also reflect the interpersonal relationships that create ethos. The whole-school feeling exists to such an extent that it drives the school as a community towards achieving goals. An intangible relationship between local and school communities and school ethos may exist but the link could be difficult to define. Yet the importance of ethos in the learning community is widely accepted. McLaughlin (2005, 306–7) highlights the better performance of schools which develop a strong ethos. He further suggests that ethos is becoming more prevalent in education policy. Donnelly (2000, 135–6), by offering two definitions which *reflect either a positivist or anti-positivist view,* highlights the difficulty in delineating ethos. A positivist would view ethos, she suggests, as *a formal expression of the authorities' aims and objectives for an organisation.* Anti-positivists on the other hand *see ethos as something which is more informal emerging from social interaction and process* (Donnelly 2000, 150). The resultant reality in the learning community she suggests is that *ethos is not a static phenomenon* but rather… *a 'negotiated' process whereby individuals come to some agreement about what should and should not be prioritised.* Leaders, managers, practitioners, parents and pupils, teachers and all staff create a school ethos through values and behaviours that reflect values portrayed in policies and practice.

_____ The school environment _____

There is a distinctive link between the culture and ethos created in schools and their environment. An uncared-for school building, regardless of age, will reflect an uncaring community. Working in an environment that is in need of repair (as most schools are) creates stress before any consideration of workload. As *Every Child Matters* recognises, working in an environment that is unhealthy is not conducive to healthy development. Recognising the impact of the physical environment on learning outcomes, the government set up the Building Futures Group in 2004, a joint project between the Commission for Architecture and the Built Environment and the Royal Institute of British Architects to address the future structure of school buildings. Findings from the project showed the *impact of school design on the effective delivery of teaching and learning.* Although the project highlighted the need for *inspirational learning spaces,* it recognised that school buildings *do not exist in a vacuum. The way that teachers are developed professionally,* it further suggested, *the school curriculum, management, assessment and testing systems, parental engagement, expectations and entitlements all intermesh with the design of schools to create the learning environment* (*Building futures*, 2004, 6–9). To realise this vision, the government has committed further funding to build or design all secondary schools in England. Members of the school community need encouragement in order to fulfil their potential; a stimulating environment will produce stimulating results. They also need to consider how to create a positive environment. This may include:

- good quality displays of pupils' work and achievements covering the full range of ability
- bright, open spaces with carpeted floors and plants, pictures and photographs
- clean buildings: no litter, adequate bins that are emptied, working toilet facilities
- supervised areas for study
- adequate facilities for every subject, (e.g. physical education and music store areas)
- the opportunity to use outside places and spaces.

The management of the school environment is the responsibility of everyone in the school community. The development and maintenance of the internal and external environment can be a key activity within the school and can help with remodelling.

School, home and the community

The connection between the school and the community is not fixed but exists on a continuum. There are three possible patterns of connection between the school and the local community described as follows.

1 The closed door pattern

The school deals with all the child's educational and social problems, whilst community involvement and intervention is minimal. Within a closed system as in the second law of thermodynamics, the total energy of the system will deteriorate. According to Friedman (1986), the closed door policy towards the community lacks feedback and will waste energy without the right guidance. In the absence of input from the parents and the community, the school will be unaware of changes occurring in these systems, and hence will be unable to adapt itself and its curricula to these changes, so will keep degenerating.

2 The open door pattern

The school and the parents operate as open systems, so that information flows freely in both directions. The school with an open door policy makes the parents partners in their children's educational process and strives to become an influential factor in the life of the community. A basic assumption of systems theory is that the open system is designed to process the inputs of its external environment and return the processed product to the environment for its use and benefit. The exchange of energy occurs in a cyclic nature. The final and improved product serves as a new source of energy passing from the environment to the system. In this way the deteriorating process is stopped (Katz and Kahn, 1978). According to Friedman (1986), the school with an open door policy receives its pupils from the parents, teaches them and raises their level of education, in order to return them to their community. In their adult life they will produce a new generation of pupils, whose contribution to their children's education is expected to be greater than that of their parents' generation.

3 The balanced pattern

The school and the parents set the degree of closeness or distance between them, in order to achieve their educational and social goals to the optimal extent. When the distance is large, the school has to bridge the gap and reach out to the community; when the distance is small, the school has to some extent to close its gates.

MIDDLE LEADERSHIP QUESTIONS

1 How would you describe your school community?

2 How does your school participate in the community in which it is located?

3 What are the values that underpin practice in your school?

4 Does your school have an open or closed door policy? Or both?

Parental involvement

Parental involvement in the school enriches the pupils' world and extends their horizons because when parents take part in the educational process, pupils are exposed to a variety of individuals who represent different worlds in terms of life experience, age, occupation, interests and attitude; these encounters afford many opportunities for learning, enrichment and identification (Noy, 1984). Since the late 1990s there has been a strong movement in England by the government to encourage parents to become more actively involved in their children's learning. Busher (2000b, 90) suggests that this coincided with the increasing body of recent research highlighting the impact parents have on enhancing their children's learning. The benefit of parental involvement is also manifested in the pupils' personality and behavioural variables, such as improvement of self-image and learning habits, reduction in disciplinary problems and absenteeism, and rise in motivation (Raywid, 1984).

Parents will also benefit from their involvement, which enables them to deepen their knowledge of their child's world, the subjects taught, the teaching methods and effective forms of negotiation with children. Involvement in their child's education may help parents to develop their own personalities and satisfy their needs. In the school they may find an outlet for their talents that are not expressed in other places. By 2010, all mainstream and special schools should provide access to or be delivering extended services which include:

parenting support including information sessions for parents at key transition points, parenting programmes run with the support of other children's services and family learning sessions to allow children to learn with their parents.

(DfES, 2005f, 8)

Parents gain satisfaction from the experience of expressing their needs and skills, from the new opportunities opened to them for self-expression and realisation, and from the chance to share in the educational process and the gratitude and praise they receive for their participation and involvement (Noy, 1984; Hituv, 1989).

Teachers benefit from parental participation in the educational work of the school. Noy (1984) reports on four main areas in which parental involvement makes a substantial contribution: physical help, connections and contacts, the educational sphere and creativity. This also strengthens the teachers' professional, social and personal image, relieves the feeling of solitude that accompanies the teacher's work and increases their motivation to persevere and refresh their professional knowledge.

MIDDLE LEADERSHIP QUESTIONS

1 Do parents have a voice in creating the school community?

2 Does your school have a range of activities that involve parents?

3 How does your school encourage parents to participate in extended activities within the school?

4 Is your school welcoming to all who visit?

Remodelling

From the National Remodelling Team (NRT) website **www.remodelling.org**, case studies provide examples of practice that have engaged professionals and parents in the common goal of preparing pupils for their role in society. This is not new, the 1996 National Commission on Education (NCE) study of effective schools in disadvantaged areas provided several examples where good practice and a common goal had motivated the local community. The NCE refers to the ten success features in *Success Against the Odds* (NCE, 1996), which formed the basis for the proposals for raising achievement in schools. Each resonates strongly with the aims and purpose of the remodelling agenda:

■ strong, positive leadership by the head and senior staff

■ a good atmosphere or spirit, generated by shared aims and values and by a physical environment that is as attractive and stimulating as possible

- high and consistent expectations of all pupils
- a clear and continuing focus on teaching and learning
- well-developed procedures for assessing how pupils are progressing
- responsibility for learning shared by the pupils
- participation by pupils in the life of the school
- rewards and incentives to encourage pupils to succeed
- parental involvement in children's education and in supporting the aims of the school
- extra-curricular activities that broaden pupils' interest and experiences, expand their opportunities to succeed and help to build good relationships within the school.

In the course of the study, NCE researchers visited a school in the West Country which had a positive, highly motivated staff where the ten features of success were in evidence. The research team was able to observe each of the above in practice:

We were impressed by the positive attitude of staff, including teaching support staff, and by their dedication. It is surely a central part of successful school management to create the conditions to enable the staff to make this kind of commitment. One example of the school's success in this respect is the range of after-school provision which is provided by teachers out of sheer commitment to the school.

(NCE, 1996)

MIDDLE LEADERSHIP QUESTIONS

1 What leadership and management skills can your school provide for the broader community?

2 What activities within your school could be extended to involve more members of the school community?

3 How can your school become an extended school?

_____ Partnership – a code for practice _____

Extended schools, in fulfilling the outcomes of *Every Child Matters*, will move education beyond the classroom to involve parents and families, childcare, health and social care, youth services, community activities, community renewal and lifelong learning. In May 2005, Stephen Twigg, the then Minister for School Standards, commented that the government recognised the impact schools have on local families and communities and the importance of forging effective partnerships at a local level to achieve mutual benefits.

There is a clear recognition of the need to fund activities beyond the classroom. This is to be welcomed but, if it is to be successful, values and attitudes will need to be determined and addressed. This can be achieved through transparency of governance and leadership, which has clarity of purpose with a vision for partnership that is sustainable, supported in part, by *Extended Schools: A Code of Practice* (Sandwell, 2005).

The intentions of the authors of the code of practice were that it should be a flexible self-evaluation tool for self-review, planning and quality assurance. It is designed to accommodate the extensive range of activities and services provided by schools contributing to community development. It acknowledges that growth takes place when people have opportunities to set their own goals. The code is therefore a framework for all extended schools that recognises the continuing and developmental nature of the process as an extended school which:

- identifies common principles drawing on examples of good practice from around the country
- provides a common framework with identifiable success criteria which all schools can use to evaluate and improve practice
- establishes a clear process for self-review, evaluation and recognition at one of three levels of good practice.

Using the Code of Practice as a framework for self-evaluation may bring important tangible benefits which can:

- ensure that activity is closely linked to overall purposes and is really targeted at identified needs
- identify areas for development and set priorities for future action
- ensure that all stakeholders are involved in extending activity
- provide a foundation for building partnerships with other agencies and services including youth and community, social, health and other services based upon recognised standards of good practice
- provide a benchmark for internal and external comparison.

The Code of Practice (Sandwell, 2005) identifies three categories of good practice:

- **Emerged:** *There is a clarity of purpose, coherent planning and provision which meets local needs and which demonstrate a clear link with the purposes, goals and targets of extended schools across more than one area of activity or service.*

- **Established:** *Schools have demonstrated a commitment to continuing improvement and increasing community ownership. They are self-critical, able to address weaknesses and build on strengths, with an understanding of self-evaluation and the ability to use it effectively in realising their goals. They will have widened provision across several areas of extended school activity or service.*

- **Advanced:** *Provision represents the leading-edge of practice, involving young people, parents and the wider community in goal setting, planning and developing the provision. Schools will have the conviction, confidence and expertise to train and to lead others and to become national centres of excellence, in the majority of extended school areas of activity/service.*

Managing extended schools

As the NRT advises, the management of extended schools is a role that should not be taken by a teacher or school leader engaged in teaching and learning during the traditional school day (NRT, 2005); this could be in conflict with workforce reform. The management of an extended school programme requires training to prepare managers and staff to develop an understanding and the skills needed for the role.

The Education Act 2002

The Act stipulates that schools must *consult widely before providing extended services*. As a *minimum* they need to consult parents, children, staff and LAs (DfES, 2005a, 17).

This will involve working in partnership with a range of other agencies in order to provide services and activities that extend beyond the traditional school day to meet the needs of children and young people, their families and the wider community.

Since 2003, the NRT has been running a pilot in a range of extended schools that provides an opportunity for the practical implications of this initiative to be worked through. Further guidance is being developed by the NRT with current information found at websites for *Every Child Matters* **www.everychildmatters.gov.uk** and remodelling **www.remodelling.org**.

Enrichment activities

Within the remodelling process, the range of available roles for each school will depend on the size and potential scope of activities. Sports, arts, language enhancement and other activities, which were often delivered through clubs and extra-curriculum programmes, may be introduced into the timetable. If carefully planned and integrated into the curriculum, there is huge potential for the growth of such activities. Partnerships with neighbouring schools may also facilitate the transfer of talent within these areas. There is no statutory planning, preparation and assessment (PPA) entitlement for these specialist staff although schools may choose to provide time. Enrichment activities should be designed to enhance the quality of the curriculum and learning experience of all learners. The importance of enjoyment in learning should not be overlooked and health and safety must also be considered when planning such activities.

MIDDLE LEADERSHIP QUESTIONS

1 Have you delegated management and leadership of extended schools?

2 Have you negotiated/received additional funding?

3 What support has been provided by the LA?

4 How is the extended school agenda being monitored and evaluated?

Community schools

Each area of current innovation and development was a feature of community schools when they were first conceived in the 1950s (Poster, 1982). The shared drivers for community and/or extended schools are:

■ school improvement –

breaking through barriers

parental engagement

■ children –

preventative strategies

children's services

childcare strategies

- the regeneration of communities –

  supporting independence.

LAs are now proposing to create shared structures and systems that will underpin collaboration and partnership between schools and other agencies; the intention is to support the community leadership role of schools whilst raising attainment and attendance. As outlined in DfES and inter-agency policies, the objectives are to:

- enhance the relationship between schools and their communities by extending the use of schools as a resource for the wider community to address educational and social needs

- improve each school's capacity to remove the barriers to success (which include economic, health and social factors), and

- promote parental engagement in children's learning.

Within the core offer, government, regional and local funding will be provided to support building links with local business, the strategic co-ordination and planning for community engagement and multi-agency work and to provide project management support. As with extended schools, the key elements of community schools include multi-agency family and child support services, study support, family learning and community use of facilities. LAs recognise that this will mean a culture change for heads of service and, in some cases, heads of schools, from management and control to leadership and influence. Figure 2.1 illustrates the range of potential services on offer through community schools.

FIG. 2.1   Community schools

The many partners who are in support of effective community schools are illustrated in Figure 2.2. Community and extended schools have to address a range of issues beginning with a change in culture. This will involve the building of trust and confidence in and with new partners, in order to realign services nearer to the point of delivery. This is set within the context of demographic changes that include: new housing developments; the reduction in the number of school-age learners; a further need for children's centres and family liaison officers, and an increase in the capacity or need for voluntary and community sector support. With an availability of services and support, schools need to understand which extended and/or community initiatives might be beneficial.

FIG. 2.2 Community support

_____ Building with the community _____

All new community and/or extended school strategy policies recognise that each school exists in a distinctive social context that ultimately impacts on the culture and ethos experienced by staff and children. If schools are to develop within the community and for the community, school leaders will need to engage with that community. Working collaboratively at strategic and operational levels is essential for school improvement and community development. Middle leaders will need to be aware of current issues and future trends that will affect the school and community whilst developing the community and/or extended school. In communities, there is a rich and diverse resource that can support opportunities for pupils and other learners. Models of collaboration are strategies already in place that encourage parents to support learning.

Middle leaders will contribute to building a school culture that utilises the richness of the resources that exist within and beyond the school, and ensure that learning experiences are integrated into the wider community. The change in culture will also contribute to the development of an education system that will lead to innovation in all areas through sharing good practice. The effectiveness of building partnerships with the community is based on long-term planning through consultation and identification of needs. Innovation is pro-active, as well as reactive, where multi-agency teams work across boundaries.

MIDDLE LEADERSHIP QUESTIONS

1 Is there a shared vision across services with regard to providing the best for all children?

2 Will the main partners (education, health and social services) become an integrated service?

3 What are the staffing and resource implications?

4 Who do we need to communicate with in our community?

CASE STUDY

Community music centres

Many schools and communities have a history of making music. These music facilities have been established over time through church and faith groups, the voluntary sector, schools and philanthropists. This case study describes a local centre and an international centre that have provided many opportunities for volunteers and students to develop a range of skills. The local centre originated in a large, co-educational, 11–18 comprehensive school in southern England; the other is a music centre in Lisbon, Portugal.

Within the school, community music started with a choir for pupils and children from neighbouring schools. This led to the formation of a school wind band which evolved into a community music centre (CMC) and now exists as an independent charity within the local community. In Portugal, the music centre provides an opportunity for young people to join a musical ensemble that rehearses in the languages with which participants are most familiar, i.e. English and Portuguese. The centre sympathises with the internationally mobile student and caters for students from a variety of musical backgrounds. As a community group, the international music centre is unrestricted by involvement in a national music system and open to all.

Blandford and Duarte (2004) found that the social benefits motivated and sustained membership of both centres. Social skills are enhanced by participation in a musical community through the development of friendships, improved self-confidence and, in many cases, facilitated transition into a new environment.

In terms of learning, participants developed transferable skills associated with learning and taking responsibility. Through teaching and guiding younger members, the participants were able to gain understanding of their own needs particularly in the areas of intonation, aural perception, notation and ensemble proficiency. The experience of inclusion moves beyond notions of class, ability, race or creed as has been demonstrated by research, practice and music-making. In terms of inclusion, it would appear that by moving out of school and into the community, the codes that limit our understanding of community are broken.

Participation in a musical community is fully inclusive. Children with learning and physical disabilities are supported and stimulated by the group. Students from different nationalities, cultural backgrounds, abilities and a wide age range are able to combine their efforts to the common good of the community.

All players reported how much they had enjoyed the experience of participating in a musical community. Reflected in the words of the music educator, Isaac Stern (Guaspari, 1999), the aim of music-making is:

> ...not to make 'musicians' out of everyday performers, but more important, to make them educated, alert, caring, inquiring young people, who by playing music feel a part of the connective tissue between what the mind of man has been able to devise and the creativity of music... in other words, become literate, and part of the culture of the whole world.

Sports centres

The government has stated that schools could reach out to their communities through sport and that there are real opportunities for joined-up approaches to extended schools within the context of *Every Child*

Matters (DfES, 2003b). Many consider that sport within schools is in decline with a high proportion of the population being inactive, so there is a clear need to encourage future generations. This can happen through school/club links, Step into Sport, the QCA PE/Sport Investigation, the Gifted and Talented intitiative and swimming.

The government's white paper on *Choosing Health* (HMG, 2004) has recommended a need for a decrease in the number of people who smoke or are obese and an increase in the number of people who exercise and are encouraged to support sensible nutrition and drinking habits. Extended schools can reach out to their local communities through sport by:

- maximising physical activity by embedding these intentions into the school's improvement plan
- letting the school premises to establish strong links, communication and participation in local sports teams
- inviting parents to be involved, and
- making all visitors feel welcome.

There are real opportunities for a joined-up approach that responds to the needs of *Every Child Matters*.

MIDDLE LEADERSHIP QUESTIONS

1 Why do you offer extended activities and how are they co-ordinated?

2 How did you decide what to offer?

3 What partnerships exist and how do they support the extended school?

4 Why do young people, adults and service providers want to be involved?

5 Who is doing what and what resources are available?

6 Who participates in activities?

7 How do you let people know about these?

8 Who currently delivers activities and services and how are they selected?

9 How can you develop the range of your activities/services?

10 What evidence do you need to collect to show that activities/services are worth the cost?

11 How could you use the *Extended Schools* code of practice?

Summary

Relationships with parents and the broader community are central to the effectiveness of an extended school. All members of the school, as participants in the school and local community, should be encouraged to have a shared commitment to the school community.

Schools, like other communities, have their own characteristics and personalities. The culture of each school is determined by individual and collective beliefs and values. Differences between schools may be explained in terms of organisational and social structures which reflect the interpersonal relationships that contribute to ethos. The management of the school environment is the responsibility of everyone in the school community.

The relationship between school, home and the community will have a significant impact on learning and teaching. The connection between the school and the community is not static but develops on a continuum.

There are almost as many definitions of extended schools are there are schools engaged in this aspect of the remodelling agenda. Extended schools are based on standards of leadership and management but also recognise that to achieve the highest standards and sustain improvement, the curriculum and other learning experiences of the child support should be co-ordinated as a whole, contributing to, and being sustained by, the local community. The management of an extended school programme requires training that prepares managers and staff to develop an understanding and the skills needed.

The effectiveness of developing schools with the community will lead to long-term planning through consultation and identification of needs. Building schools with communities will bring schools to the heart of each community, offering a wide range of services to support the wider community.

REVIEW QUESTIONS

1 What is meant by community?

2 What is an extended school?

3 Who are the partners in an extended school?

4 What will be the effect on pupils?

5 What can be learnt from community and social initiatives practised elsewhere in education?

6 How can the culture and ethos of the school impact on remodelling?

7 What factors influence culture and ethos?

8 How can the community engage in remodelling regarding workforce reform, extended schools and *Every Child Matters*?

_____ **SECTION 2:** _____

PLANNING

Chapter three: School organisation: vision, mission and aims

As a precursor to planning, this chapter provides guidance on vision, mission and aims in school settings leading to examples of good practice.

Chapter four: Strategic plans: policy, creation and implementation

This chapter focuses on how leaders develop and implement plans and policy. Building on the previous chapters it provides a framework for the development of policies.

Chapter five: Planning

The relationship between department and school plans is shown by theoretical and practical evidence. The chapter concludes with an example of good practice.

School organisation: vision, mission and aims

Effective schools

Organisational structure and culture

Collaborative framework

Cultures – the theory

Defining vision and mission

Aims

Summary

——————— Effective schools ———————

A measure of a school's effectiveness is the ability of the staff to work as an organisation towards achieving the school's vision underpinned by a shared set of values and beliefs. A **vision** embeds the philosophy underlying professional and organisational practice within the school. Vision statements are critical to the effectiveness of strategic and operational plans. A vision moves an organisation forward from where it is now to where it would like to be. A vision would be reflected in the school's aims and organisational practice. Visions are notably achievement-orientated, inspirational and aspirational and, as such, should be shared by all members of the school community.

The **missions** that follow visions provide a clear sense of direction and purpose. These are a means of creating operational plans: objectives or targets to be met by members of the school community within departments and year teams. This chapter considers schools as organisations and the centrality of a school's vision and mission statements in moving the educational establishment forward.

Following vision and mission statements will be **aims**. These provide measurable goals or targets against which the school and teams can monitor, review and evaluate effectiveness.

——— Organisational structure and culture ———

For all schools, large or small, the organisational structure and culture of the school will determine its effectiveness. Fidler (2002, 46) suggests that organisation structure *assumes an ordered internal situation in which people act in accordance with policies and work towards agreed organisational goals.*

There are several models of organisations; a middle leader will know which model applies in their school and where they are placed within the structure. Figure 3.1 illustrates a model whereby different parts of the organisation are interlinked.

Figure 3.2 illustrates a more hierarchical, tall model which, in practice, distances senior leaders from middle leaders. In recent years, models of school management have tended to become flatter. This has avoided the problems of tall structures where there are too many layers of management and a tendency for needless bureaucracy. Flatter organisations (see Figure 3.3) can change and react more quickly in the increasingly dynamic and ever-changing working environment of education. Interestingly, flatter organisations have a tendency to force managers into delegation, because of the enlarged managerial span of control.

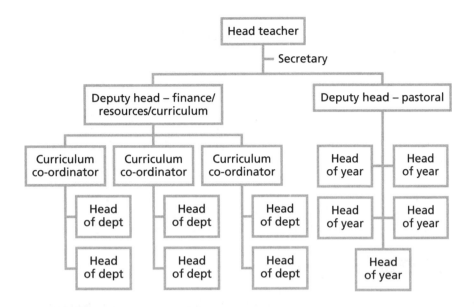

FIG. 3.1 School leadership – interlinking model

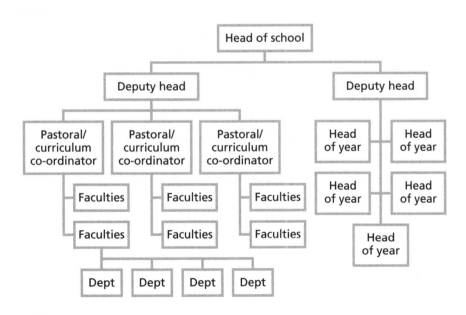

FIG. 3.2 School leadership – tall model

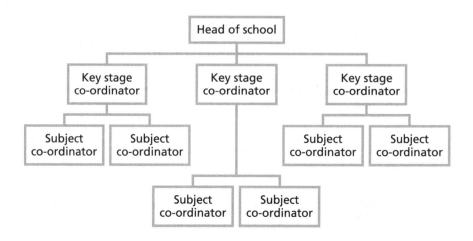

FIG. 3.3   School leadership – flat model

The specific purposes to be achieved in collaborative decision-making at school level are (Spinks, 1990, 122):

1 *to provide an approach to school management which clearly focuses on learning and teaching (the central issues of any school);*

2 *to facilitate sharing in the decision-making processes and the involvement of all possible participants in appropriate ways;*

3 *to identify clearly the management tasks and to provide direct and easily understood links between them and information about them;*

4 *to identify clearly responsibilities for decision-making and activities and to demonstrate lines of accountability;*

5 *to provide a means to relate resource allocations of all kinds to learning priorities for students;*

6 *to facilitate evaluation and review processes with the emphasis on further improving opportunities for students;*

7 *to limit documentation to simple, clear statements that can easily be prepared by those involved in their already busy schedules.*

Collaborative framework

A collaborative framework designed by Caldwell and Spinks (1988 in Chapman 1990, 124) is the most effective approach to school organisation (see Figure 3.4).

FIG. 3.4 Collaborative framework, (Caldwell and Spinks 1988, Figure 3.1)

In the context of structures for school culture, the collaborative model is more flexible and would be appropriate for the majority of schools but as Spinks (1990, 145) stated, *the model [. . .] is just a starting point*. Harris and Lambert (2003, 96) suggest that schools focused on continual and sustained improvement to build communities that are *collaborative and empowering*. In such communities, they further suggest, *positive relationships* are encouraged and *all voices* are *heard and acknowledged*. If school leaders are to make it work they need knowledge and skills related to 'learning and teaching', curriculum design and development, the gathering of information for programme evaluation and the capacity to exercise leadership.

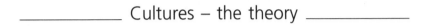

Cultures – the theory

The culture of a school is its 'personality', the way that work is done. Every school is different and has slightly different expectations of its management. Sergiovanni (2001, 76) comments that *a school has character when there is consistency between that school's purposes, values, and needs, and its decisions and actions*. The culture of each school is determined by individual and collective beliefs and values. Schools do not consist of homogenous groups of people with shared identities; schools are collections of individuals within a shared culture. The modelling of a school will require improvement plans and policies that acknowledge established practice. In her article, 'To strengthen the mixture, first understand the chemistry', Foy (1981) suggested reasons why leaders should try to understand the culture of their organisation. In brief:

- leaders will be better able to relate to the organisation if they appreciate its nature
- leaders may be able to predict the behaviour of people in the organisation, thereby making the managers more effective.

A school culture will manifest itself in many forms:

- **practice** – rites, rituals and ceremonies
- **communications** – stories, myths, sagas, legends, folk tales, symbols and slogans
- **physical forms** – location, style and condition of the school buildings, fixtures and fittings
- **common language** – phrases or jargon specific to the school.

Within each culture, sub-cultures exist with their own sets of characteristics. The school culture may be the dominant culture or subject or year teams may create their own sub-cultures.

Handy offers a means of understanding the culture of organisations by identifying common characteristics. In *Understanding Organisations* (1993) he identified three concepts of organisations: power, people and politics. Handy believed that the concepts should:

- **help to explain the past**, which in turn
- **helps to understand the present**, and thus
- **to predict the future**, which leads to
- **more influence over future events**, and
- **less disturbance from the unexpected**.

He stated that the analytical task of the manager is to:

- *identify the key variables of any situation*
- *predict the probable outcomes of any changes in the variables*
- *select the ones [s/]he can and should influence.*

More specifically, Handy perceived organisations as:

- *collections of individuals*
- *political systems*

joined together by:

- *power and influence.*

Handy (1993, 182) described how organisations differ according to the way they work; their levels of authority, formality and control; how much planning they undertook; and in terms of financial matters, rules and results. Handy also described the impact of the buildings; schools can certainly offer variety here.

Most significantly, Handy focuses on the people within organisations, as it is people who create and work within the culture of an organisation. Handy (1993, 183–91) defined four cultures which could provide a framework for analysing practice:

- power culture
- role culture
- task culture
- person culture.

Each list may contain elements that apply to a particular school. There may be other characteristics which could be applied. Equally, the characteristics may be more observable at different periods of the school day, week or year!

1 The power culture

FIG. 3.5 The power culture

Characteristics of a power culture (see Figure 3.5) are:

- small entrepreneurial organisations
- web shape in design
- patron god would be Zeus – the god of the broad light of day
- culture depends on a central power source, rays of power and influence spreading out from the central figure
- organisation dependent on trust and empathy for effectiveness
- communication dependent on telepathy and personal conversation
- if whoever is at the centre of the web chooses the right people, they can be left to get on with the job
- few rules and procedures – little bureaucracy
- control is exercised by the centre, by occasional forays from the centre or summonses to the centre
- proud and strong, can move quickly in response to threat or danger – the type of movement will depend on the person(s) at the centre
- the quality of the person(s) at the centre is of paramount importance
- individuals employed by them will prosper and be satisfied, if they are power-orientated, politically minded and rate risk-taking as important
- resource power (financial and human) is the major power base
- limited security
- size – the web can break if it seeks to be involved in too many activities
- faith in the individual not in committees

- judges by results and is tolerant of the means
- low morale and high turnover in the middle layers – too competitive.

2 The role culture

Characteristics of role culture (see Figure 3.6) are:

FIG. 3.6 The role culture

- stereotyped as bureaucratic
- can be pictured as a Greek temple
- patron god is Apollo – the god of reason
- logic and rationality
- strength is in its pillars
- the work of pillars, and the interaction between the pillars, is controlled by:
  procedures for roles (job descriptions, authority decisions)
  procedures for communications (required sets of memos)
  rules for the settlement of disputes
- co-ordinated at the top by a narrow band of senior managers
- role or job description is more important than the individual
- individuals are selected for satisfactory performance in the role
- performance over and above the role is not required
- position power is the major power source
- personal power is frowned upon and expert power is only tolerated
- rules and procedures are the major methods of influence
- needs a stable environment (e.g. civil service)
- offers security and predictability – clear career path
- economies of scale are more important than flexibility

- slow to perceive the need for change
- change may lead to collapse and the need for new management.

3 The task culture

Characteristics of task culture (see Figure 3.7) are:

FIG. 3.7   The task culture

- job or project-orientated
- structure best described as a net
- some strands of the net are thicker and stronger than others
- emphasis on getting the job done
- influence is placed on expert power more than on person power
- utilises the unifying power of the group to ensure that individuals identify with the objective of the organisation
- groups, project teams or task forces for a specific purpose
- high degree of control over work
- easy working relationships within the group with mutual respect based upon capacity rather than age or status
- appropriate where flexibility and sensitivity are important
- limited depth of expertise
- thrives where speed of reaction, integration, sensitivity and creativity are important
- control is difficult – by allocation of projects
- little day-to-day management
- preferred by middle leaders
- lack of resources can lead to political problems
- not always the appropriate culture for the climate and the technology.

4 The person culture

Characteristics of person culture (see Figure 3.8) are:

FIG. 3.8 The person culture

- unusual, individuals may cling to its values
- the individual is the central point
- it exists only to serve and assist the individuals within it
- structure best described as a cluster
- control mechanisms are impossible
- influence is shared; the power-base is usually expert, individuals do what they are good at
- generally only the creator achieves success
- individuals may exist in other cultures – not easy to manage
- little influence can be brought on them, not easily impressed.

Organisational culture will vary; schools are complex organisations with management structures that are determined by and are a reflection of the dominant culture. Peters and Waterman (2004, 75) highlight the *dominance and coherence of culture* in strongly performing companies, where all employees share a common set of values. In most schools, middle leaders will need to understand the culture in the same way that they need to understand their own personalities. Middle leaders will need to identify the culture of the schools in which they work; they should also identify the culture in which their team works. This will be according to the collective beliefs and values of the school community and their relationship to the community's own beliefs and values. As a sub-culture, do the characteristics and practice of the team reflect the culture of the school or do they differ in any way? Middle leaders represent the school through their team. School and team culture ought to be compatible.

A middle leader will not be in a position to change the school's culture. However, as a manager of a team or department, middle leaders are in a position to influence or change its sub-culture. Effective schools require collective practices. Individuality may generate creativity; however, if the individual's values and beliefs are the antithesis of the organisation's values and beliefs, this will result in negative behaviour. Conflict will inevitably ensue!

 Defining vision and mission

Vision

The head teacher has responsibility for collaborating with the school community in the generation of its vision. This emphasises a collegial approach to writing and achieving a vision; as each school's ethos is distinctive, school vision or mission statements will also be distinctive. If a school is to be successful, it has to be effective. A measure of a school's effectiveness is the ability of the staff to work towards achieving the school's vision, i.e. working towards a shared set of values and beliefs. Fidler (2002, 105) suggests that staff could contribute by writing down their hope for the future of the school. *Bringing different ideas together,* he further suggests, *should produce a composite. Some components will be incompatible with others and discussion should help to resolve these.* The vision statement should be succinct and should contain, within a few words, the philosophy underlying professional practice within the school.

Although management literature emphasises the need for vision in organisations, vision is often an intangible, difficult and ambiguous concept. Fidler (2002, 105) describes vision as:

… the creative 'double-loop' thinking of trying to envisage how things might be different in the future. It leaps the present and the short term. It looks 10–15 years ahead, sufficient time that things might change radically, and tries to vision the organization in a new and successful future… the vision is not just a projection forward of the present but it does bear some relation to the starting conditions

A vision will move an organisation forward from where it is now to where it would like to be. A precise goal is more credible than a vague dream. A vision should be realistic and attractive to all members of the organisation. As a condition, a vision should be more desirable in many important ways than that which currently exists. A specific definition of vision within the context of schools would be the school's aims. These are notably achievement-orientated and, as such, should be shared by all members of the school community.

Missions will provide a clear sense of direction and purpose. These are a means of creating operational plans: objectives or targets to be met by members of the school community.

A vision must be clear and comprehensible to all: teachers, parents, pupils, governors, visitors, etc. School vision statements should direct the school's population towards a common purpose.

Identifying shared values is the starting point when generating a vision for the school. Based on past and present values the vision might reflect what is **good** within the school. A genuinely **good** school with shared values and beliefs will be an effective school.

As stated, a vision must be shared, but it is the responsibility of leaders to ensure that visions 'happen'. Knowledge and understanding of a school's vision by staff is central to the success of the school. A shared vision will provide a framework for practice. When shared, the vision can be debated and developed. Monitoring and evaluation of values and beliefs through the sharing process should be common practice in schools.

Mission

A school's mission statement will provide the framework in which a vision can become a reality. A mission statement is therefore operational. Grace (1998, 120) suggests that school mission statements are of crucial importance in the context of developing an effective and inclusive school. Mission statements set out what a school's intended outcomes are for its pupils, their development and overall attainments – academic, social and personal. In practice, it is very easy for a school to lose its overall direction because it is unsure about what kind of school it is, and what it is trying to do. Middle leaders have a significant role in the realisation of mission statements, ensuring that things get done and that aims are achieved. Figure 3.9 illustrates the relationship between vision, mission and aims.

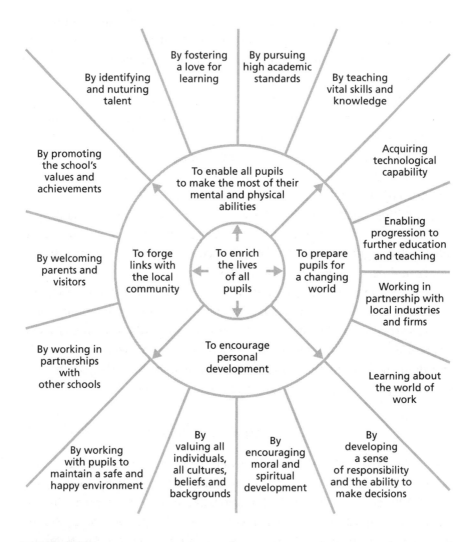

FIG. 3.9 School vision and mission statements (Blandford, 1997)

Mission statements

When preparing the school prospectus, head teachers need to create statements which reflect the ethos of the school. Davies and Ellison (1997, 147) advocate stating the school mission at the start of the prospectus. *If a sense of purpose and a clear message are to be communicated,* they suggest, *readers need to know straight away what the school stands for.* They further advocate reinforcing *key words from the mission statement* within *sub-sections* of the prospectus.

A mission statement (see Table 3.1) describes the way in which an organisation has chosen to conduct its activities. The extent to which the middle leader participates in this process will be determined by:

- how much authority the leader has to make decisions
- how many staff each leader has to manage
- level of staff specialisation
- clear job descriptions for all staff
- clear lines of communication relating to the team.

TABLE 3.1   Mission statement

As managers we are committed to:

- improving the quality and delivery of care
- ensuring that staff are briefed on the school's objectives and are clear about their own limits of authority
- utilising to the maximum the skills of our staff
- encouraging staff to take decisions for themselves within the limits of their authority
- concentrating on achievement
- encouraging individuals to find solutions rather than putting forward problems
- fostering the building of teams to promote achievement increased participation in CPD
- encouraging a sense of belonging to a unit/department
- being supportive of staff in their endeavours, allowing them an opportunity to put forward their views and encouraging their initiative.

Several examples of mission statements are provided in Table 3.2: from a specialist school, a Church of England primary school, a Catholic secondary school and a girls' grammar school respectively. Whilst faith schools tend to provide clear mission statements within their prospectuses, other schools incorporate their mission statements into a general educational and pedagogical philosophy. Further examples of mission statements are shown in Table 3.3.

TABLE 3.2   Mission statements from a variety of schools

- To promote and celebrate excellence and achievement through: development of high-quality teaching and learning; creation of a caring environment based on trust, respect and equality of opportunity; integration of schools and pupils into the wider life of the community.

- To create a stable, ordered and balanced community which will foster each child's intellectual, physical, aesthetic, spiritual, emotional, moral and social development.

- To provide for learning to take place within a broad and balanced curriculum of both academic and practical work, which gives pupils not only experience of the major subject disciplines but also a sense of satisfaction in their achievements.

- To encourage each child throughout their school life to develop an enquiring and receptive mind as well as the ability to reason. In this way the child will acquire the skills and knowledge necessary to develop their potential and enable them to take their full part in society.

- To develop as a community of faith, one in which the teaching of Jesus Christ is at the foundation of all that we undertake. The principal aims of the statement are as follows:
  - To develop the whole person in the image of Christ
  - To allow young people to be formed according to a Christian view of the world
  - To teach pupils following Christ's own teaching, and through the advancement of knowledge, to understand god and humanity better.

We value and uphold the traditional values of good manners and hard work and have high expectations of all our pupils. We aim to instil in them a positive attitude which seeks out and relishes an academic or social challenge and overcomes it.

TABLE 3.3   Further examples of mission statements

- To ensure that each child has a command of language and the ability to communicate effectively and confidently in reading, writing, speaking and listening

- to develop a knowledge and understanding of basic mathematical facts and concepts and of how to use them

- to encourage scientific curiosity and to organise observational studies, particularly in the local environment

- to awaken children's awareness to their heritage, both local and national, and to give some understanding of their place in the world

- to give an understanding of moral and ethical codes, religious beliefs and ideas, and of how to live with others
- to teach skills and the appreciation of aesthetic qualities in the creative arts: art, craft, music and drama
- to develop and maintain a healthy body by providing enjoyment in physical activities
- to create a happy school environment
- to help children learn that courtesy, good manners and consideration for others are very important qualities and to make each child a responsible member of the school community and also of the wider community
- to encourage children to develop a habit of learning and to develop a lively enquiring mind and a co-operative attitude towards all the people who are working for the successful achievement of these aims.

Aims

Each school will have aims which are demonstrated in Table 3.4.

TABLE 3.4 Example of school aims

We seek to:

1 Create a happy, friendly, caring and welcoming school that will provide for pupils' needs in a sensitive way.
2 Foster a positive self-image in pupils, building self-confidence through priase and encouragement.
3 Encourage a positive attitude to life and learning, enabling each pupil to reach their full educational potential.
4 Prepare pupils for leaving and participation in society by teaching the appropriate social, independence and academic skills.
5 Ensure that all pupils and staff feel valued, and that any prejudice is challenged on all levels.
6 Promote an atmosphere of co-operation, with governors, staff, parents/carers and pupils working together as a school.
7 Develop links with the wider community, exploring integration for pupils wherever possible.
8 Provide a broad curriculum which encourages aesthetic, physical, academic and social development while meeting the requirements of the national curriculum.

Strategic planning in schools will occur annually through the school improvement plan (SIP). As an operational tool, the value of a SIP will rest with the senior leadership team and their ability to work collaboratively with others. Within the content of the SIP, vision, mission and aims will lead to aims and objectives as illustrated in Figure 3.10.

FIG. 3.10   Vision to objectives

Summary

The culture of a school is its 'personality', the way that work is done. Every school is different and has slightly different expectations of its management. A school culture will manifest itself through practice, communication, physical forms and a common language. Handy (1993) defines an organisation according to its culture. His definitions of power, role, task and person culture provide a framework for middle leaders. It is highly unlikely that you will be able to influence or change the culture of your school.

Middle leaders will be part of the school organisational structure. Theorists suggest that an interlinked span of control is the most effective structure for schools. This contrasts with tall and flat structures currently found in schools.

A specific definition of vision within the context of schools is reflected in a school's aims. A vision will move an organisation forward from where it is now to where it would like to be. Visions are set within the culture and organisational structure of a school. Vision statements must be realistic and attainable. Visions must be shared; the monitoring and evaluation of values and beliefs through the sharing process should be common practice in schools.

Missions provide a clear sense of direction and purpose. These are means of creating operational plans; objectives or targets to be met by members of the school community. A school's mission statement will provide the framework in which a vision can become a reality.

Vision and mission statements are critical to the effectiveness of strategic and operational plans.

———————————

REVIEW QUESTIONS

1 Why are school visions central to planning?

2 School organisation structure determines effective leadership. In your opinion, which organisation structure model might, in practice, be more effective? Why?

3 How would you define culture within the context of the school?

4 How would you ensure that the culture of your team reflected the culture of the school?

5 How would you ensure, as a middle leader, that you were continuing to make the school's vision 'happen'?

Strategic plans: policy creation and implementation

Strategic planning

Operational planning

The planning process

The school improvement plan (SIP)

Implementing the SIP

Developing a policy: professional development

From theory to practice

Creating and implementing an inclusion policy

Monitor, review and evaluate

Summary

_____ Strategic planning _____

An effective school will have plans and policies that support the leadership and management of learning. This chapter focuses on the development and implementation of strategic plans and policies.

A strategic plan is an expression of how an organisation intends to achieve its vision, mission and aims in a deliverable form for a period beyond the current school or financial year. In an effective school a strategic plan will be a working document used by staff and governors in the delivery of agreed aims and objectives. The plan will consider where the school wants to be and how it aims to get there. A deliverable plan will encompass all the activities of the school.

Strategic or long-term planning takes into consideration the strengths and weaknesses of the school as an organisation and also external factors such as government directives. Fidler (2002, 13) suggests that *strategic thinking is a mental attitude which tries to keep long-term objectives constantly in mind and considers all short-term decisions in this long-term perspective.* School leaders have a critical role in articulating organisational goals. These goals will reflect personal values as determined by vision and mission. Preparing a strategic plan might encompass a framework for all activities which might also relate to the remodelling process, as shown in Figure 4.1.

FIG. 4.1 Strategic plan

The format of the strategic plan will depend upon the individual needs and circumstances of the school. Ideally the plan should cover a period of three to five years and be reviewed and modified on an annual rolling basis so that a medium-term planning horizon can be maintained. It should, as Fidler (2002, 25) suggests, *include implications for both what to do and also what not to do. In short*, he continues, *it should indicate (implicit) priorities*. It should be a coherent and comprehensive document showing the relationship between financial and academic years. Schools should develop their own planning cycle and timetable which allows for:

- a review of past activities, aims and objectives – did we get it right?

- definition or redefinition of aims and objectives – are the aims still relevant?

- development of the plan and associated budgets – how do we go forward?

- implementation, monitoring and review – how do we make the plan work and keep it on course?

- feedback into the next planning cycle – what worked successfully and how can we improve?

Operational planning

Operational planning is about tasks underpinned by policies and targets and relates directly to the role of staff, leaders and managers: who does what, when and how? Operational planning is detailed. It aims to achieve a particular set of objectives within a given time and is concerned with making things happen in the short-term, for example how to run a department or team over a period. The planning, implementation and evaluation of professional development programmes at school should take account of the school's strategic plan, priorities and available resources. A useful framework for developing and implementing an operational plan is provided by the National Occupational Standards (Management Standards Centre, 2004). For effective outcomes the standards recommend the following:

- *Balance new ideas with tried and tested solutions*

- *Balance risk with desired outcomes*

- *Make sure your plans are consistent with the objectives*

- *Make sure the plan is flexible and complements related areas of work*

- *Develop and assign objectives to people together with the associated resources*

- Win the support of key colleagues and other stakeholders

- Monitor and control your plan so that it achieves its overall objectives

- Evaluate the implementation of your plan and make recommendations that identify good practice and areas for improvement.

Each layer of leadership in a school requires operational planning with defined targets linked to who does what, when and how? Operational planning provides the details that turn strategies into actions and aims to achieve a particular set of objectives within a given time. The process of developing a school's operational plan should be collaborative.

The process of planning is often more important than the plan. In terms of the innovation itself, an action plan might address a range of questions including who will benefit from the plan – pupils or colleagues? What will the costs be for those affected? Will additional resources be required to monitor the additional resources? It is also worth considering: is the change easy to communicate to those concerned and will they see its purpose? If this is not agreed, will it be possible to adapt what is intended to suit specific circumstances? Whose support will be needed? Will key people have a sense of ownership of the change? Given opportunities provided by *Every Child Matters, Extended Schools: Access to Opportunities and Services for All: A Prospectus* (DfES, 2005f), and the remodelled workforce, middle leaders will need to consider how these will impact on their team.

_____ The planning process _____

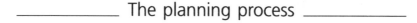

West-Burnham (1994b, 157) defines effective planning as a three-part process: plan, act, review (see Figure 4.2).

FIG. 4.2 The management cycle

As shown in Figure 4.3 the key features of good planning are:

- Everything is driven by the values and mission of the organisation and these have been developed and are owned by all staff.

- Strategic planning has a three- to five-year time-frame, i.e. beyond the contingent and reactive, and is primarily the responsibility of senior staff and community representatives.

- Once agreed, strategy has to be translated into a policy which serves as the basis of decision-making, notably for annual budgets and the deployment and development of staff.

- Medium-term planning is primarily concerned with translating policies into action, most significantly through annual development plans, objective budgeting and planning for the deployment and development of staff.

FIG. 4.3 Strategic planning in context (West-Burnham, 1994a, 80; after Davies and West-Burnham, 1990)

- This, in turn, facilitates the negotiation of short-term targets so that each individual is working to optimum effect.
- Because the vision has been translated into individual activities, evaluation is based upon the aggregation of specific outcomes, allowing the matching of intention and actual achievement.

_____ The school improvement plan (SIP) _____

The SIP provides a framework for strategic planning in which staff can identify long- and short-term objectives to manage themselves effectively. A SIP should relate to the school vision or mission.

A School Improvement Plan is a plan of needs for development set in the context of the school's aims and values, its existing achievements and national and LA policies and initiatives.

School Development Plan Project (DES, 1991)

The SIP should be central to the management of the school, involving all teachers. The extent of a middle leader's involvement will be determined by the head teacher and/or senior leadership team. In practice, middle leaders will need to know and understand the content of the SIP. As the leadership structures of schools change, increased collaboration may lead to a greater involvement in policy-making for middle leaders. Hargreaves and Hopkins (1991, 4) argue that:

The production of a good plan and its successful implementation depend upon a sound grasp of the processes involved. A wise choice of content for the plan as well as the means of implementing the plan successfully will be made only when the process of development planning is thoroughly understood.

The main purpose of a SIP should be to improve the quality of learning for pupils. Stoll *et al.* (2003, 153) underline the need to *see patterns and discern connections between seemingly unconnected events* in improvement planning. They further suggest that effective school improvement plans consider *connectedness*, where they get *below the surface of the actions or explore what happens when all of the priorities are being worked on at one time*. In practice, all leadership activities should relate to the SIP if they are to have a central role in school life. Effective middle leadership will depend on the knowledge and understanding of the SIP in directing the school towards its vision. Skelton *et al.* (1991) advocate that the format of SIPs should:

- demonstrate involvement
- provide a focus for action
- provide a means of presenting the plan
- provide a link to staff development
- provide a means of assessing progress.

The value of a SIP as an operational tool will rest with the senior leadership team. Middle leaders, as West-Burnham indicates, will have greater involvement at the operational level.

An understanding of the planning process is a necessary prerequisite to participation in the development of the SIP. A model of the planning process will aid development planning, illustrated in Figure 4.4.

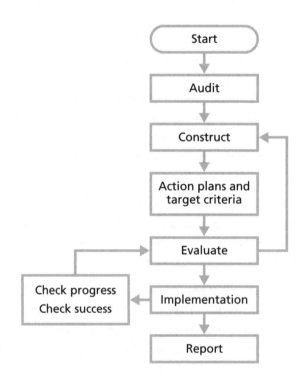

FIG. 4.4 The planning process

The audit

To begin, SIPs might identify strengths and weaknesses in the various relevant areas. In essence an audit will provide a basis for selecting priorities for development. The context of the audit will be:

- values, vision, missions, aims and objectives of the school
- policies and initiatives
- inspections and reviews
- staff appraisals
- views of all stakeholders: staff, governors, parents, pupils and community.

A full audit will be time-consuming; a programme of specific small-scale audits may be more practical and achievable within the school setting. As a middle leader you may be allocated responsibility for an area associated with your work. An audit might include:

- interviews with colleagues
- lesson observation, where appropriate
- review of documentation
- writing-up findings.

The outcomes of an audit should reveal strengths and weaknesses in order to provide a basis for action planning. The audit will also identify priorities for development.

Uniqueness of each SIP

It is critical that each SIP should be unique. As Skelton *et al.* (1991, 166–7) advised, SIPs should:

- demonstrate involvement
- provide a focus for action
- provide a means of presenting the plan
- provide a means of assessing progress.

The success of an improvement plan will depend upon the planning process. Fidler (2002, 26) suggests that developing a SIP involves a hierarchial planning process. He recommends, at the first planning level, a consideration of the impact of the strategic plan on the *organisational structure and the decision-making* processes within the school. There are several examples in school management literature of what should be included in the SIP. Fidler (2002, 26) identifies the following areas, where detailed sub-plans need to be drawn up:

■ *curriculum (and pupil outcomes) plan (what we intend to contribute to children's learning)*

■ *staff planning (how we intend to recruit and develop people with the skills to do it)*

■ *financial (and material resources and premises) plan (how we intend to acquire and spend the money to help us achieve it)*

■ *marketing plan (how we intend to obtain the resources and support of others to enable us to achieve it).*

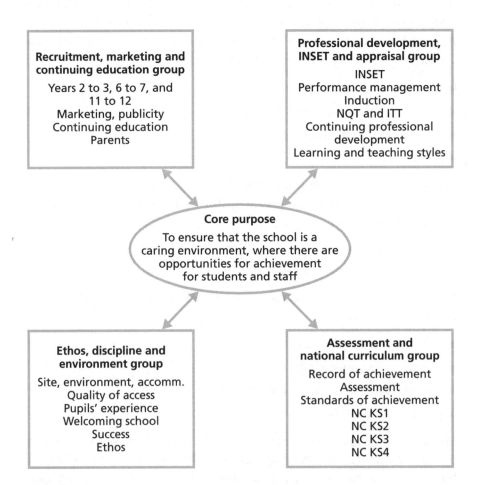

FIG. 4.5 Effectiveness: school improvement plan

The plan might include:

- aims of the school
- proposed priorities and their time-scale
- justification of the priorities in the context of the school
- different aspects of planning drawn together
- methods of reporting outcomes
- broad financial implications of the plan.

As a strategic plan, the SIP should consider the changes needed to improve the effectiveness of the school shown in Figure 4.5. Planners should recognise that the urgent and unavoidable linking of priorities will lead to increased collaboration between staff and other stakeholders.

CASE STUDY

Preparing a school improvement plan

Plans had previously been formulated on a three-yearly cycle in 1992, 1995, 1998 and 2001. The move towards school improvement rather than development has led to the school improvement plan (SIP) which was piloted from 2002. The SIP was developed with the aim of making it:

- more accessible to those who use it
- more relevant to those planning it
- easier to develop
- easier to monitor and evaluate in terms of its impact on teaching and learning.

FIVE STAGES IN CONSTRUCTING THE SIP

1 In 2002, the senior leadership team (SLT) reviewed the school's current SIP and assessed where the school was in terms of its aims and values, and pupils' achievement. A SWOT analysis was undertaken. This assessment enabled all staff and governors to express their ideas, concerns and anxieties about the SIP.

2 SLT collected information, discussed and decided objectives and priorities with all who should be involved, focusing attention on only those areas requiring action. This included asking the questions 'How well should we be doing?' and 'What more can we aim to achieve?' in comparison with similar schools. An initial audit focused on standards, teaching, the curriculum, schemes of work and assessment, student care and discipline, leadership and management, parents and community partnerships, premises and the school environment, budget costs and projections.

3 Analysis of where the school was then and where it needed to be was provided on the basis of a draft overview. Targets included in the plan reflected the needs identified by staff and governors and set out what was needed to make it happen. An INSET day was held where all staff were involved in planning the short-term (one-year) goals of their areas of responsibility.

4 Support for teachers, including time to work together on implementing the plan, and the appropriate resources, including materials and equipment, were essential in order to ensure that everybody involved was aware of the part they would play. Monitored implementation was essential to ensure that what was intended to happen would happen.

5 Progress was to be evaluated through SLT, line and performance management assessments. The ultimate question for any change or development is: what is the effect on the pupils' learning? The consequences need to be beneficial or the SIP will need to be adapted. Once the evaluative outcomes are known, these will form the basis for repeating the five-stage construction procedure.

SCHOOL IMPROVEMENT PLAN
VISION

SCHOOL IMPROVEMENT IN ORDER TO BE AN 'EXCELLENT SCHOOL'

We wish to build on current successes by planning. To promote and celebrate excellence and achievement through:

- development of high-quality teaching and learning

- creation of a caring environment based on trust, respect and equality of opportunity

- integration of the school and its pupils into the wider life of the community.

These aims should be enshrined in everything that the school does. Ultimately, the school strives to be an 'excellent school'.

AIMS

Following INSET and discussion with staff, parents, children and governors the senior management team met to discuss the way forward for the school. Through this process, a plan consisting of new aims was formulated in order to continue the improvement that the school had enjoyed over the previous seven years. These aims are at the centre of all that we do in order to raise standards and take into account the aims of the sports college development plan (SCDP). Planning at all levels is expected to link in with these areas and their sub-sections. The school improvement plan is a working document that provides a broad framework of actions, needs and intentions where all staff have been involved in its compilation. The plan has a broad long-term outline for developments planned over three years, with a more detailed list of action intended to enable attainment of set targets during the year.

OBJECTIVES

The development of high-quality teaching and learning

- Creation of a highly skilled and specialist workforce to facilitate learning in the modern environment

- Integrating modern technologies to transform teaching and learning

- To create a school that enables pupils to learn in the most effective style according to their needs

- To raise levels of attainment at KS3, KS4 and KS5.

The creation of a caring environment based on trust, respect and equality of opportunity

■ To offer a curriculum accessible to all

■ To improve management of pupil behaviour, attendance and attitudes while continuing to improve overall levels of achievement

■ To develop accommodation to meet the needs of the curriculum

■ To maintain and develop the ethos of 'learn, participate, perform and excel'.

Integration of the school and its pupils into the wider life of the community

■ To meet the community aims in both the sports college and advanced school plans

■ To work with our partners in PE, sport and the wider community

■ To create communities of school through collaboration

■ To increase out-of-hours learning.

Each of the aims and objectives is now at the operational stage of development, owned and managed by senior leaders, budgetholders, teachers and members of the school community.

SCHOOL IMPROVEMENT PLAN

WHERE WE WOULD LIKE TO BE

During a senior leadership meeting, it was agreed that we want to:

■ be re-designated as an Investor in People

■ become a training school

■ continue to raise standards

■ become an inclusive learning community

- develop teaching and learning

- employ and train high-quality staff

- work in collaboration with key partners (especially at key stage 5)

- ensure a high-quality environment

- use the specialism of PE and sport to support whole school improvement

- use ICT to support whole school improvement

QUESTIONS

1 Can this case study be used as a template in your school?

2 Is your school's vision clear and concise?

3 Are the objectives acceptable with the current level of funding?

4 How are the objectives monitored?

5 Having read this case study, what can you do to improve financial management in your school?

Implementing the SIP

Once the SIP has been completed, detailed action plans can be drawn up. This will involve middle leaders and colleagues deciding on the way forward to implement the SIP. Action plans are a means of making the strategy operational. Action plans should contain:

- the agreed **priority** area
- the **targets** – specific objectives for the priority area
- **success criteria** against which progress and achievement can be judged
- the **tasks** to be undertaken

- allocation of **responsibility** for tasks and targets – with **time-scales**
- **resources** required.

Action plans should prepare the way forward for the implementation of the SIP. How this will work will depend on several factors. Hargreaves and Hopkins (1991, 65) identify the activities required to make the plan work:

- sustaining commitment during implementation
- checking the progress of implementation
- overcoming any problems encountered
- checking the success of implementation
- taking stock
- reporting progress
- constructing the next development plan.

People management is the key to successful implementation of the SIP. Middle leaders have a critical role in this process.

___ Developing a policy: professional development ___

An effective and improving school as a learning organisation will have clear policies relating to the management of learning, people and resources. As an example, a professional development policy should reflect a school leadership team's desire to value and support its staff (Figure 4.6). It is self-evident that staff development needs to be placed at the centre of school improvement and effectiveness.

The National Occupational Standards (Management Standards Centre, 2004) cover the following areas of management and leadership, which can be employed as an appropriate framework for professionsl development in schools:

- *managing self and personal skills*
- *providing direction*
- *facilitating change*
- *working with people*
- *using resources*
- *achieving results.*

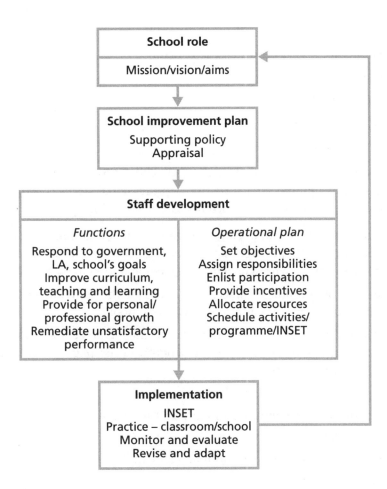

FIG. 4.6 Professional development policy

Each school should have a professional development policy that defines aims and describes how these will be implemented.

A professional development policy will include details of:

- staff performance management targets related to school development targets
- individual needs, as identified by the performance review process
- training opportunities through –

  in-school activities

  whole-school INSET

  LA courses

national initiatives

accreditation and award-bearing courses

■ resources available from –

within the school

funding agencies

external bids.

Once targets have been identified, each school has to plan, implement and evaluate a programme for CPD. A professional development policy will include statements that encompass the following:

■ The aim of CPD within a learning organisation is to improve the quality of learning and teaching. The immediate aim is to improve the performance of those with school management and teaching responsibilities.

■ The CPD programme balances the needs of the individual with the institutional developmental needs of the school.

■ The school will have some systematic diagnostic process for individual needs (e.g. appraisal) and for the school's needs (e.g. self-evaluation in relation to the SIP).

■ Sets of needs to be balanced are –

needs of head teachers, senior staff and teachers

needs arising from SIPs

needs of the LA – subject and management

needs of LA policy

needs of government policy.

The model starts with the roles of the school, as stated in the mission and vision statements and aims. The General Teaching Council (1993) produced guidance on statements that could be found in a staff development policy (see Table 4.1).

A guiding model for a staff development policy that relates to the institutional development plan and review is shown in Figure 4.7. The model illustrates the need for teaching and non-teaching staff to have a range of knowledge and understanding, skills and abilities to meet the needs of their pupils. Each area details what is required for staff development, subjects, teaching and learning styles, elements of learning attitudes and areas of experience. The model also indicates the need for training and development to be: relevant, balanced, broad, differentiated and reflected in the institutional development plan. The model is comprehensive and applicable to both primary and secondary schools.

TABLE 4.1   Staff development policy

What is a staff development policy?	Features
A staff development policy should be:	broad
	differentiated
	relevant
	balanced
Staff should be trained to deliver:	subjects
	elements of learning
	areas of experience
Staff should have the opportunity to develop skills in:	communication
	observation
	study
	problem-solving
	literacy
	numeracy
Staff should have an understanding of:	equal opportunities
	economic awareness
	health education
	environmental education
	information technology
Staff should have the opportunity to develop:	teaching styles
	learning styles
	team work
	resource management
	collaborative working

Source: General Teaching Council (1993)

As shown in Figure 4.7, personal and professional development are directly related to school improvement/development. Too much emphasis on meeting school needs may deskill and demotivate teachers and support staff, and lead to staff wastage.

Specifically, leaders should reflect on what choices are available within the context of professional development, identifying:

■ what is required to improve performance

■ how this will be done

■ when this will be done.

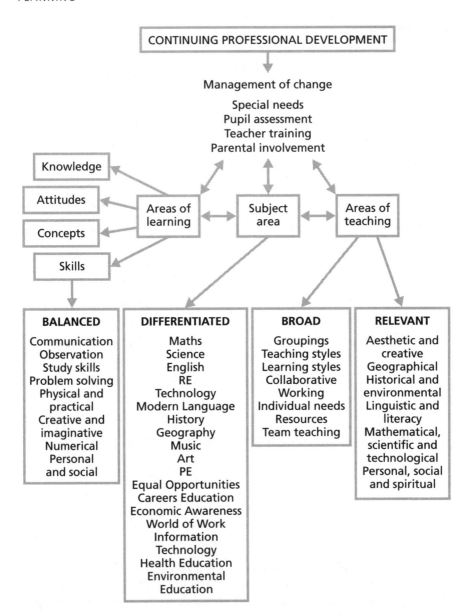

FIG. 4.7 Model for professional development within the context of school

The checklist that follows for the preparation of a staff development policy reflects the need for breadth and depth in professional development.

CHECKLIST

A good professional development ethos is critical to the effective implementation of the professional development policy. Activities important to establishing an environment favourable to CPD are:

■ the establishment of a positive professional development attitude by all members of the community of learners and acceptance of the idea of professional development throughout working life, i.e. lifelong learning

■ instilling the need for continuous learning into new practitioners during their initial professional education and, ideally, to establish a synthesis of initial and continuing education

■ enabling practitioners to learn effectively, i.e. by applying the knowledge of cognitive psychologists to the needs of the practitioner and professional development. Adult learning is about learning to learn rather than simply being taught

■ providing expert support and guidance on professional development issues for all parties, and especially for practitioners.

—————— From theory to practice ——————

A self-developing school will have targets that provide adequate time, resources and follow-up support for staff development. These will include:

■ an emphasis on development of the individual within the school's organisational context

■ more individuals undergoing professional development

■ professional development not isolated from other developments

■ professional development related to the context of the school/college

■ professional development about both individual and organisational needs

■ professional development opportunities as the result of collaboration, participation and negotiation.

Figure 4.8 provides a flow-diagram on how to implement school and professional development plans and policies. Each process begins with an audit of practice and need, through the school auditing procedures and performance management. Targets are then set, based on identified needs. This leads to policies, planning and resourcing. Documents that are a record of policies, procedures and practices, the SIP, and CPD/INSET

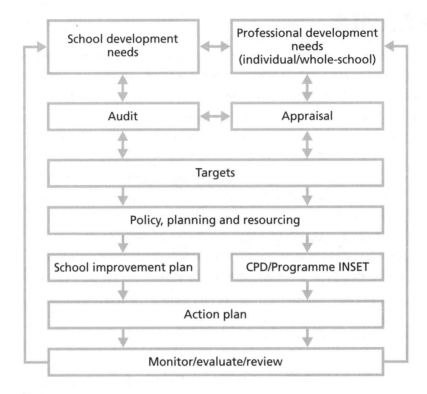

FIG. 4.8 Implementation: school and professional development policies and plans

programmes are then compiled. Action plans provide the detail identifying what needs to be done, by whom and when. The cycle is completed with monitoring, evaluation and review.

___ Creating and implementing an inclusion policy ___

As with professional development an inclusion/SEN policy will be linked to a SIP. The inclusion policy will relate clearly to the school's vision and be central to school leadership by involving all teachers in the process of identifying its aims and objectives. The implementation plan should also identify with other school initiatives. All policies need to reflect school, LA and government policies. The main purpose of any plan should be to improve the quality of teaching and learning for all pupils.

Middle leaders will need to consider how SEN contributes to the development of a learning environment for a community of learners. A fundamental element of learning and teaching is the self-esteem of pupil, teacher and senior leadership team. Without self-esteem, pupils and teachers will not function in the school community. There is a need for every school to have an inclusion/SEN policy that focuses on personal development and growth. Busher (2000b, 52) underlines the importance, *in creating an inclusive school, of developing staff abilities to improve the quality of learning opportunities students have*. An inclusion/SEN policy should reflect the ethos of the school and contribute to the fulfilment of its mission.

As with SIPs, an inclusion/SEN policy will reflect the values and beliefs of the school community. It should also relate to the social development of pupils as appropriate to their age and personal needs. Each school will need to have a view on what it particularly wishes to encourage but all schools will need to foster the development of desirable attitudes and personal qualities which can relate to the knowledge and understanding, skills and abilities of the members of their community.

Schools complement and extend the functions of the home and wider community by helping to prepare all pupils to live in society. Pupils need to learn the obligations that go with membership of a group and a community. The development of personal values is an outcome of an effective inclusion policy that relates to the social function of each school. Pupils also need to become aware of their own identity as individuals and of the importance of taking account of the feelings and wishes of others.

In practice, teachers provide a range of opportunities for pupils to learn and develop social skills and attitudes. The process of social development is continued throughout primary and secondary education, in school rules and codes of practice, in school councils and clubs and in the encouragement of pupils' responsibility for themselves and others.

Teachers will benefit from a clear and agreed inclusion/SEN policy that has expectations of them as practitioners. Effective teachers operating under clearly understood guidelines feel confident when giving clear instructions and will be able to develop targets for pupils and teachers.

What makes a good inclusion/SEN policy?

The precise content of an inclusion/SEN policy must be determined by the school community. The recommendations from the DfES (2001a) indicate that whole-school SEN policies are based on a clear set of principles and values.

There is a huge difference between simply having an inclusion/SEN policy on paper, and having one that actually works well in practice. Some factors that go towards making a policy work are when the policy is:

- not just a paper exercise, but is used effectively on a daily basis and across the whole school
- created in consultation with teachers and pupils
- reviewed and updated to ensure that any parts which do not work are altered
- clear to pupils, parents and staff
- a clear and effective part of the whole school ethos
- one that puts the emphasis on positive aspects
- one which lets teachers know what to do, and who to turn to, if additional help is needed
- one which encourages consistency, but also allows for individual approaches to SEN.

In practice, an inclusion/SEN policy will be a comprehensive and assertive statement intended to guide the school community (Johnson *et al.*, 1994). The policy will be the outcome of a democratic decision-making process involving all members of the school community; participation is the key to an effective policy. Senior leaders might begin the process of developing a policy by:

- identifying the stages of development
- identifying key personnel; SENCO and a SEN team responsible for writing the policy
- deciding on a time-scale for short-, medium- and long-term objectives
- identifying achievable outcomes related to the school vision and development plan
- identifying professional development support and INSET needs for the whole staff.

_____ Monitor, review and evaluate _____

Inclusion is not something that can be made to happen from outside a school or even by the commitment of a few dedicated individuals. It requires ownership by the head teacher and senior leadership team, governors and all staff. It also requires willingness on the part of schools to look at their own practice and to identify areas where they could do better. Inclusion must be an integral part of whole school self-evaluation and improvement.

Schools now have self-evaluation frameworks. The following range of tools can be used by schools to assess how well policies are serving different groups of pupils:

- Ofsted's inspection handbook
- *Evaluating Educational Inclusion* (Ofsted, 2000)
- *Primary National Strategy* – materials to link with existing self-evaluation frameworks for subject leaders and key stage co-ordinators
- *Index for Inclusion* – designed to help schools assess how inclusive they are and to support their development, explains the concepts behind inclusion and provides a detailed framework for self-review and supporting materials (CSIE, 2004).

If a policy is not monitored and evaluated it will not be possible to determine whether objectives have been achieved. Monitoring and evaluation are critical to the successful implementation of a policy for inclusion. This will involve senior and middle leadership teams, teachers, teaching assistants, parents, pupils, governors and the LA. The process of monitoring will also enable members of the school community to move further towards agreed objectives. Having adopted a collegial approach to policy development, monitoring and evaluation, the school community can move forward with confidence.

Monitoring must be based on practice and outcomes, and related to agreed criteria/set targets. Furthermore it should provide a framework in which teachers can reflect on their own practice and professional needs.

 Summary

A strategic plan is an expression of how an organisation intends to achieve its aims and objectives in a deliverable form for a period beyond the current school or financial year. To secure effective leadership of the school it should be used as a working document for staff and governors to establish commonly shared and accepted aims and objectives. Ideally it will contain a practical and deliverable mission statement to define the essential purpose of the school. The plan will consider where the school will realistically want to be and how to aim to get there. A deliverable strategic plan ought to encompass all the activities of the school.

In successful schools, school development/improvement plans (SIPs) focus on strategies to improve the quality of teaching and learning and thereby raise pupil achievements. These successful schools often display: a shared vision and high expectation about pupil achievement; an agreement on effective teaching practices and their benefit for pupil achievement; agreed and acknowledged arrangements to ensure the school is managed effectively and efficiently; a strategy to develop, monitor and review curriculum policies and schemes of work; and a coherent approach to monitoring and evaluation, assessing pupils progress and recording and reporting their achievements. In such schools, staff development is placed at the centre of school improvement and effectiveness.

The SIP will also ensure that barriers are removed so that all pupils have an equal opportunity to succeed at school. Strategies for managing the curriculum, organisation and staffing will make the best possible use of resources to improve pupils' learning and promote inclusion and achievement, in line with the school's stated aims, as long-term vision is turned into short-term goals. A SIP clarifies collective thinking so that there is a shared purpose in the school and a consistent interpretation by all staff and governors.

REVIEW QUESTIONS

1 How does an operational plan differ from an improvement/strategic plan?

2 How does an internal audit inform a strategic plan?

3 The main purpose of a SIP is to improve the quality of learning for pupils. What should inform the planning stage for a focused and effective SIP?

4 What are the aims of CPD? What factors need to be considered for effective school CPD?

5 A middle leader will have responsibility for team development. How would you as a middle leader identify your team's needs and communicate these to senior management?

6 How might a middle leader monitor an inclusion/SEN policy?

chapter five

Planning

What is planning?

Strategic and operational planning

The department improvement plan (DIP)

Decision-making

Curriculum planning

Timetabling

Summary

_____ What is planning? _____

Planning is a messy, repetitive and confusing aspect of a middle leader's life. This chapter focuses on the elements that will assist middle leaders in determining a good plan. As planning is a practical activity the chapter begins with three established principles.

1 As a **process**, planning consists of the stages shown in Table 5.1:

2 Planning involves two aspects of leadership practice which should be adopted by a leader from the start:

  ■ **Analytical** – thinking things through involving calculation and individual reflection.

  ■ **Social** – motivating and drawing on the contributions and commitment from colleagues.

3 When determining objectives be **SMART** (Tuckman, 1965). Remember, objectives should be:

Specific

Measurable

Attainable

Relevant

Timed.

Problems and constraints

Planning may involve going around in circles (see Figure 5.1) as various combinations of objectives, actions and resources are considered, whilst ensuring that all elements are included. In successful schools, school improvement plans (SIPs) focus on strategies to improve the quality of teaching and learning and thereby raise pupils' levels of achievement. Successful schools often display:

■ a shared vision and high expectation about pupil achievement

■ an agreement on effective teaching practices and their impact on pupil achievement

■ agreed and acknowledged arrangements to ensure the school is managed effectively and efficiently

TABLE 5.1 Planning stages

Objectives	Stage 1	*Define the objectives*	What are are you aiming to achieve?
	Stage 2	*Generate and evaluate*	What are the courses of action *objectives/actions* available? Which one will best achieve your objectives?
Actions	Stage 3	*Identify the actions*	What is required to implement your objectives?
	Stage 4	*Sequence the actions*	What is the best order?
Resources	Stage 5	*Identify the resources*	What resources are required?
Review	Stage 6	*Review the plan*	Will it work? If not, return to stage 2 or 3.
Preparation	Stage 7	*Prepare plans and schedules*	Who will do what and when?
Audit	Stage 8	*Monitor and evaluate*	Re-plan if necessary.

- a strategy to develop, monitor and review curriculum and associated learning and teaching policies and schemes of work
- a coherent approach of monitoring and evaluation, assessing pupils' progress and recording and reporting their achievements.

Planning can be challenging, enjoyable even, but it can also be difficult (LaGrave *et al*, 1994, 5–24). Middle leaders need to be able to plan a variety of events that happen in the life of the school, and specifically within their area of responsibility. The majority of middle leaders will experience the limitations of finance and other resources. There will also be time factors to consider in the preparation and implementation of the plan. It may be necessary to alter the plan in order to accommodate these challenges.

Planning will also be constrained by the need to meet deadlines. This must be included in the development of plans. More specifically, problems may arise if objectives are vague, circumstances change, or if there are difficulties with people and local politics.

FIG. 5.1 The planning cycle

_____ Strategic and operational planning _____

In brief, strategic planning is a broad statement which relates the overall approach and direction to the achievement of a mission. Developing and maintaining a strategy involves establishing a framework within which an operational plan can take place. Strategic planning is long-term planning, which takes into consideration the strengths and weaknesses of the organisation and external factors such as government directives. A SIP is a strategic plan.

As discussed in Chapter 4, operational planning is about tasks and targets and directly relates to the role of a school's middle leaders: who does what, when and how? It is concerned with making things happen in a short time-scale; how to run a department or team over a short period of time (up to 12 months). Operational planning is detailed. It aims to achieve a particular set of objectives within a given time. A department improvement plan (DIP) is an operational plan.

_____ The department improvement plan (DIP) _____

If it is to be effective, the DIP should be placed in the context of the school, LA and national planning. Figure 5.2 illustrates the position of the DIP within the school structure.

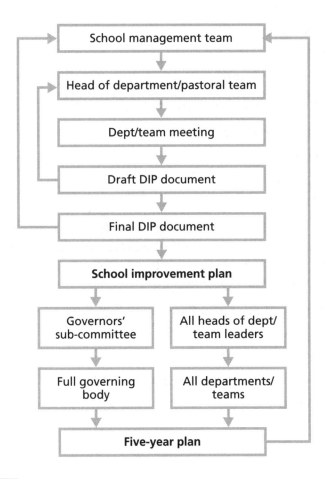

FIG. 5.2   Position of DIP in SIP

A DIP is similar to the SIP. The DIP should reflect the aims of the SIP and provide an operational framework for implementing the action plans emanating from the SIP. In brief a DIP should contain the following:

- a summary of the department's aims and objectives
- a method of achieving the aims and objectives
- monitoring and evaluation.

The DIP will enable staff to work together towards a common goal. The plan will have a sense of direction and purpose, the central aim being to improve the quality of teaching and learning within an area of responsibility. Points for consideration are:

- aims and values
- schemes of work
- policy documents
- teaching and learning
- assessment and reporting.

A DIP will also include statements on:

- special educational needs
- equal opportunities
- differentiation
- resources.

If a plan is to be effective it will need to be developed collaboratively. As Caldwell and Spinks (1988, 37) indicate in their model for *The Collaborative School Management Cycle* (see Chapter 3), in this model, staff as team members participate in:

- goal-setting and need identification
- policy-making
- planning of programmes
- preparation and approval of programme budgets
- implementing
- evaluating.

Decision-making

There are 'peaks and troughs' of administrative activity that occur in every academic year. Time-tabling, assessment and inspection are key events in each school's programme. Identifying when such events occur is essential to the successful management of a department or school.

Planning involves decision-making, individually and collaboratively. If department planning is to be effective, middle leaders will need to understand how to prioritise and how to make decisions. Warwick (1983, 3) states that:

Decision-making is so much part of daily life in any school that it can easily be taken for granted. Only when things go wrong; when bad decisions have been taken or the consultation process has broken down, do most teachers become aware of it.

Hall and Oldroyd (1990b, 16) advised that *decision-making is intimately bound up with every individual manager's personal values, personal goals and management style.* Essentially middle leaders have to 'think on their feet', making decisions at frequent intervals throughout the working day. In order to make quality decisions Hall and Oldroyd (1990b, 16) suggest that managers should have:

- *clear personal values*
- *clear personal goals*
- *problem-solving skills*
- *high creativity*
- *high influence.*

A middle leader will develop the skills and abilities required to determine when to act on their own and when to collaborate with others. Adopting a structured approach to decision-making will aid the process. This involves:

- Clear analysis of the learning purpose: context, resources, outcomes.
- Clear specification of the criteria for the plan as determined by the SIP, the LA and government initiatives.
- Systematic research.
- Testing decisions against likely outcomes to assess the quality of teaching and learning.

Deciding when to consult the team will affect:

- the quality of the decision
- staff's acceptance of the decision
- the amount of time involved in the decision-making process.

Fidler (2002, 51) states:

Involvement in decision-making has two major benefits:

a) an improvement in the quality of the decision.

b) improved motivation and commitment of those involved.

However, as Fidler further states, *involvement is not without its drawbacks.* These include:

- *it is slower than autocracy;*
- *it consumes a great deal of staff time;*
- *the pattern of decision-making is less predictable;*
- *the pattern of decision-making is less consistent;*
- *the location of accountability may be less clear;*
- *some decisions are expected to be taken by senior managers and participation may be seen as abdication.*

In conclusion, middle leaders should build on their team's ability to participate in the management of the school. A sudden transition to full staff participation will not happen, although middle and senior managers should be developing teachers' management skills within the context of CPD. The transition should be supported by appropriate training and a climate where risk-taking is accepted. Monitoring and evaluation of such processes are necessary for success.

—————— Curriculum planning ——————

Final decisions on the curriculum plan will be made by senior leadership. Middle leaders should be involved in the process of planning the delivery and content of the curriculum. The process is as shown in Figure 5.3.

Having gone through this process, estimates of the number of periods will be required. This should then be checked with staff who will be able to identify potential problems. For example, in secondary schools there will be the added dimension of examination options. The role of middle leaders is critical to the successful development and implementation of an effective curriculum plan.

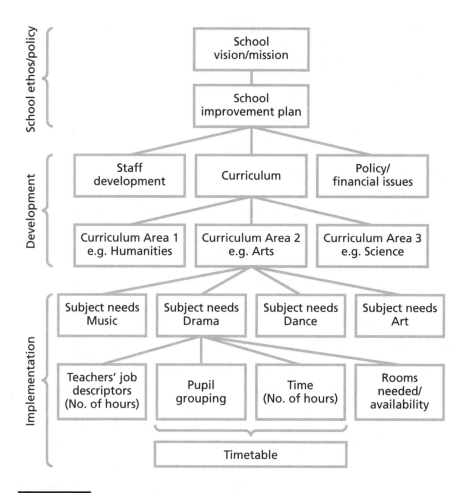

FIG. 5.3 Curriculum plan – process of development and implementation

The introduction of Citizenship Education in 2000 and eight new vocational GCSEs in 2002 increased the demand on curriculum planning. In the primary sector the need for specialist subject teachers has led to significant changes in the structure of the school day in both infant and junior schools. The White Paper, *14–19 Education and Skills* (HMI, 2005) sets out further reforms for the national curriculum and qualifications to be phased in between 2008 and 2013. The proposed reforms are designed *to ensure that every school is a good school and that every child receives increasingly tailored support* (DfES, 2005g). Although the proposed changes – *fourteen sets of specialised diplomas, at three levels up to advanced level, covering the occupational sectors of the economy* (the first five of which will be available in 2008), the introduction of functional skills into GCSEs and an extended project at advanced level (DfES, 2005g) – will undoubtedly increase the pressures on curriculum planning, schools are to be supported in the implementation of the reforms at the local level by LAs and the Learning and Skills Council.

Timetabling

Timetabling is an administrative and team management process. The national curriculum provides a curriculum framework for all schools. Guidelines are given on the number of subjects taught and recommendations of allocated time. This applies to all schools across all phases. The final decision as to how time is distributed is at the discretion of all school leadership teams. How the school is managed will determine the degree of staff involvement in timetabling. Middle leaders need to be able to know and understand the concepts and procedures involved in timetabling and curriculum planning.

- **Curriculum content**, the number of subjects is determined in part by how the school interprets the national curriculum. The content of a school's curriculum should also reflect the ethos of the school. Schools may place an emphasis on technology, sport, expressive arts or languages. This will be reflected in the number of additional periods on the timetable which are allocated to those subjects.

- **Teacher availability** will also determine the content of the curriculum and timetabling. There would be little point deciding to place an emphasis on music without a music specialist. Staff availability is important. The majority of schools employ part-time staff; team leaders need to identify when they are available.

- **Pupils** need to be organised into groups prior to timetabling. Policy decisions will need to be made, i.e. are pupils grouped according to age, ability, group/class size? Such decisions will reflect the ethos of the school. In larger schools, middle leaders and their teams may elect to organise pupils differently to other areas in the school. This will need to be considered within the timetabling process.

- **Time is important!** The use of time on a timetable is often neglected. How the school day is divided is relevant to how pupils learn. Equally relevant is when pupils are taught. Practical considerations should also impact on the timetabling process, for example, movement around the school site and changing for physical education activities. The carrying of kit, books, materials for technology and musical instruments to school on the same day may be a physical impossibility for some children.

■ **Rooms**. Middle leaders may have responsibility for a suite of rooms within the school. The availability of each room and the position of the room will be relevant to delivery of the curriculum. Shared rooms will only 'work' if managed sensitively. Staff needs should be considered. The availability of relevant equipment and access for preparation are both necessary considerations for timetabling.

Before scheduling the timetable, middle leaders should always be asked by the senior leadership team to identify timetabling needs. Keep copies of memos and details of conversations held. Timetabling is a detailed process, aspects of which even the most efficient deputy head teacher may forget!

A timetable for the forthcoming academic year will be written during the summer term once pupil numbers and staffing have been agreed. Leaders will need a clear summary of subjects, teachers, pupils, time and rooms. In order to gather this information, senior leaders will consult with middle leaders who, in turn, meet and discuss all issues and their implications with their team. Analysis of staff needs is essential. All requirements should be listed and presented in a clear format to the senior manager responsible for writing the timetable.

The key to the process is *negotiation*. It may be necessary to manage changes to the timetable over a number of years. There are aspects of the national curriculum and assessment practices which are subject to legislation and must therefore take priority. Other areas might be more flexible, for example in a music department; Table 5.2 highlights where changes might be needed in this specific area.

As the Table 5.2 indicates, the ramifications of change to the structure of the timetable in any of the areas could be considerable. Middle leaders need to know the component parts of the timetable and understand the effect their decisions will make on other subject areas. 'Defending your corner' may not be the most profitable way of approaching timetabling. Compromise is essential; there may be more than one approach to achieving the intended aim. Work with the timetabler and appreciate the enormity of the task.

The following case study is an example of good practice in a co-educational comprehensive school and illustrates the need for a detailed DIP:

TABLE 5.2   Timetable changes – music department

Area	Change(s)	Implications
Subjects	Integrated courses modular curriculum	'blocked' timetable additional staff
Teachers	additional SEN support increased music provision	financial staff development team-building management
Pupils	re-grouping mixed ability teaching additional subjects	rooms financial management management
Time	increased music provision	reduction of time allocated to other subjects staff rooms management
Rooms	specialist rooms, e.g. for music, computers, labs, workshops	financial need for rooms non-sharing management

CASE STUDY

Creative arts development plan 2006–10

This framework is intended to focus the DIPs over the next five years. Towards this we propose to develop in four areas:

- to ensure that the creative arts are recognised as central to the school community

- to enable the creative arts to flourish within the department

- to ensure opportunity for all

- to monitor the resources and funding available to the department in ensuring this development.

Ensure that the creative arts are recognised as central to the school community by:

- raising the profile of the work done by students in the creative arts department through presentation, performance, exhibition and display

- providing the accommodation necessary for the creative arts and the study of the creative arts, and investigating the possibility of shared access to specialist designated arts facilities with other institutions

- providing useful academic and vocational courses and routes through the school, into post-16 and advice for beyond school courses, in all areas of the creative arts

- providing career advice, work experience and information on further and higher education opportunities within the creative arts and cultural industries

- raising the standards of achievement and expectations among students in the work they produce

- supporting new types of creative art, new ways of presenting and interpreting the arts, working with new technologies and monitoring the existing work done in the department

- ensuring well-qualified, informed and trained staff are available to students, whether through staffing of specific short-term projects, or buying in experience for longer term and continuing projects, INSET to meet the needs of permanent staff, and full involvement of all staff in the department in its continual development

- creating manageable teaching group sizes, through rationalising the delivery of the creative arts subjects to all pupils at KS3 and KS4.

Enable the creative arts to flourish within the department by:

- ensuring that opportunities to enjoy and participate in the creative arts are increased and spread more widely through the school

- promoting diversity and variety in the creative arts

- imaginatively managing the greater flexibility available within the curriculum, vocational courses and GCSE, allowing the possibility of extending learning and a commitment within the school to the delivery of creative arts education

- encouraging pride and developing a critically appreciative audience for the creative arts

- encouraging artists-in-residence, student-led work, audiences within the school and participants to raise standards in the creative arts

- working with the LA, local advisers and inspectors, and local and national bodies to develop new opportunities for creative arts projects, cross-curricular links and schemes of work within the creative arts and other departments at the school, and with other schools in the LA

- maintaining, and extending where possible, instrumental music tuition, with particular attention to including instruments from different cultures

- an expectation that students will receive formal exposure and experience in all creative arts practice

- ensuring that all students have experience of professional specialisms, whether outside school, or through workshops and performances by individuals and groups within school.

Ensure opportunity for all by:

- promoting all forms of cultural diversity within the creative arts
- promoting all forms of participation in the creative arts
- developing and updating staff experience through INSET
- recognising the actual and potential contribution of community groups from ethnic minorities to the creative arts, and seeking ways of capitalising on this resource
- making more resources available to groups from ethnic minorities with the potential to extend their creative arts education
- building and developing links with these community groups.

Ensure greater funding for the creative arts from all sources:

- from the allocation of departmental budgets, curriculum development bids, LA, DfES and charitable funding, based on a clear set of costed options
- from the allocation of local educational grants and funding projects, from trust funds, grant agencies and other philanthropic sources, and in partnership with other schools and colleges of further and higher education.
- from partnerships with the private sector, commercial and industrial organisations
- from broadcasting agencies, art centres, galleries, museums, exhibition and concert halls, and theatre companies.

As advised this also contains detailed aims and objectives for a five-year period:

Creative arts development plan aims and objectives related to school aims and objectives

Standards of achievement

To raise the levels of achievement of all pupils through a curriculum within the department that reflects and caters for the needs of an individual student in a multi-cultural, multi-ability school, irrespective of that student's starting point.

Assessment, recording and reporting (ARR)

To continuously develop and implement a departmental system of ARR in line with the whole school system of ARR which provides pupils, parents, staff and other agencies with formative and summative outcomes.

Curriculum

To have in place a curriculum within the department that fits the needs of the students at the school and which takes into account statutory orders and establishes a continuum that opens progression routes post-16.

Creative arts objectives relating to SIP – standards of achievement

Academic year 2006–07

GCSE, vocational and AS and A2 grades to be raised by 5 per cent on previous year. Improve pupils' grades at KS5, KS4, KS3 measured relative to their achievements at KS4, KS3 and KS2.

Building on existing development strategies to facilitate pupils' performances on the NC approaching the national norm at KS3.

Academic year 2007–08

GCSE, vocational and AS and A2 grades to be raised by 5 per cent on previous year. Improve pupils' grades at KS5, KS4, KS3 measured relative to their achievements at KS4, KS3 and KS2.

Building on existing development strategies to facilitate pupils' performances on the NC approaching the national norm at KS3.

To further implement strategies to facilitate students' performances on the NC approaching the national norm at KS3.

Academic year 2008–09

GCSE, vocational and AS and A2 grades to be raised by 5 per cent on previous year. Improve pupils' grades at KS5, KS4, KS3 measured relative to their achievement at KS4, KS3 and KS2.

To have evidence that students' performances on the NC reflect or exceed the national norm at KS3.

Creative arts objectives relating to SIP – assessment, recording and reporting

Academic year 2006–07

To comply with examples of good practice in ARR and modify ARR policy as necessary.

To ensure department compliance with the whole-school ARR policy.

To assist in the evaluation of processes and outcomes of the pilot projects on self-assessment in the creative arts.

To assist in the implementation of the whole school (Year 7–12) National Record of Achievement (NRA) accreditation action plan.

Academic year 2007–08

To build upon and enhance the practice and process of self-assessment within the department.

To continue to monitor department assessment policy, practice and process.

To assist in the continued implementation of the 14–19 action plan.

Academic year 2007–08

To have a system in place to monitor and map the progress of a pupil through the department which provides formative and diagnostic feedback to pupils, parents and staff.

To have a system in place to monitor and map the progress of a pupil across the curriculum which provides summative feedback to pupils, parents and staff.

To evaluate the implementation of the assessment programme at KS3.

To have in place a reporting process which matches the school's 14–19 assessment process that is fully accredited and meets externally validated criteria.

Creative arts objectives relating to SIP – the curriculum

Academic year 2006–07

To review what and how we teach KS3 creative arts.

To establish a KS4 curriculum within creative arts which develops a vocational programme.

To offer creative arts within the options that best meet the needs of pupils who choose these subjects.

To make short-term decisions about vocational qualifications.

To be fully involved in the monitoring and evaluating of the curriculum and to review the creative arts curriculum regularly.

Academic year 2007–08

To establish a KS3 curriculum that improves the continuity of progression from KS3 to KS4 within the creative arts.

To evaluate transition and continuity from KS2 to KS3.

To review what and how we teach KS4 creative arts, vocational and AS/A2 awards.

Academic year 2008–09

To establish a curriculum offer within the department at KS3 that improves continuity of progression from KS3 to KS4.

To evaluate the vocational programme for possible introduction at KS4 within creative arts.

———— Summary ————

Planning is a messy, repetitive and confusing aspect of a managers life. Planning may involve 'going around in circles' as you consider the various combinations of objectives, actions and resources. On balance, leaders who spend time planning on their own will feel resentful when other people become involved and 'spoil' what was a 'good' plan.

The terms 'strategic planning' and 'operational planning' are relatively new concepts in school management. A strategy is a broad statement which relates the overall approach and direction towards the achievement of a mission. Operational planning is about tasks and targets and directly relates to the role of a school's middle leaders – who does what, when and how? Strategic planning is therefore central to the process of managing.

If it is to be effective, the DIP should be placed in the context of the school, LA and national planning. A DIP is similar to the SIP. The DIP should reflect the aims of the SIP and provide an operational framework for implementing the action plans emanating from the SIP. The DIP should enable staff to work 'together' towards a common goal. The process by which the DIP is constructed will reflect management style. Consulting colleagues may be time-consuming. However failure to do so may also be time-consuming.

Planning involves decision-making, individually and collaboratively. A middle leader needs to develop the skills and abilities required to determine when to act on their own and when to collaborate with others. Planning requires collaboration if planned objectives are to be achieved. Middle leaders will build on their team's ability to participate in the leadership and management of the school. A sudden transition to full staff participation will not happen, but middle and senior leaders should be developing teachers' skills within the context of continuing professional development. The transition should be supported by appropriate training and a climate where risk-taking is accepted. Monitoring and evaluation of such processes are necessary for success (see Chapter 10).

REVIEW QUESTIONS

1 What are the essential planning stages in the development of a SIP?

2 SIPs focus on strategies to improve the quality of teaching and learning to raise levels of pupil achievement. What characteristics are common to schools which produce effective SIPs?

3 DIPs are similar to SIPs. What issues need to be considered by a department leader in developing an effective DIP?

TASKS

Chapter 6: Leading teams

Team leadership is pivotal to the success of an effective school. Principles and practice provide guidance for middle leaders in a variety of settings.

Chapter 7: Management of change

Change management is central to all school and college settings. A theoretical approach to this challenging aspect of educational management will provide practitioners with clear guidance and examples of good practice.

Chapter 8: Learning organisations: inclusion, individualised learning and collaboration

How to collaborate within teams, beyond teams and beyond the institution is a key feature of organisational life within the government's agenda for schools. This differs from the market-led ideology of the 1980s and early 1990s which created competition and tension in educational settings.

Chapter 9: Administration and communication

Management of the wider workforce is a feature of current developments in the working practices of teachers and lecturers. This chapter will focus on the administration needed to support these developments.

Chapter 10: Monitoring and evaluation

This chapter will focus on internal and external monitoring and evaluation. The new Ofsted framework will be considered as will LA and school review processes.

chapter six

Leading teams

Effective teamwork

Developing team leadership skills

The team

Motivation

Middle leadership in practice

Middle leadership responsibilities

Summary

_____ Effective teamwork _____

Teams are necessary within the context of schools as organisations and effective teamwork within schools should be valued. Everard *et al.* (2004, 163) stated:

A team is a group of people with common objectives that can effectively tackle any task which it has been set to do. The contribution drawn from each member is of the highest possible quality, and is one which could not have been called into play other than in the context of a supportive team.

Features common to all school leadership teams, across all phases of education, include: structures and roles, and size of team. This chapter defines structures and roles in primary and secondary schools. In the majority of schools middle leaders work in teams (Figure 6.1) the size of which will reflect the size of the school. Subject co-ordinators in small primary/secondary schools may be in a department of one: themselves! Ultimately the place of the middle leader within the structure of the team is that of team leader.

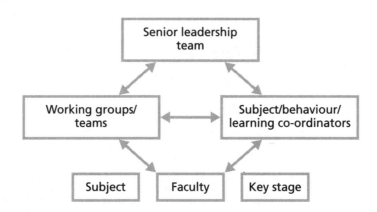

FIG. 6.1   School leadership teams

Trethowan (1985, 3–4) in Coleman and Bush (1994, 265) offers the classification of teams shown in Table 6.1.

TABLE 6.1 Membership of leadership teams (Trethowan, 1985)

Team	Membership
Senior leadership teams	Head teacher and deputy head teacher
Middle leadership teams	Head of department, heads of year
Staff teams	Subject or pastoral staff
Project teams	Ad hoc groups established to achieve short-term goals
Interdisciplinary teams	Compromised of members from various departments to deal with long-term issues

Teams do not act as teams simply because they are described as such. Teams need to work together on a common task. Northouse (2004, 210) ✱ emphasises the need for team leaders *to focus on what makes teams effective or what constitutes team excellence. Leaders, he continues, cannot cognitively analyse and then appropriately function to improve groups without a clear focus on team goals or* outcomes. Employing the criteria for group effectiveness proposed by Hackman and Walton (1986) and characteristics for team excellence proposed by Larson and LaFasto (1989), Northouse (2004, 211–15) advocates the following in the implementation of effective teams:

■ *Clear elevating goals – the team should be kept focused on the goals and outcomes can be evaluated against the objectives.*

■ *Results-driven structure – teams should find the best structure to accomplish their goals.*

■ *Competent team members – team members need to be provided with the appro-* ✱ *priate information and training to carry out their job effectively and to be able to* CA *work collaboratively within the team*

■ *Unified commitment – effective teams do not just happen. They are carefully designed and developed. Involving team members in the various processes can enhance the sense of unity.*

■ *Collaborative climate – founded on trust out of which develops honesty, openness, consistency and respect, where integration of individual actions is seen as one of the fundamental characteristics of effective teams.*

■ *Standards of excellence – need to be clear and concrete where team members feel a certain pressure to perform well. An effective leader can facilitate this process by: requiring results – make expectations clear; reviewing results – provide feedback to resolve performance issues; and rewarding results – acknowledge superior performance.*

- *External support and recognition – provide teams with the necessary resources to carry out the required tasks and reward team member performance, rather than individual achievement.*

- *Leadership-effective teams – are founded on effective team leadership. Leaders influence teams through four processes: cognitive – helps the team to understand the problems with which they are confronted; motivational – unites the team and helps the members to achieve the required standards; affective – helps the team to cope with difficult situations by providing clear goals, assignments and strategies; and co-ordination – matches individual skills to roles, provides clear objectives, monitors feedback and adapts to changes.*

Middle leaders in schools will inevitably work in two types of team: structured teams and those created for specific purposes. Determining the purpose of the team is critical to effective management. Handy (1993) suggested the following functions or purposes of teams which can be applied to schools as organisations:

- *distributing and managing work*
- *problem-solving and decision-making*
- *enabling people to take part in decision-making*
- *co-ordinating and liaising*
- *passing on information*
- *negotiating or conflict resolution*
- *increasing commitment and involvement*
- *monitoring and evaluating.*

———— Developing team leadership skills ————

Developing team skills will involve a balance between concern for team, concern for the task and developing the individual. Few middle leaders are able to achieve this effective balance. Everard *et al.* (2004, 163) highlight the ineffective way *tasks are handled* when teams do not *'gel'*. They further suggest that *when many groups in the school fail to work at peak efficiency the effectiveness of the whole organisation suffers*. West's (1995, 84) model of team leadership which shares many of the characteristics of Northouse's (2004) later delineation of effective teams, provides a practical framework for schools (see Table 6.2).

TABLE 6.2 Leading teams (West, 1995)

KEY FUNCTIONS/ ACTIONS	TASK	TEAM	INDIVIDUAL
Define goals	Clarify goals Establish time-scale Gather information Identify requisite resources Establish parameters of authority	Select/assemble team Explain goal and rationale Generate commitment Encourage questions	Check that individuals understand goals Respond to questions and expressions of concern Involve each person
Plan and decide	Identify options Investigate how to make best use of skills of members Plan timing of events Check resource needs Identify success criteria Generate ownership of plan	Consult with team Brainstorm ideas List suggestions Agree priorities Agree success criteria	Listen to suggestions Identify/assess abilities relevant to the task Coach relevant skills as required
Organise and brief	Establish procedures Draw up brief and action plan Check individual understanding of roles and tasks Listen to and respond to feedback	Set up appropriate structures and agree on sub-tasks Communicate agreed plan Take questions and queries Delegate tasks Finalise plan	Check understanding of individual roles Reward commitment and enthusiasm Reward good ideas Invite feedback

Control, support and monitor	Report progress to key stakeholders at agreed intervals Amend action plan as necessary Set examples Maintain commitment to goals	Co-ordinate work of sub-groups Check resources are in use Provide feedback on tasks Deal with disagreements/conflict Celebrate sub-goal achievement Resolve emergent problems	Provide support to individuals Encourage disclosure of problems Recognise individual achievements Reassure where necessary Check agreed deadlines are on course
Evaluate/ review	Evaluate goal achievement by applying agreed success criteria Report on team performance Consider future action Note potential improvements Recognise and celebrate achievement	Give feedback on achievement Invite team to review their effectiveness Identify learning/ insights gained	Provide individual feedback on goal achievement Recognise individual development Recognise contributions made to the team Gather individual perceptions of team's effectiveness

The team

A middle leader may find identifying the characteristics of their team difficult. The nature of the task and the ethos of the school will influence the working habits of team members. Equally, pressure from external agencies will affect the quality of teams in schools. Family commitments, hobbies and political initiatives are areas of influence on teachers' lives; these, in turn, will influence the individual's commitment to the team. In essence, the quality of the relationships within the team will determine the quality of the task.

Essentially, successful teamwork depends on a clearly defined set of aims and objectives, the personalities of team members and the team manager. Team work is, as with all aspects of effective management, time consuming. Tuckman (1965) defined the stages of team development as:

- **Forming:** The team is not a team but a set of individuals. The focus is on the team purposes, composition, leadership and life-span. Individuals are concerned to establish their personal identities in the team and make some individual impression.

- **Storming:** Having reached a consensus on the team's purpose, conflict arises as assumptions are challenged. Personal agendas are revealed and some inter-personal hostility may be generated. Successful handling enables the team to reach fresh agreement on purpose, procedures and norms.

- **Norming:** The team seeks to establish its norm and practices: when and how it should work. As working procedures are established there will be a communication of feelings, mutual support and sense of team identity.

- **Performing:** Solutions to problems emerge, the team is mature and productive. Individuals and team are relaxed and confident.

Middle leaders should aim to lead and participate in effective teams which agree aims, share skills, realise potential and reduce stress and anxiety. A middle leader should avoid the pitfalls of weak management which include:

- over-emphasis on people
- over-emphasis on task
- over-emphasis on agendas, not processes
- reacting to events, not anticipating them
- failure to celebrate success, individual and team.

The complexity of the middle leader's role is further illustrated by West-Burnham's nine components of team effectiveness as presented in Coleman and Bush (1994, 279–80):

1 **Explicit and shared values**. No team can operate effectively unless it is working in a context where the values are clear and agreed, and translated into a mission.

2 **Situational leadership**. The team is sufficiently mature to base leadership on function and needs rather than power and status. Skills are more important than hierarchical factors. This requires a willingness by the designated leader to stand back and allow other team members to assume control according to the needs of the situation.

3 **Pride in the team**. This implies commitment and involvement and is manifested in high morale and loyalty. Team members have self-belief, and confidence in others and the team as a whole.

4 **Clear task**. The outcome which the team is created to achieve is clear, realistic and understood. Teams are motivated by tangible goals, clear outcomes and a firm time-scale.

5 **Review**. Effective teams learn and develop by a process of continuous feedback and review. Team review is a permanent feature of every activity and leads to more effective working.

6 **Openness**. Teams achieve a high level of candour in review and exchange. There are no 'hidden agendas' and there is praise and criticism. The latter is frank and direct, but constructive rather than negative.

7 **Lateral communication**. Team members are able to communicate with each other without reference to the team leader. Networks are formed and nourished by the team.

8 **Collaboration**. Decisions are shared and have full commitment. Quality decisions emerge from the full utilisation of the knowledge and skills of team members.

9 **Action**. Team decisions are expressed in terms of action. Each team member knows what has to be done, by whom and when. Effective teams issue agreed actions after their meetings.

Motivation

Perhaps the most important element of team leadership is the ability to motivate others. Staff who are motivated and committed to educational excellence create an environment which motivates pupils. Managers who know and understand this will enable staff to develop professionally. Team leaders should create conditions which focus on achieving excellence. A middle leader should encourage participation and facilitate teamwork. As a team leader, a middle leader will serve as a role model to team members. Stoll *et al.* (2003, 122) suggest that o*ne of the most powerful ways* *leaders can lead others' learning is through modelling.* Middle leaders should inspire and motivate others to achieve high standards and to work towards fulfilment of the school's aims. In practice this will require middle leaders to:

- provide staff with challenges and intellectual stimulation
- celebrate the ways staff help pupils
- practise participatory decision-making
- encourage teamwork and collegiality
- develop positive appraisal systems
- enhance individuals' self-esteem
- articulate performance expectations
- be aware of and use the rewards that staff members value
- be aware of and use various types of feedback systems.

Clearly motivation is more than satisfaction; it also requires knowledge and understanding of what is expected. The most important aspect is sharing a common goal which is highly valued by the team.

Middle leadership in practice

The emergence of middle leaders in primary schools has been a response to the needs of primary teachers, who have experienced immense curriculum change and associated administrative burdens. As a consequence, there has been a need to promote the development of common understanding and good relationships (Knutton and Ireson, 1995, 60). New initiatives have to be addressed by head teachers. These focus on the need to facilitate the development of middle leaders in their institutions. Bradley *et al.* (1983) comment on the need to support school leadership by:

- *fostering a collaborative and participative approach;*
- *making maximum use of the talents of each member of staff, by creating an efficient structure of responsibilities within the school and then delegating effectively;*
- *encouraging staff to take responsibility for their own development.*

Primary school middle leaders will understand the processes involved in developing management skills. This section has shown, albeit briefly, that there are general skills which can be identified in primary and secondary schools. The key difference between leadership of primary and secondary schools is that secondary schools perceive leadership posts as points on a hierarchical scale. In contrast, primary colleagues perceive management as curriculum-focused and task-orientated.

Bennett (1995, 101) sustains the view that many middle leaders in primary schools deny the validity of the concept. Bennett (101–4) does, however, acknowledge that there are five characteristics that generate a need for middle leaders. Briefly:

1 **The size of the school**, the smallest secondary school is larger than *most* primary schools. In addition to the teaching staff, there is a body of technicians and support staff. The organisation is larger, needing greater administrative and managerial support. There is also the need for communicating information to a larger number of pupils, parents, outside agencies and employees than the number involved in primary schools. Some arrangement has to be made to communicate.

2 **The nature of the work** is determined by the national curriculum.

3 **How the work is organised**. The pastoral system with a combination of guidance and disciplinary functions has a significant role in secondary schools. There has been a move since the 1980s to strengthen the guidance function and develop a teaching focus through programmes of personal and social education, passing the disciplinary function to subject departments as a teaching issue. In contrast, a primary teacher has a responsibility to relate to all subject co-ordinators of the subjects they teach, thus creating a complex web of formal relationships. In both primary and secondary schools, teachers can be both superordinate and subordinate to each other. However, in secondary schools teachers may work in isolated teams and are less likely to experience close collegial working relationships with the whole staff.

4 **The national funding structure for schools** has also had a significant impact on secondary school middle management. Since the ERA (1988), schools are funded on a formula based largely on the number of pupils of particular ages on the roll. Subject departments are similarly funded to a formula encompassing the number of pupils for each age being taught and its subsequent resourcing needs. As a consequence, departments will compete with each other to gain the maximum number of students.

5 **Teachers' status**. Teachers' salaries, status and promotion prospects are also affected by the size of the school. Changes to school leadership have created the need for teachers to be responsible for the sub-units of the school.

Middle leadership responsibilities

Middle leaders will have specific responsibilities identified in the job description for each position within the structure of the school. The statutory *School Teachers' Pay and Conditions Document* (STPCD) (DfES, 2005e) gives guidance, in line with the *National Agreement*, of the duties of a main pay grade (MPG) teacher. *The National Agreement* aims to raise standards and tackle workload in schools. It is the function of the Workforce Agreement Monitoring Group (WAMG) to monitor the implementation of the *National Agreement*. On a regular basis, WAMG issues guidance notes, which reflect the agreed position of all the signatories, to support schools in implementing the *National Agreement*. By June 2005, 12 notes, which are updated online, had been issued. However, additional advice is given by a number of agencies including:

- National Remodelling Team (NRT)
- National Joint Council (NJC) for government initiatives
- governors' associations
- individual trade unions
- LAs.

Additional responsibilities

A middle leader will also have the additional responsibilities, which are adapted from those described by Armstrong *et al.* (1993b, 28–9), shown in Table 6.3.

TABLE 6.3 A middle leader's additional responsibilities

Staff (teaching and non-teaching)	■ Selection, including job specification in consultation with the head teacher, compilation of advertisements, selecting the short list and interview procedure
	■ Deployment, including equitable distribution of classes and timetabling
	■ Appraisal
	■ Support, including induction of new staff and students on teaching practice
	■ Staff development and in-service training including contribution to school improvement plans
	■ Maintaining morale

	■ Supervision
	■ Organisation of departmental meetings
Curriculum development	■ Aims and objectives: their statement, evaluation and modification
	■ Syllabus, selection and design
	■ Monitoring, including the recording of progress of new courses
	■ Evaluation
	■ Methodology
	■ Responding to national and local initiatives
	■ Implementing school policies and curriculum statements (e.g. equal opportunities, information technology, language across the curriculum and special needs)
Curriculum management	■ Schemes of work
	■ Examination administration – internal and external (excluding invigilation)
	■ Setting cover work for staff absence
	■ Continuity and progression – KS2 to KS3 and KS4 onwards
Resources	■ Management of equipment and stock
	■ Security, especially of hazardous substances
	■ Organisation of field trips and visits
	■ Development of teaching resources
Pupil progress	■ Assessment – development and supervision of formative and summative profiling systems, including those related to national testing
	■ Internal and external moderation procedures
	■ Grouping – organisation of student groups to encourage effective learning and progression
	■ Motivation, discipline and welfare
Record keeping	■ Co-ordination and upkeep of departmental records, group lists, staff and pupils' records, including profiles and records of achievement
	■ Compilation, collation and security of records of examination assessments
	■ Administration of national tests

Liaison	■ With members of the department
	■ With parents, employers, industry, etc.
	■ With senior management, heads of year, other departments, ancillary staff
	■ With feeder schools and colleges
	■ With officers, advisers and Inspectorate
	■ With external moderators and assessors
	■ With governors
Safety	■ Overall responsibility with the department
	■ Checks on implementation of LA policy
	■ Reporting problems to the head teacher and LA
	■ Liaison with schools' safety officer and LA safety officers

Table 6.3 refers to a department or subject-based area. Schools also have highly complex pastoral teams. Although the *National Agreement* exempts teachers from certain pastoral responsibilities (counselling), Calvert and Henderson highlight the demands placed on middle leaders by pastoral duties (1995, 70):

[. . .] pastoral [care . . .] places special demands on managers to provide a supportive framework, which will equip pupils to cope with the ever-increasing pressures of life. Often under-valued and misunderstood, inadequately resourced and prepared for, pastoral provision can be patchy.

All teachers are involved in pastoral care as it permeates every aspect of school life. Formally there are two pastoral roles experienced by the majority of teachers and co-ordinated by middle leaders: heads of year and personal social and health education (PSHE) co-ordinators. Form tutors have responsibility for administration, discipline and welfare of pupils. PSHE teachers (who may be the form tutor) are responsible for teaching a set syllabus encompassing a range of issues: personal, social, vocational and moral.

A strong framework to co-ordinate those involved in the different aspects of pastoral care is needed. Middle leaders of pastoral teams need to be good managers, capable of building teams, resolving conflicts and providing support. Pastoral teams will need to have a shared commitment to the needs of pupils and teachers. If senior leaders are to recognise the developmental needs of pastoral co-ordinators and teams, training should be provided.

Change management teams

The following case study is taken from the NRT website at **www.remodelling.org**. The LA remodelling adviser for Buckinghamshire, Steve Edgar, writes about the deployment of remodelling consultants as a team to support schools in remodelling which includes:

- supporting schools in implementing the contractual change
- increasing capacity to meet remodelling targets
- creating a team of remodelling consultants
- evaluation of remodelling events
- delivery of school PPA training
- sharing expertise across the LA.

I was appointed initially as a senior adviser within the School Improvement Service in January 2003 and assumed responsibility for remodelling, alongside my other responsibilities, after a few months in post. Throughout 2003–04 the number of colleagues supporting remodelling within Buckinghamshire was very small.

A small number of advanced skills teachers (ASTs) with expertise in 'Working with Support Staff' had been appointed in the LEA in early 2003 and the schools where a number of these ASTs taught featured within the group of schools who were the first to remodel. These ASTs provided effective links between teachers and support staff in their schools, they had capacity to support change, including where appropriate the school change team.

The key role of the central team has clearly changed over a very short period. The role has moved from direct delivery to co-ordination, the challenge will be the need to ensure consistency and quality and to ensure that the wider programme is monitored and the quality continuously improves.

It is too early to have completed an evaluation as to the overall benefits and concerns of working with this extended team. The immediate challenge is maintaining a consistent approach given the size of the team and developing effective strategies to monitor activities during very busy weeks. One surprising early observation has been the reaction of some head teachers when their tranche leader turns out to be a head teacher from a different school. Learning from others is however a central process within networked learning communities and perhaps in years to come, the remodelling process will be shown to have been instrumental in leading the way here as well.

Question

Having read this case study, what can you do to develop teams within and beyond your school? List your suggestions under the following headings.

To do	Action

Summary

There are many features common to all school management teams, across all phases of education. In the majority of schools middle leaders work in teams. The size of each team will reflect the size of the school. It is axiomatic that teams are necessary within the context of schools as organisations. As a middle leader, it is critical to understand that teams do not act as teams simply because they are described as such.

Middle leaders in schools will inevitably work in two types of team; structured teams and those created for specific purposes. Essentially, successful teamwork depends on a clearly defined set of aims and objectives, the personalities of team members and the team manager. Developing middle leadership skills will involve a balance between concern for team, concern for the task and developing the individual. A middle leader may find identifying the characteristics of their team difficult.

Middle leaders should aim to lead and participate in effective teams which agree aims, share skills, realise potential and reduce stress and anxiety. Perhaps the most important element of team leadership is the ability to motivate others. As a team leader, a middle leader will serve as a role model to their team members. Middle leaders should inspire and motivate others to achieve high standards and to work towards fulfilment of the school's aims.

REVIEW QUESTIONS

1 What characteristics delineate an effective team?

2 As a middle leader how would you form and manage your team effectively?

3 One of the principle issues underpinning team leadership is motivation of the team. As a middle leader how would you ensure that your team is motivated?

4 What are the key areas of responsibility for a middle leader?

chapter seven

Management of change

Why change?

Middle leaders and change

Change management teams

Analysis of change

Resistance to change

Choosing a change strategy

Implementing change

National Remodelling Team approach to change

Evaluating change

Summary

——————— Why change? ———————

Since the introduction of compulsory education in the 19th century there has been continuous change within the education system. The underlying assumption is that change is necessary in order to respond to other circumstances that happen within society. Schools, as organisations, develop, mature and adjust to both internal and external changes. Drucker (1980) stated that:

All institutions live and perform in two time periods, that of today and that of tomorrow. Tomorrow is being made today, irrevocably in most cases. Managers therefore have to manage both today – the fundamentals – and tomorrow. In turbulent times, managers cannot assume that tomorrow will be an extension of today. On the contrary they must manage for change; change both as an opportunity and as a threat.

Change is important and complex; whilst it can be unsettling, threatening and unpredictable it is also an opportunity for creativity and learning. For the school, team and individual change provides the opportunities to:

- acquire/practise new skills
- increase job satisfaction
- improve working practices
- work with new people
- improve use of time and skills
- increase responsibility
- increase reward
- increase efficiency.

With change comes accountability. Following Callaghan's Ruskin College speech (1976) education has become more accountable for the way in which it serves society.

As shown in Table 7.1, the government began workforce reform with the 2002 Education Act, *Extended Schools* (HMG, 2003; DfES, 2005f) and *Every Child Matters* (DfES, 2003b). The government established remodelling advisers (now extended schools remodelling advisers) to help LAs support schools with the implementation of the *National Agreement: Raising Standards and Tackling Workload* (WAMG, 2003).

TABLE 7.1   Key developments and policy documents

2002	Education Act
	Extended schools
2003	National Agreement
	Time for Standards: Transforming the School Workforce
	National Remodelling Team
	School Teacher Pay and Conditions
	Every Child Matters
2004	Children Act
	Five year Strategy on Education
2005	*Every Child Matters: Children's Workforce Strategy*
	Common Core of Skills and Knowledge
	Common Assessment Framework

In addition, supplementary policies on finance (DfES, 2003c), skills and knowledge (DfES, 2005b) and a common assessment framework (DfES, 2005c) have been produced as well as further government legislation and details of earlier policies. Each new document contributes to school practice but has also swamped practitioners with ever more advice to be absorbed. In 2005, further advice was also provided by the TDA (Developing Multi-agency Teams) and the Study Support Team's Extended Schools Framework. There are also local policies which supersede or supplement the national policies in the context of LA reform; the creation of Children's Trusts is an example of such change. This is to replace LAs bringing together services that embrace the social, educational and economic well-being of children as determined by *Every Child Matters* (DfES, 2003b). Other measures to support the change process include:

■ a concerted attack on unnecessary paperwork and bureaucratic processes, through the establishment of the Internal Review Unit (IRU), with a practitioners' panel including a senior school administrator

■ recruitment of new managers from outside education who can contribute effectively to schools' leadership teams

■ additional resources and support from a national 'change management' programme to help delivery of the reforms.

Change is a theme which remains constant in all areas of educational practice and children's services. Schools are at the centre of these changes as they embrace and respond to social, technical, environmental, educational and political (ideological) changes that are the make-up of the society in which we live.

Change means different things to different people depending where they are placed in relationship to the change. Dame Pat Collarbone (*Guardian*, 2005) outlines change in relation to remodelling:

Workforce remodelling is about enabling teachers to deliver even better education for pupils than they do at present. It's putting in place new ways of working that enable people to have a better work–life balance. It not only focuses teachers on teaching and learning but it also opens a new world of opportunities for staff other than teachers... Remodelling is about forming fresh working relationships, about getting the whole system geared up to working in new ways.

Collarbone further advises (Ibid.) that we do not want to fall into the trap of creating more work for ourselves. It is really an opportunity to say how we might work more effectively with the child as the focus. Remodelling will encourage further changes; each school is now responsible for a self-directed approach in partnership with other agencies. This will involve the whole school community in equipping itself for change. The wider workforce and wider network is intended to provide additional support as required. The aim? To raise achievement in order to improve results.

Remodelling provides the challenge and opportunity for schools to set their own agenda. Given the scope of the change, the remodelling process will include the community within and beyond the school gates. Schools are not alone but part of a wide network of support involving LAs, the NRT, GTC(E), CWDC and NCSL. Schools can *develop the core offer of extended services by working in partnership with existing local private or voluntary sector providers or by building on existing links with other local schools and working as a cluster*. Although LAs provide advice as to which services/agencies are willing to work in partnership with schools, Education Improvement Partnerships offer a means of bringing together local providers. Their prospectus can be obtained through the following website: **www.standards.dfes.gov.uk/sie/si/ educationimprovementpartnerships** (DfES, 2005f, 19).

The NRT suggest that for schools engaging with the remodelling process, they might expect:

- *teaching and learning is the main focus*
- *the workforce is involved in making decisions*
- *tasks and activities are undertaken by the appropriate people within flexible working patterns*
- *managing change is a normal part of school life*
- *the school shares experiences and learning with other schools*

- *the work–life balance is acceptable to the whole workforce*
- *all workforce and other stakeholders are aware of the direction of the school.*

(NRT website **www.remodelling.org**)

Remodelling will impact upon the school community as a whole; it is axiomatic that remodelling should benefit learners. The positive outcomes of remodelling might include raising achievement, partnership, increased interest and/or motivation of staff and pupils, improved learner social skills and behaviour, attendance and punctuality.

——————— Middle leaders and change ———————

Middle leaders need to enable their teams to accommodate change. This should be a collaborative process involving innovation, implementation and adoption. The real problem is how to manage change effectively. Remodelling is a mixture of top-down, bottom-up and expert changes, each of which is discussed below.

Top-down

When someone in a position of authority introduces change, there is little the middle leader can do to influence the proposals. This scenario involves a clear statement by the decision-maker(s), followed by action and dissemination. The national curriculum is an example of the top-down approach. Leadership, collaboration and a willingness to take (not make) decisions will make the difference between poor and excellent practice. A top-down model will allow changes to be made quickly, efficiently and with authority.

Bottom-up

A consequence of collaborative management is a bottom-up approach to the management of change. Remodelling has the potential to be bottom-up. This approach involves teams and will therefore concern middle leaders when:

- the need is to address a problem which remains unclear to those not involved
- a school- or department-specific solution is required.

A disadvantage to this approach is that it is time consuming to plan and implement, as there is a need for consultation and agreement. Most phases of remodelling will require involvement of all staff, especially those involved in the classroom.

Expert

A leader may approach an expert if unsure how to tackle an issue. The expert could be a member of the senior leadership team, colleague or external agent. The expert approach may offer a quick and cost-effective means of bringing about change but could mean loss of influence and control.

Middle leaders need to take a broad view in order to achieve the best possible outcomes. Experts may be among the team, which might maintain the team's and the school's objectives.

Middle leaders may be unable to effect change due to the constraints of their position. A middle leader will need to ascertain:

■ Who are the main players involved – staff, pupils, parents, governors?

■ Who will manage the change process – senior management, middle management, colleagues, external agents?

■ How will the change be evaluated – time-scale, questions?

■ Does the change relate to school/department improvement plans?

■ Who will be responsible for recognising the need for change and making it happen?

_____ Change management teams _____

It is clear that remodelling and other changes will require the use of external agencies and experts. The expert could be a member of the senior leadership team or external agent such as an LA remodelling adviser. The introduction of an expert for remodelling could mean loss of influence and control. Consequently the school will need to ensure that the change process is managed by the change management team (CMT) so that it can be evaluated in terms of impact.

The NRT considers that the result will be rising standards, measurable through:

■ pupils' exam results

■ improved behaviour and attendance

■ staff recruitment, retention and morale

- school is more popular
- stakeholder expectations met
- *Every Child Matters*.

Developing the remodelled workforce/managing change

- The range of activities for the remodelled workforce must be determined by all staff.
- The remodelled workforce must be engaged according to school needs and priorities.
- Training and resources are essential to effective change.
- Government initiatives include dedicated time for planning, preparation and assessment.
- Workload planning can assist with the implementation of school workforce reform.
- Professional development for managing the new workforce is required.

Analysis of change

Change can take place at different levels, which need to be identifiable. The level of change will impact on those who are involved in the process of change. Factors influencing change (see Table 7.2) may also create barriers to change. So, what will change involve?

Middle leaders will need to reflect on their own attitude towards change. This will influence their team. Generally people who have a sense of commitment and are in charge of their lives will see change as an opportunity. Those who are uncomfortable with their role will view change negatively. Every school will have a combination of people who view change on a continuum from threat to opportunity! There may be individuals who will not be threatened by the change, but will feel threatened by the change process.

TABLE 7.2   Factors influencing change

Factor	Result
Technical	Change in process or use of equipment (e.g. management procedures or computers).
Social	Changes to beliefs and values, creation of a group (e.g. religion or football team).
Power	Changes in political leadership at a macro and micro level (e.g. political party, head of school or head of department).
Financial	Change in funding mechanism (e.g. availability of resources).
Personnel	Change in status, family or own (e.g. marriage, divorce, children).
Physical	Change in school site (e.g. condition of buildings, available facilities).

In the context of remodelling and workforce reform, some staff will be enthusiastic, whilst others may view it with fear, or as a threat. As with other aspects of the school, staff reaction to change will reflect the ethos of the school. Oldroyd and Hall (1990) identify settings where staff response was poor, which should be considered as part of the remodelling process:

■ *morale is low*

■ *change agents are not respected*

■ *there is a track record of failed innovation*

■ *risk-taking is discouraged*

■ *leaders are inflexible in their attitudes*

■ *there is little outside support . . .*

. . . teachers will be less motivated to support change strategies *which*

■ *are unaccompanied by practical training and support*

■ *do not adapt to developing circumstances*

■ *do not recognise local needs*

■ *offer no sense of collective 'ownership'*

■ *do not build a 'critical mass' for change.*

Neither will they commit themselves to innovations which:

■ *are not seen as beneficial*

■ *cannot be clearly understood*

■ *are at odds with their professional beliefs*

■ *are inadequately resourced.*

_____ Resistance to change _____

People will resist change, especially if it is someone else's change that has been forced upon them. Resistance to change can be a major restraining force that can be overcome with understanding. Change may incur resistance due to self-interest, misunderstanding, different assessments of the situation or, as stated, a low tolerance for change. Common responses to change are 'political' behaviour, rumour, disagreement and/or excuses.

Westhuizen (1996) identified the resistance factors from his survey of all school principals in secondary schools in the Free State Province of South Africa. These are grouped in response to the key areas of change in the context of the remodelling process in Table 7.3.

TABLE 7.3   Remodelling barriers to change (adapted from Westhuizen, 1996)

Workforce reform

- fear that change will cause a loss in job security
- the loss of established customs which provide security
- a disruption of the status quo (existing practices) which provides satisfaction
- fear that change will not succeed
- a low tolerance for change
- the lack of resources to facilitate change
- insufficient evaluation of the progress of the change
- the lack of a positive climate for change
- poor performance motivation
- the lack of support from the management team of the school during the change process
- weak strategies for managing resistance to change
- the absence of participative decision-making

Extended schools

- the perception that change is not regarded as an improvement
- increased work pressure
- the lack of creative power
- authoritarian leadership
- the lack of courage to take risks

- unclear role definitions
- wrong timing for the implementation of change
- previous experience reveals no need for change
- application of the wrong strategy for change
- a high level of organisational conflict
- insufficient communication between the school principal and staff
- staff distrust in the management team of the school

Every child matters
- fear of the unknown
- the absence of a need to change
- an inability to handle uncertainty during the change process
- an irreconcilability of cultural characteristics with the proposed change
- a workforce who do not understand the aims/purpose of the change
- doubt about own abilities

Negotiation can be a relatively easy way to avoid major resistance. However, team leaders must be sure of the parameters in which they are working to avoid a negative outcome. The government's intention is that all schools have the necessary structures and tools to successfully implement change and be supportive through training, listening and providing time during busy periods.

 Choosing a change strategy

Strategies for implementing change can be summarised as follows:

- **Directed** – imposing change by management, top-down, hierarchical
- **Negotiated** – concedes everyone's wishes
- **Action-centred** – as a consequence of action research.

In order to choose an effective change strategy the CMT will need to:

- identify the level of complexity and time needed
- identify resistance and analyse
- select the method of overcoming resistance
- take account of their own attitude towards the change.

The choice of strategy adopted will be dependent on the pace of change, level of resistance, level of status of the initiator, amount of information required, key players and time available. Schools should not ignore these factors. A common mistake is to move too quickly and involve too few people.

Forcing change will have too many negative side effects. Equally, knowing and understanding change strategies will only go part-way to facilitating the change process.

As with all aspects of management, interpersonal skills are critical to success when managing change. The choice of strategy adopted will be dependent on:

- the pace of change
- level of resistance
- level of status of the initiator
- amount of information required
- key players
- time available.

Schools, as organisations, should not ignore these factors. A leader can improve the chances of success by:

1 Analysis	■ current situation
	■ problems
	■ possible causes of problems
2 Evaluation	■ factors relevant to producing changes
3 Selection	■ change strategy
4 Monitoring	■ implementation

As with all aspects of leadership, interpersonal skills are critical to the successful and effective management of change.

_____ Implementing change _____

Schools, as organisations, have the necessary structures and tools to successfully implement change.

Action research may provide the most appropriate way forward for managing change in a school. Action research involves identification of a practical problem/issue which is changed through individual or collaborative action, then researched. The problems may not be clearly defined and the change process may evolve through practice. As a mechanism for change, action research contains two key elements: collaboration and evaluation. By involvement, the team will try out a number of approaches to the problem and will learn from each; this will take time.

INSET

Schools can achieve change through a programme of education and training. An education and communication programme can inform and provide a platform for analysis in which resistors can engage in debate surrounding the implementation of change. This approach will require a lot of time and effort if it is to be effective. Middle leaders can (and should) play an active role in the planning of INSET programmes if they are to be relevant to practice.

Participation and involvement

As team leaders, middle leaders should encourage participation in the development and implementation process. Through participation, resistors become informed and are able to contribute to the outcome of change. The participation process can be difficult and time consuming. When change is required immediately, it may not be possible!

Support

Another means of dealing with potential resistance to change is to be supportive through training, listening and providing time during busy periods. Support is most effective when fear and anxiety lie at the heart of resistance. Again, this can be time consuming and does not always produce positive results.

Negotiation

A middle leader will need to be a skilled negotiator. All but major resistance can be costly and is therefore best avoided, negotiation can be a relatively easy way to avoid major resistance. However, managers must be sure of the parameters in which they are working to avoid a negative outcome.

Co-option

A form of manipulation is co-option, inviting resistors to join as change agents. Often the change will occur without the individual noticing. This will be difficult to maintain in the long-term as people do not enjoy being manipulated.

Coercion

This is a risky process, as inevitably people will become resentful and the costs are high.

Successful approaches to change will often involve a combination of the above. Middle leaders will require the knowledge and understanding, skills and ability to approach change.

___ National Remodelling Team approach to change ___

To guide schools in their remodelling, the NRT is promoting a change process based on the techniques and experience gained in business and education, and tried successfully with pilot schools. CMTs and collaboration are two of five key elements that the NRT is recommending for successful remodelling. The NRT recognises that schools are not all the same and that each school is in a position to create a change environment that suits it.

The following boxed extract outlines the NRT stages for the remodelling process as adapted from business models. Schools need to use the remodelling process to help identify and agree where change is necessary, facilitate a vision of the future which is shared across whole school communities and create plans for change in an atmosphere of serious consensus. It is important to remember that remodelling schools apply a generic process with the aim of producing unique outcomes.

> **The mobilise stage** – Schools recognise the need for change. School representatives attend remodelling training events organised on a local or regional basis by LAs working individually or collaboratively. At these events schools are introduced to the remodelling process and to the tools and techniques which remodelling deploys. Key to the success of remodelling is that the nature, scope and goals of remodelling are effectively communicated to school communities.
>
> **The discover stage** – Once the school has been mobilised and an inclusive change team has been formed the remodelling process begins

to focus on uncovering the issues around workload and other school priorities. The discover stage involves identifying and acknowledging what works well within a school as well as recognising issues and challenges which the change process should aim to address. This often involves holding workshops with staff members to discover why some elements of school practice are more successful than others. Throughout the change process it is important that the work of the school change team is transparent and that there are good channels of communication which allow the team to feedback to the whole school.

The deepen stage – When the school change team acquires a greater understanding of the scale and scope of the change issues. Teams use the remodelling tools and techniques to help identify the root causes of issues and understand which staff members are most affected.

The develop stage – The school change team uses problem-solving techniques to develop strategies and solutions to address the issues identified at previous stages. Although learning from other schools can be of vital assistance, remodelling allows schools to develop plans which are 'made-to-measure', and which will be effective and sustainable.

The deliver stage – When plans are confirmed and start to be implemented. It is essential that there is a continuing review process which ensures that as change happens it meets the original goals identified at earlier stages and moves the school towards the shared vision of the future. There may be a need for solutions to be modified as they are put into practice.

Source: NRT (2003) website http://www.remodelling.org/

Evaluating change

It is often difficult to test the outcome of change against the original objectives. There are often unintended outcomes, and defining criteria for success is problematic. If the objectives have been carefully constructed, evaluation should be possible. As change agents, middle leaders will set objectives which can be measured after the change has been implemented. Evaluation can often proceed simultaneously with the change programme; this should not be left until the end.

Managing change

The NRT website **www.remodelling.org** contains several case studies on how various schools have coped with the remodelling process. Below is one reflecting creative interpretation of the changes resulting from workforce reform at Whittingham C of E First School.

In our remodelling journey, we have been able to look deep down and reassess the core purpose of our jobs – that is to provide excellence in teaching and learning and raise the standards of pupil achievement in all that we do. This focus has been of prime importance to the school, which has launched itself into the true spirit of the remodelling process.

Once staff understood the concept of workforce reform, they embraced it wholeheartedly. This was most evident in the formation of the change team – every member of staff wanted to be involved. The school has grown quite substantially over the last few years from four members of staff to 15. With greater numbers in the change team, there are now also more dynamics at work. There is a greater emphasis on making sure we all have the time to meet.

Getting it right in remodelling

At the 'deepen' stage – where we really looked into the emotional and political issues involved in the process – we realised that we really had to get it right if remodelling was to work. That meant being comfortable talking about our issues. What came out of that was really useful since it highlighted particular areas concerning time management – all issues were personal to each member of staff but many commonalities were drawn up at this stage. Since we were all together, we could prioritise this and look at individual workloads. Our workforce reform adviser gave us the idea for the picture frame exercise: this is where you have picture frame boxes one inside the other and each one has a different level of task. Staff were asked to identify what tasks they always found time to do in the centre frame, tasks sometime addressed in the next frame and so on. Then we reflected on what our role really should be and soon arrows and rubbings out were appearing all over the picture! This proved to be a really useful and empowering exercise, enabling us to really examine what the core purpose of our jobs should be.

Being inventive about cover and PPA

We have to be very inventive when it comes to providing time for cover and for PPA. This has involved a mixture of getting funds that pay for cover, being creative with the timetable and taking on additional part-time teaching staff. Lead teaching by subject specialists within school, supported by two TAs with three small year groups has proven a really successful way of addressing PPA time – while ensuring that the pupil continues to receive a consistent level of learning. At the beginning of the session, the subject leader teacher will introduce the learning objectives for the two classes and will then leave to take their PPA time. The two classes will then continue to be taught by the remaining teacher with two TAs in support, having already been briefed on the key objectives and lesson plan. At the end of the session, the lead teacher will come back to go through the learning objectives and assess what has been achieved.

As a teaching head, I was class-based every morning. By increasing my class-share teacher's hours and changing our working week, parents are now beginning to perceive the class as my responsibility on a Monday and Friday and my share teacher's during the rest of the week. This frees me up at the beginning and end of the day on those occasions to deal with any issues arising.

Good at innovation

Class responsibility is one of the major workload issues for teaching heads – being well-planned, prepared and flexible are all 'musts', however leading by example is also easy, because if I ask a member of staff to do something, I also have to do it! In small schools, we have to be good at innovation – that means sharing the planning, making sure we've covered the curriculum and so on. I am particularly pleased with how parents perceive us and the amazing support they give to their children's learning, both in and out of school.

Remodelling has certainly taken longer than we expected, but we feel that now we are getting somewhere. I think that one of the main hurdles was getting over to the teachers the fact that they could come out of the classroom and take their PPA time. We could only achieve this by guaranteeing high-quality supervision in the classroom. The staff's attitude and understanding has been a really big enabler of the change process. It helps that they all care for each other in the first place, but we also have a very high level of support staff. We viewed the starting point as not getting rid of the 24 tasks but to look at our support staff and see how they could help, first acknowledging the re-organisation of their timetables.

A positive experience

Everyone values everyone else's position in the school. We now do half-term training – termed Buddy training – where key stage 2 staff team up with early years teachers and get to appreciate and understand other staff member's jobs. It's always difficult getting everyone together, but by utilising post-entry training funds, we are all able to go to a country house hotel twice a year to focus on school improvement plan issues.

Remodelling has been a very positive experience in our school. We have everyone on board – staff, parents and governors are involved at all stages. It does make you look hard at the way you do things. As our remodelling adviser once said: 'Take a risk – think outside the box.'

Question

Having read this case study, what can you do to manage change? Set your answers out in a table with the following headings.

Middle leader: action points	Team: action points

——— Summary ———

Management of change is a recurring theme in education. The reason for change is that education has to respond to the circumstances and events that happen in society. It is axiomatic that in society, change is on the increase. Change is important and complex.

Before implementing change it is important to consider whether the change is necessary. A middle leader is in a position which will enable them to identify and implement change as a positive tool in strategic planning.

Change will occur as a consequence of external pressures. Middle leaders need to enable their teams to accommodate change. As a middle leader you will encounter three types of internal pressures for change:

- top-down
- bottom-up
- expert.

Middle leaders need to take a broad view in order to achieve the best possible outcomes. Change can take place at different levels, which need to be identifiable. Some staff will be enthusiastic, whilst others may view change with fear, seeing it as a threat.

Middle leaders should reflect on their own attitude towards change. People will resist change, especially if it is someone else's change that has been forced upon them.

When change is implemented in the school, a disturbance of the status quo occurs.

Action research may provide the most appropriate way forward for managing change in a school. As a mechanism for change, action research contains two key elements: collaboration and evaluation. Schools, as organisations, will have the necessary structures and tools to successfully implement change:

- INSET
- participation and involvement
- support
- negotiation
- co-option
- coercion

and, of course, change management teams.

REVIEW QUESTIONS

- Remodelling embraces workforce reform, *Extended Schools* and the principles that underpin *Every Child Matters*. What is the role of the middle leader in the remodelling process?
- As a middle leader how might you develop a positive attitude to change amongst your team members?
- What should leaders of change do at the outset to avoid a negative outcome?
- Which strategy for change would you employ? Why?
- What factors would you consider to be important for the effective and successful implementation of change?

chapter eight

Learning organisations: inclusion, individualised learning and collaboration

The inclusive practitioner

An inclusive approach to learning and teaching

Creating inclusive classrooms

Individual learning plans

Collaboration

Working in partnership with local authorities

LAs and children's trusts

Challenges and opportunities

A common assessment framework

Summary

_____ The inclusive practitioner _____

Teachers are responsible for the development of pupil knowledge, citizenship and values. Teachers are responsible for embedding notions of inclusion and lifelong learning in pupils. Middle leaders and teachers need to be developed as holistic practitioners within schools as learning organisations.

This chapter examines the role of the teacher as an inclusive practitioner (providing suggestions for the implementation of the theory of inclusion in the classroom. Links between policy and practice are critical to the implementation of effective inclusion. Stainback *et al.* (1994, 489) suggest that:

the goal of inclusion is not to erase differences but to enable all students to belong within an educational community that validates and values their individuality.

The chapter further considers the principles underpinning collaborative, multi-agency practice in schools, focusing specifically on the role of external agencies.

___ An inclusive approach to learning and teaching ___

The initial question is how to make education more responsive to an individual child or how to deliver personalised learning. This means:

- having high expectations of all children
- building on the knowledge, interests and aptitudes of every child
- involving children in their own learning through shared objectives and feedback
- helping children to become confident learners
- enabling children to develop the skills they will need beyond school.

Developing good learning relationships is fundamental to effective teaching. Moreover, learning behaviours are integrated components of the classroom rather than fragmented attributes of the child (Cornwall and Tod, 1998). The social context of the classroom has long been researched and the importance of wider influences on learners' behaviour should not be ignored. Case study research suggests that the quality of the relationship between teacher and learner is very significant (Cline, 1992). Stoll *et al.* (2003, 137) advocate *positive relationships* as a *secure basis for learning*. Earlier research (Serow and Solomon, 1979; Prawat and Nickerson, 1985) suggests that children are more likely to develop positive attitudes and behaviours when they experience positive relationships with their teachers. Teachers' self-perception of their skills and confidence is an important consideration for the management of relationships in the classroom. A consequence of teacher lack of confidence could be unskilled teaching and increased disaffection and challenging behaviour in the classroom.

Active learning of the kind that is to be encouraged, if learners are to be motivated and take responsibility for their own achievements, asks learners to be self-motivated and collaborate with others to construct their knowledge. Moll and Whitmore (1998) describe the teacher's roles as guide and supporter, active participant in learning, evaluator and facilitator.

All of these activities are part of the relationship between teacher and learner but there are many less definable or measurable facets to the relationship, such as the ability to encourage the learner or providing responsive instruction. Castelikns (1996) states responsive instruction is typified by teachers showing that they:

- are available for support and instruction
- are willing to take the learner's perspective on work problems
- are willing to support the learner's competencies
- will challenge the student to be active and responsible in choosing, planning, executing and evaluating the activity and its outcomes.

Involving learners in the planning of their study or learning objectives is not a new strategy and was reaffirmed in the revised CoP (DfES, 2001a). The benefits to learners range from ownership of targets to more accurate judgements, and hence assessment, of their own performance (Munby, 1994). To achieve this kind of learner involvement presupposes an encouraging relationship between teacher and learner.

Relationships with peers are also considered to be important factors in school learning. In recent years an emphasis on inclusive environments has resulted in increased mixed-ability classrooms and schools. Research indicates that traditional whole class instruction that is teacher-directed to all class members, with uniform academic tasks and ways of performing, is inappropriate as a primary mode of instruction in heterogeneous classes since it fails to cope with the differences between pupils in terms of needs and abilities (Ben-Ari and Shafir, 1988). Vygostsky (1962) emphasised the pivotal contribution of social interaction to cognitive development and the view that cognitive development is a process of continuous interplay between the individual and the environment. It follows that classroom groupings for teaching and peer relationships could have a significant impact on learning. It is important for teachers to recognise and foster the possible mechanisms for improved learning behaviour (Hertz-Lazarowitz and Miller, 1992). The lack of appropriate social and inter-personal skills and competencies can result from any home background so it is necessary to enhance positive learning behaviours by encouraging:

- high feelings of self-worth
- a robust sense of self
- self-reliance
- autonomy
- a positive view of the world
- a sense of personal power.

_____ Creating inclusive classrooms _____

The following practical suggestions for a framework for inclusive teaching and learning are taken from Cheminais (2004):

1 *A welcoming, friendly, supportive and emotionally literate classroom climate is of prime importance; where pupils and staff feel secure, are able to share feelings and ask questions; where misunderstandings are dealt with sensitively, and used as positive teaching points and where put-downs are not permitted.*

2 *Teachers and teaching assistants who have high expectations, making these clear to pupils, and incorporating the learning cycle structure in all lessons. This entails establishing a positive mind-set and readiness for learning; connecting pupils' previous learning to new learning; giving pupils the big picture, sharing the lesson objectives and expected outcomes with pupils; breaking learning down into achievable steps, as well as providing extension activities, utilising multi-sensory teaching and learning approaches; ensuring pupils are active participants throughout the lesson; providing opportunities for pupils to demonstrate their knowledge and understanding, and to review and reflect upon their learning at the end of the lesson, in order to ensure new knowledge is not lost.*

3 *The teacher and teaching assistant modelling effective learning strategies and expected outcomes. This would also entail pupils being provided with a range of learning and curriculum access resources that would enable them to extend their research and study skills, and to produce learning outcomes in a variety of alternative formats, in ICT, digital technology, multimedia, as a regular feature of lessons.*

4 *Providing opportunities for pupils to talk about their learning, e.g. describing the different ways they talked through a problem; asking open questions to prompt alternative solutions and approaches; and ensuring that pupils work in a variety of ways, in pairs and small groups, as a whole class or independently, during the lesson.*

5 *Encouraging pupils to assess their own learning and that of their peers sensitively and constructively; teachers commenting on pupils' work, indicating clearly what each pupil needs to do in order to improve, or make their next piece of work of 'premier league' quality.*

6 *Teaching assistants being empowered to utilise their strengths; being clear about their role in relation to the effectiveness of their VAK (visual, auditory, kinaesthetic) support strategies, in consolidating and extending pupils' learning. Teaching assistants who can differentiate 'on the spot' using both hi-tech and lo-tech aids, are a powerful learning resource*

—————— Individual learning plans ——————

The remodelling process (workforce reform, extended schools and *Every Child Matters*) also requires schools to create individual learning plans for all pupils.

Individual learning embraces every aspect of school life including ICT, curriculum choice, organisation and timetabling, assessment arrangements and relationships with the local community. The initial question is how ILPs will make education more responsive to an individual child and how to deliver personalised learning. The answer is having high expectations of all children so that staff can build on the knowledge, interests and aptitudes of every child whilst involving children in their own learning through shared objectives and feedback. This process helps children to become confident learners, enabling them to develop the skills they will need beyond school; it sets learning situations and provides resources.

Since the 1960s, classroom practice has been influenced by the child-centred theories of Piaget, Montessori and Frobel. These emphasise a need for teachers to reflect on classroom organisation and approaches to learning and teaching. Solity (1992) provides a useful summary:

The classroom is then geared to stimulate children, to encourage interest and for their learning to be based on their experiences. The teacher is a facilitator, promoting learning and acting as the child's guide in the learning process.

Active learning of this kind is to be encouraged if learners are to be motivated and take responsibility for their own achievements; it asks learners to be self-motivated and collaborate with others to construct their knowledge. Moll and Whitmore (1998) describe the classroom staff's roles as guide and supporter, active participant in learning, evaluator and facilitator. These roles contribute to the relationship between teacher and learner but there are many less definable or measurable facets to the relationship, such as the ability to encourage the learner or providing responsive instruction. Castelikns (1996) states that responsive instruction is typified by teachers and classroom support staff showing that they are available for support and instruction, willing to take the learner's perspective on work problems and support the learner's competencies. This challenges the learner to be active and responsible in choosing, planning, executing and evaluating the activity and its outcomes.

Collaboration

Meeting the educational needs of all pupils requires statutory agencies to work flexibly. Schools need to develop policies and protocols that ensure that there is a seamless service. Working supportively, and in partnership with parents and pupils, will ensure everyone involved understands the responses of the professionals concerned, and will lead to a better quality, more meaningful provision. Maintained schools must publish information on the school's arrangements for working in partnership with LA support services, Health and Social Services, the Connexions service and any relevant local and national voluntary organisations. It should be recognised that external support services can play an important part in helping schools identify, assess and make provision for all pupils. It is self-evident that all services for all pupils should focus on identifying and addressing needs to enable them to improve their situation through:

- early identification
- continual engagement with the child and parents
- focused intervention
- dissemination of effective approaches and techniques.

The objective is to provide an integrated, high-quality, holistic support that focuses on the needs of the child. Such provision should be based on a shared perspective and should be built on mutual understanding and agreement where all voices are heard. Services should adopt a flexible pupil-centred approach to service delivery to ensure that the changing needs and priorities of the pupil and their parents can be met at any given time.

All agencies will need to recognise the need for effective collaboration of services involving pupils and parents. Consultative responsibilities and effective communication systems at management and practitioner levels will then be clearly identified. Developments in organisational structures and working practices will need to reflect this principle. Joint planning arrangements would then:

- take account of good practice
- ensure consultation with all relevant services
- agree priorities
- publicise decisions to parents and professionals
- regularly review policies and objectives.

____ Working in partnership with local authorities ____

The framework for change is developed from the 2004 Children's Act which focuses on five outcomes that are the key to well-being in childhood and later life (DfES, 2004c). The following sections focus on the policies and practices that will help to facilitate these five outcomes. The government proposed radical changes to the whole system of children's services which include (DfES, 2004e):

- *the improvement and integration of universal services...*
- *... specialised help to promote opportunity, prevent problems and act early and effectively*
- *the reconfiguration of services around [children] and [families] in one place, for example, children's centres, extended schools and the bringing together of professionals in multi-disciplinary teams*
- *dedicated and enterprising leadership at all levels of the system*
- *the development of a shared sense of responsibility across agencies for safeguarding children and protecting them from harm.*

Government publications set out a vision for integrated services beginning with advice for early years and school-aged children and young people. They identify that early years and childcare provision gives a good start to young children's development as well as appropriate support for parents. The government's ten-year strategy for early years and childcare intends to provide more integrated services for young children, as well as childcare and family support services based for older children in schools. Many schools already offer a wide range of extended school sporting and cultural activities. However, community participation is key to both the short- and long-term success of the extended school.

LAs and children's trusts

The government intends that children's trust arrangements are to be developed in most areas by 2006 and all areas by 2008. For schools this will mean that (DfES, 2004c):

■ *children's trust arrangements involving schools in local partnerships so that schools can feed their views into local service planning and, if they wish, provide services individually or in partnership with other schools;*

■ *children's trust arrangements and schools working together to find places for hard-to-place pupils...*

■ *local authorities working closely with schools in fulfilling their duty to promote the educational achievement of looked-after children.*

It is intended that integrating services will mean more effective support for pupils with complex needs who require multi-agency support. Two processes are available (DfESD, 2004c):

■ *a Common Assessment Framework to help schools identify when a pupil's needs can be met within the school and to enable better targeted referral to other specialist services when needed so they can respond more effectively*

■ *cross-government guidance on information-sharing to improve the sharing of information between schools and other agencies about individual children with additional needs.*

LAs and children's trusts will also engage with schools and other providers to ensure that all children in their local area are being effectively supported. Head teachers will be key strategic partners in shaping the pattern of local services. Schools may want to develop their role in delivering services through foundation partnerships and other clustering arrangements.

The delivery of more integrated services will require new ways of working and a significant culture change for staff used to working within narrower professional and service-based boundaries. Easy and effective communication across current organisational and professional boundaries is a strong foundation for co-operation. One way to manage this is the co-location of managers and frontline staff from different services working together in multi-disciplinary teams in an extended school.

Practice within LAs is varied and experience has shown that several have complex support structures that remain unknown or unclear in practice to practitioners in schools. Central to the effectiveness of LA support teams and other support agencies is their ability to communicate their role to classroom teachers. Often the point of contact in schools is the special educational needs co-ordinator (SENCO). Rather than leaving the SENCO to deal with pupils who may have SEN, all teachers should consider their responsibilities to pupils in their classrooms. LA support services can provide advice to practitioners (e.g. teaching techniques and strategies, classroom management and curriculum materials) as well as:

- support for curriculum development
- direct teaching or practical support for class teachers
- part-time specialist help
- access to learning support assistance.

Table 8.1 considers the management and range of pupil support.

TABLE 8.1   **Pupil support** (Blandford and Gibson, 2005)

The direct support to pupils will be managed in a range of ways by:

- gathering information from the pupil, school, home, community, other agencies
- assessing the pupil by identifying patterns
- understanding and observation
- planning for school, home and the community
- defining intervention procedures, including group work, work in classroom, work off-site, continued observation, a combination of approaches and a watching brief
- reviewing dates planned well in advance, especially those required in the code of practice (DfE, 1994, DfES, 2001a).

The range of pupil support includes:

- classroom observation
- lunchtime and break observation
- one-to-one counselling
- social and interpersonal skills group work
- anger management and conflict resolution group work
- friendship groups support work
- lunchtime clubs and playground support

- therapeutic use of art, drama, play and music
- co-operative games
- home–school liaison
- support for parents
- classroom-focused support work
- off-site curriculum-focused work at child and family support centres.

As stated, LAs should provide full information to all schools about the range of locally available services and how they can be secured. Leadership teams should be aware of the LA's policy for the provision of support services and how the school can access them. Whether or not funding for particular support services is delegated to schools, it may be helpful for schools and LAs to draw up agreements for such services, specifying the scope, quality and duration of the service to be provided. When schools enter into contracts with private or voluntary sector providers, they should also satisfy themselves of the qualifications and experience of the specialists involved, that the service represents good value for money and carry out appropriate police checks.

It is most likely that schools will consult specialists when they take action on behalf of a child through *School Action Plus* (DfES, 2001b). Nevertheless, the involvement of specialists need not be limited to children receiving provision through *School Action Plus*. Outside specialists can play an important part not only in the early identification of SEN but also in advising schools on effective provision designed to prevent the development of more significant needs. They can also act as consultants and be a source for in-service advice on learning, teaching, behaviour management and specialist strategies for all teachers.

MIDDLE LEADERSHIP QUESTIONS

1 How does your school engage with external agencies?

2 Is there a school policy on identifying support for pupils?

3 How involved are parents in determining support for their child?

4 Does the LA provide adequate information on the support services available for all pupils?

5 What are the school's staff development needs?

———— Challenges and opportunities ————

Raising achievements through meeting the needs of individual pupils requires flexible working of statutory agencies. From September 2005, maintained schools must publish information on the school's arrangements for working in partnership with LA support services, health and social services, the Connexions service and any relevant local and national voluntary organisations; Ofsted inspection teams will be seeking evidence of this practice. It should be recognised that external support services can play an important part in helping schools identify, assess and make provision for all pupils.

The objective is to provide an integrated, high-quality, holistic support that focuses on the needs of the child. Such provision should be based on a shared perspective and should build on mutual understanding and agreement where all voices are heard. Services should adopt a flexible pupil-centred approach to service delivery to ensure that the changing needs and priorities of the pupil and their parents can be met at any given time.

All agencies will need to recognise the need for effective collaboration of services involved with pupils and parents. Consultative responsibilities and effective communication systems at all levels can then be clearly identified. Developments in organisational structures and working practices need to reflect this collaboration.

———— A common assessment framework ————

A common assessment framework (CAF) has been created (DfES, 2005c) to support the five outcomes of *Every Child Matters*. Its aims are, where appropriate, to provide an assessment of a child's individual, family and community needs, which can be built up over time and, with consent, shared amongst practitioners. It is intended to:

- improve the quality of referrals between agencies
- help embed a common language about the needs of children and young people
- promote the appropriate sharing of information, and
- reduce the number and duration of different assessment processes.

The government intends that the CAF will help practitioners undertake an initial holistic assessment of a child or young person's needs to determine the level of need and identify an appropriate response. It consists of a common process for understanding and articulating the range of needs of an individual child involving the child, their parents or carers and other practitioners, as appropriate, with a common format:

- to help practitioners record the findings from the assessment in terms that are helpful in determining the most appropriate response to future needs, and

- for sharing assessment information with other practitioners and services as appropriate, while assuring the necessary levels of confidentiality and security.

The aims of the CAF are to:

- provide a method of assessment to support earlier intervention

- improve joint working and communication between practitioners by helping to embed a common language of assessment and a more consistent view as to the appropriate response

- improve the co-ordination and consistency between assessments leading to fewer and shorter specialist assessments

- inform decisions about whether further specialist assessment is necessary and if necessary provide information to contribute to it

- enable a picture of a child or young person's needs to be built up over time and, with appropriate consent, shared among professionals

- provide better, more evidence-based referrals to targeted and specialist services.

The following case study provides an example of inclusive practice in organisations.

CASE STUDY

Partnership project

Social inclusion was well developed within School C. It had a strong focus, with high-quality professional input by school staff, but it also recognised that sustained response to social need required a partnership with other agencies. This partnership involved staff from the local support unit, Education Welfare Office service, school psychologists, school nurse health workers, child protection staff and social services.

Increasingly, staff were aware that many of the problems being encountered by pupils in the 11–19 age group were a continuation, and a consequence, of much earlier social and educational concern. In 2001–02, the school addressed this situation by defining social inclusion work in the broader context of nursery, infant, junior and primary school children and their families, and outside agencies.

The leadership group recognised that the success of its work required an integrated response across the local community. To this end, the school's focus provided a vehicle for different agencies to combine in meeting the needs of children and their families.

The relationship between eight local nursery/primary schools and the school was well established. The project identified and targeted staff in each of the eight local schools to work specifically with the most needy children and, through this work, to access their family situations. The head teachers of the schools involved formed a social inclusion management group. The project established operational modes, provided funding and met the professional development costs for all staff concerned.

The management integrated response team provided the strategic direction for the project. Through the work of the staff in each school, staff had lists of needy children and families. In a co-ordinated way, the necessary support groups were identified in response to these needs. Managers distributed responsibilities according to expertise, to secure resources for families as appropriate, define follow-up procedures and, crucially, ensure respective area teams were informed about the work.

The costs associated with this project were to fund workers in the schools. This was a front-line team. Essentially, the project focused on breaking the cycle of accumulative disadvantage by placing pupils at the core of this work, recognising that families in the community need to have frequent and trusting relationships with the school. The work supports parenting skills programmes and brings staff into contact with the full range of family needs and concerns.

Summary

Developing good learning relationships is fundamental to effective teaching. Stoll *et al.* (2003, 137) advocate *positive relationships* as a *secure basis for learning*. Earlier research (Serow and Solomon, 1979; Prawat and Nickerson, 1985) suggests that children are more likely to develop positive attitudes and behaviours when they experience positive relationships with their teachers.

Involving learners in the planning of their study or learning objectives is not a new strategy and was reaffirmed in the revised CoP (DfES, 2001a).

The benefits to learners range from ownership of targets to more accurate judgements, and hence assessment, of their own performance (Munby, 1994). To achieve this kind of learner involvement pre-supposes an encouraging relationship between teacher and learner.

Meeting the educational needs of all pupils requires flexible working of statutory agencies. Schools need to develop policies and protocols that ensure there is a seamless service. Working supportively, and in partnership with parents and pupils, will ensure that everyone involved understands the responses of the professionals concerned, and will lead to a better quality, more meaningful provision.

A CAF has been created (DfES, 2005c) to support the five outcomes of *Every Child Matters*. Its aims are, where appropriate, to provide an assessment of a child's individual, family and community needs, which can be built up over time and, with consent, shared amongst practitioners.

REVIEW QUESTIONS

1 What factors would you consider when trying to make education more responsive to an individual child?

2 Developing good learning relationships is fundamental to effective teaching. How might the classroom practitioner encourage the learner?

3 How can the classroom practitioner enhance positive learning behaviours?

4 Remodelling of schools is not taking place in isolation from other public sector, private and voluntary services. How might you as a classroom practitioner, rather than add to the workload of the SENCO, provide for a child with SEN?

5 What is the common assessment framework?

chapter nine

Administration and communication

Efficient and effective practice

Managing the timetable

Assessment

Reporting

Inspection

Effective communication

Verbal and non-verbal communication

Information technology

Summary

_____ Efficient and effective practice _____

In 1991, Brighouse stated:

How well the school is organised and maintained – the administration of the school – vitally affects the lives of teachers. If there are constant foul-ups in the administration, it is almost impossible to avoid staff stress and loss of morale accumulating during the school year; moreover it saps the highest common factor of shared values and common purpose which should be that of a good school.

Teachers and middle leaders are aware that there are 'peaks and troughs' of administrative activity that occur in every academic year. Timetabling, assessment and inspection are key events in each school's programme. Identifying when such events occur is essential to the successful management of a department or school. Fidler (2002, 33) suggests that *in the steady state, administration should work efficiently and effectively to ensure that routine operations run smoothly.* He highlights the need for good record-keeping which can provide valuable information in informed decision-making.

There are few differences between primary and secondary practice. All middle leaders need to understand and be skilled in administration and communication if they are to operate effectively as a leader and teacher.

This chapter opens with a consideration of general issues relating to the control of documentation, highlighting three important aspects:

- curriculum planning (timetabling)
- assessment and reporting
- inspection.

The second part of this chapter addresses the relevance and importance of effective communication for middle leaders.

Documentation

An observable difference between classroom teachers and middle leaders is the amount of paperwork that accumulates in middle leaders' message boxes. At the start of each working day, a middle leader will have a number of administrative tasks to complete. A feature of good leadership practice is the ability to identify relevant, urgent and important documentation. In order to prioritise, a middle leader needs to know and understand the purpose of each document. A middle leader needs to keep administration under control; it should not control their actions.

Types of documentation

What documentation will a middle leader be expected to process? As indicated in this book documentation might include:

- school improvement plan
- school policy documents
- department/year handbook
- prospectus
- contributions to newsletter and senior management meetings
- timetable allocations
- resource material
- curriculum/pastoral papers
- LA papers
- pupils' reports
- assessment papers
- league table information
- department/team improvement plans
- performance management
- examination data.

A feature of good leadership practice is the ability to identify relevant, urgent and important documentation. In order to prioritise, a middle leader needs to know and understand the purpose of each document. Middle leaders need to keep administration under control; it should not control their actions.

Practical advice

Middle leaders might begin by setting aside a period in each day for administrative tasks. This may involve arriving 30 minutes earlier for work, or finding a 'window' in which they can work without interruptions by pupils, colleagues or the telephone. Good advice is to process all documentation by categorising each paper according to importance. The action plan shown in Table 9.1 may be of use and can be adapted to suit.

TABLE 9.1 Documentation action plan

Category	Content	Responses	Consultation	Action (keep a copy)
A	Team matters/pupils requiring immediate response	Within 24 hrs	Pupils, parents, head teacher, staff	Read and write
B	Team matters/pupils, senior management papers	Within 48 hrs	Team member, SLT	Meetings: read and write
C	Meetings/agendas/ reports–department/ school/LA	Within 1 week	LA/SLT	Meetings: read and write
D	Report	Within 2 weeks	Government/ SMT	Read and write
E	Documentation *not* requiring a response, but could be useful at a later date	Within 1 month		Read only/ research/ develop

The following suggestions will also help:

- **Diary** – Keeping an up-to-date diary, identifying busy periods during the term.

- **Filing** – Always file away information using ICT or paper! Check through files regularly, discarding any out-of-date or irrelevant information.

- **ICT** – Use and develop your ICT skills. Keep a catalogue of programs and files for easy reference.

- **Folder: current** – A useful 'litmus test' for each document is to create a 'current' folder referred to several times throughout the day. If a document is not relevant it can be filed away.

- **Things to do** – Add documentation to a daily 'things to do' list; where possible complete all responses in advance of the date requested. Preparing responses/reports in advance saves time.

- **Team: delegation** – There may be a specific area of work in which a team member has an interest. Develop their skills in this area and delegate some of your paperwork.

- **Reading** – When reading documentation, highlight key words and points of action. This avoids unnecessary reading and could provide the framework for your written response.

- **Response** – When responding to a document ensure that your points are relevant and relate to specific areas of the document

- **Keep a copy!** – Always keep a copy of responses, filed with related documentation.

Managing the timetable

Middle leaders will need insight into the process of translating the curriculum into the timetable to avoid any possibility of making irreversible decisions which have negative implications (Armstrong *et al.*, 1993a, 56). Middle leaders need to identify the needs of their colleagues and communicate these to senior leadership. Team leaders should always consult staff to establish their requirements.

The allocation of PPA time is an important consideration in timetabling. With increased responsibilities and the development of staff management posts in primary and secondary schools, there are timetabling implications. Agreement is needed as to how much time should be negotiated for middle and senior leadership posts. The time allocated should reflect the requirements for each responsibility and/or task. The allocation of hours for management tasks is critical to the effective leadership of schools.

Detailed job descriptions will assist the timetabler. If a member of staff has a clearly defined role which relates to hours on the timetable, there can be no doubt as to how the timetable at an individual level can be constructed. Areas of indecision, or lack of definition, will hinder the process.

Assessment

In recent years there have been many debates focusing on assessment and reporting issues in education. This has run parallel to various Ofsted reports over the last few years which have highlighted the *indifferent quality of assessment compared with other aspects of teaching in secondary school* (Ofsted, 2003, 1). Following evidence from classroom-based research, most notably that of Black and Wiliam (1998), which addressed raising standards through classroom assessment, there has been a move away from assessment *of* learning towards assessment *for* learning (Ofsted, 2003, 1). The Assessment Reform Group (2002) define assessment for learning as:

The process of seeking and interpreting evidence for use by learners and their teachers to decide where the learners are in their learning, where they need to go and how best to get there.

The group recommends that assessment for learning should:

■ *Be part of effective planning for teaching and learning*

■ *Focus on how pupils learn*

■ *Be recognised as central to classroom practice*

■ *Be regarded as a key professional skill for teachers*

■ *Be sensitive and constructive because any assessment has an emotional impact*

■ *Take account of the importance of learner motivation*

■ *Promote commitment to learning goals and a shared understanding of the criteria by which pupils will be assessed*

■ *Provide constructive guidance for learners about how to improve*

■ *Develop learners' capacity for self-assessment and recognising their next steps and how to take them*

■ *Recognise the full range of achievement of all learners.*

Building on their earlier research Black *et al.* (2002) addressed ways of improving formative assessment. Their finding highlighted the positive impact of effective formative assessment on pupil attainment. To realise this in the learning environment Black *et al.* recommend that classroom practitioners focus on the following areas (2002, 7–14):

■ Questioning – needs to raise issues about which the pupils need to think.

■ Feedback through marking – should cause thinking (pupil) to take place.

■ Peer assessment and self-assessment – provides the best means of allowing pupils to focus on aims. Clarify aims (of work) at the outset and encourage pupils to assess their own progress to meet these aims.

■ Formative use of summative tests – engage pupils in a reflective review of their work to help them plan revision (self-set questions and self-marked answers).

The benefits of assessment

Ofsted (2003), in response to advice from the QCA, underlines the significant contribution assessment can make to *raising standards in schools when the focus* (of assessment) *is placed on the professional skills of teachers.*

Considering the findings from a number of schools where recent inspections had highlighted assessment procedures as very good or excellent, Ofsted (2003, 2–3) underlines the following, as interrelated elements of a good system, where assessment focuses on helping pupils to do their best:

- *data analysis*
- *pupil planners*
- *subject targets*
- *progress reports*
- *the roles of class teachers and tutors*
- *marking*
- *additional support*
- *parental consultation.*

At the end of each key stage, the head teacher must fully comply with the arrangements for assessing pupils. Whilst this is the head teacher's responsibility, in practice middle leaders will be employed to complete each task. Ofsted (2003) recommends the following for end-of-year or end-of-unit formal assessment:

- *A shared understanding of what is to be assessed and by what criteria.*
- *Pupils need to know that formal assessment is purposeful and helpful.*
- *A shared and robust departmental understanding of national curriculum levels.*
- *Ensure that both team members and pupils know what level descriptions mean.*
- *Be specific with pupils about what they need to do to reach the next level.*

The statutory assessment arrangements involve teacher assessment of each pupil's achievements in each attainment target (AT) based on the pupil's school work over the course of the key stage, and national curriculum tests administered to each pupil and marked by their teacher.

Teacher assessment is an assessment of pupils' school work in relation to the ATs set for each national curriculum subject. The process of building up evidence of pupils' attainments over the course of a key stage is fundamental to good practice. The fundamental principles of the assessment are:

- assessment over each key stage,
- integrating assessment, teaching and learning,
- drawing on evidence from –

on-going school work

observation

homework

written classwork

- record-keeping
- retaining evidence
- school policy on assessment.

Ofsted's (2003) counsel on pupil work improvement through teaching, marking and setting targets supports the findings of Black *et al.* (2002). Ofsted suggests that the following procedures should be in place:

- *clarity in the aims and outcomes of lessons*
- *teaching methods that involve them actively and emphasis analysis, discussion, experimentation and thinking ideas through*
- *written or oral comments on their work that provide both clear evaluation of the content and structure and sensible advice that leaves them with manageable action points*
- *use of national curriculum level descriptions and GCSE grade criteria to show what needs to be done to make progress*
- *target-setting that focuses on specific, relevant and achievable goals.*

Schools may want common systems across subjects but may prefer to let key stages, faculties, curriculum areas or departments develop their own systems to agreed principles as stated in the school policy. Middle leaders may also be required to develop assessment practice within their teams. The following questions may assist in this process:

- How can marking and feedback be made purposeful and useful for assessment?
- How can previous experience be shared between year groups and subject areas?
- What recording systems in place can be adapted to current needs?
- How can the breadth of pupil achievement be celebrated, recorded and supported by evidence?
- What mechanisms can be set up to use the same work as evidence to support assessment in more than one subject?
- What is the role of the tutor/class teacher in co-ordinating assessment?
- How can secondary practice build on what partner primary schools are doing?

- How can common cross-phase practices be achieved?
- How accessible/useful will the records and evidence be to parents and pupils?

Reporting

Having established good assessment practice, middle leaders need to be aware of the legal requirements for reporting. As an administrative task, writing reports is time-consuming but pupil reports should be an invaluable tool to teaching and learning. The legal framework for current reporting practices are summarised as follows:

Introduction

(a) Reports to parents

- A written report must be sent out **at least annually** to the parents of **each pupil** for their retention.
- The report should contain at least the minimum information required by the regulations.
- The report must be sent by the required deadlines.

(b) Reports to receiving schools

- When a pupil moves school, a report containing at least the minimum requirements must be passed on to the head teacher of the new school within 15 school days.

(c) Reports to school-leavers

- Information covering at least the minimum requirements must be given to every school leaver using the mandatory format.

Guidance

(a) Reports to parents

The report must include:

- 'Brief particulars' of the pupil's progress in all subjects and activities studied as part of the school curriculum, written in the form of **succinct narrative comments** highlighting strengths and weaknesses.

- The results of all public examinations, qualifications achieved or credits towards qualifications gained. Results received after the report has been dispatched must be sent on to parents as soon as possible.

- Details of the arrangements under which the report may be discussed with teachers at the school.

- Separate 'brief particulars' for all subjects studied: where the pupil has been assessed under statutory assessment arrangements, these particulars must amplify and explain the NC assessment results.

- A record of the pupil's attendance during the year, including the total number of school sessions and the number for which the pupil was absent without authority.

(b) Reports to receiving schools

- The results of statutory assessments of the pupil under the NC by subject and attainment target at all previous key stages and the school year in which the assessments were made. The information must include that for key stages assessed by previous schools.

- The teachers' latest assessments of the pupil's progress against all applicable attainment targets since the last statutory assessment or since the pupil arrived at the reporting school (provided that the pupil was on roll for at least four weeks), whichever is more recent.

- Any public examination results, including the results of examinations leading to vocational qualifications.

(c) Reports to school leavers

- The subject and attainment target levels of every NC subject studied. The levels provided should be those achieved at the point at which the pupil was assessed in the subject for the last time under statutory arrangements.

- The results of any public examinations, qualifications achieved and credits towards qualifications gained, including vocational qualifications or credits towards vocational qualifications.

- 'Brief particulars' of achievements in all subjects and activities studied as part of the school curriculum.

Policy

In addition to managing the implementation of government guidelines on assessment and reporting, middle leaders will also participate in determining the school policy for assessment and reporting. As shown, assessment should be interpreted in its widest sense and not only in the context of the national curriculum. Assessment includes the gathering of evidence and the making of a judgement in order to provide feedback to the pupil to assist future learning and to award a qualitative value to the work or performance. The school policy for assessment and reporting should therefore:

- be understood by all participants
- begin with a review of current practice
- be developed and implemented incrementally
- support and promote equal opportunities within the school
- be integrated with or linked to schemes of work
- provide a framework for pupil continuity and progression
- be shared with all staff and governors.

A suggested framework for assessment and reporting policy is:

- Identify the stages for development of a policy for assessment and reporting
- Identify achievable success criteria in order to evaluate the process of development and implementation
- Identify key personnel: assessment co-ordinator, heads of department/subject co-ordinators, key stage co-ordinators
- Decide on the time-scale
- Identify professional development and INSET needs for key personnel and whole staff
- Ensure that all INSET needs are reflected in the school improvement plan
- Decide on a monitoring and evaluating structure.

Having considered the above, the policy for assessment and reporting should relate to the government's criteria. An assessment and reporting policy should indicate points of action, address key issues and contribute to school effectiveness by:

- supporting institutional development
- supporting institutional management
- supporting individual teacher development (CPD)
- promoting attainment
- enhancing quality of learning
- improving (changing) classroom practice.

Assessment is not an 'exact science' and the policy should be continually monitored and evaluated.

Inspection

In the context of administration, the inspection process is perhaps the most demanding of all events in the life of a school. This section will outline, in brief, the purpose of the school inspection and what it entails for the middle leader.

Background

Ormston and Shaw (1993a, 1) state:

The Office for Standards in Education (Ofsted) was set up in 1992 and has a statutory function to give advice to the Secretary of State for Education on the quality of education.

Ofsted's new inspection framework, which came into effect in September 2005, incorporates the *Every Child Matters* agenda. The aim of the inspection process remains that of giving *a clear, impartial view of the overall quality of the school;... what it does well and not so well. Inspection also provides the school with a useful check on its work and guides it towards further improvements* (Ofsted, 2005). The main features of the new inspection process, where the school's self-evaluation is central, are:

- *short, focused inspections that take no more than two days in a school and concentrate on close interaction with senior leaders in the school, taking self-evaluation evidence as the starting point*
- *short notice of inspections (between two and five days) to avoid schools carrying out unnecessary pre-inspection preparation often associated with an inspection. Short notice should help inspectors to see schools as they really are*

- *teams with few inspectors with many inspections led by one of Her Majesty's Inspectors (HMIs). Furthermore, Her Majesty's Chief Inspector (HMCI) will publish and be responsible for all reports*

- *three years as the usual period between inspections, though occurring more frequently for schools causing concern*

- *strong emphasis on school improvement through the use of the school's own self-evaluation, including regular input from pupils, parents and other stakeholders, as the starting point for inspection and for the school's internal planning and development. To facilitate this, schools are strongly encouraged to update their self-evaluation form on an annual basis*

- *a common set of characteristics to inspection in schools and other post-16 provision of education from early childhood to the age of 19*

- *there will be two categories of school causing concern, those deemed to require special measures and those requiring a notice to improve.*

(Ofsted, 2005, 1)

Everything is open to inspection including:

- documentation
- policy statements
- views of parents
- governor involvement
- school and individual planning records
- assessment procedures
- policy statements
- minutes of meetings
- budget forecasts
- resource levels
- accommodation
- staff development.

The only exceptions are where a school has special circumstances: a voluntary-aided church school, for example, will have its religious education (RE) inspected by the diocese rather than by the Ofsted team.

The *Framework for the Inspection of Schools* (Ofsted, 2005) is the instrument by which schools are inspected. Under the Education Act 2005, inspectors must report on:

- *the quality of education provided in the school*

- *how far the education meets the needs of the range of pupils at the school*

- *the educational standards achieved in the school*

- *the quality of the leadership and management of the school, including whether the financial resources made available to the school are managed efficiently*

- *the spiritual, moral, social and cultural development of the pupils at the school*

- *the contribution made by the school to the well-being of those pupils.*

(Ofsted, 2005, 5)

The process

Prior to the inspection, Ofsted prepares a pre-inspection summary employing the school's self-evaluation form (SEF), performance and assessment (PANDA) report and the previous inspection report. Information relating to the school and pupils, including a school self-evaluation is provided by the SEF. At the beginning of the inspection process the school is asked to provide its current SIP along with a copy of the timetable and a plan of the school.

During the inspection, inspectors will gather first-hand evidence by:

- *direct observation*

- *talking to staff, pupils and others in the school*

- *tracking school processes, such as evaluation and performance management*

- *analysing samples of pupils' current and recent work*

- *joining meetings such as school council or management meetings, and directly observing management processes, such as the monitoring of teaching*

- *analysing records relating to pupils with special educational needs, including individual education plans, statements, annual reviews and transitional reviews*

- *tracking case studies of vulnerable pupils such as those with learning difficulties and disabilities, and children in care.*

(Ofsted, 2005, 12)

Middle leaders will need to ensure that all paperwork is kept up-to-date. Between inspections middle leaders will be required either to contribute to or develop:

- school improvement plan

- school prospectus
- policy documents
- school timetable
- staff handbook
- schemes of work
- department handbook (including marking policy)
- department extra-curricular activities
- curriculum plan
- assessment and reporting procedures.

A further dimension to inspection is what occurs beyond the classroom in the extended school and in response to *Every Child Matters*. Consideration is given to the quality of the educational experience the pupil is receiving as a consequence of other aspects of school life, for example:

- pastoral system
- primary/secondary partnerships
- school/HEI partnerships
- INSET
- cross-curricular links
- support
- extra-curricular activities.

The introduction of the common inspection schedule for schools and other post-16 provision ensures that all aspects of the educational experience are considered within the new inspection framework. Ofsted provides non-statutory guidance on using the schedule and on conducting inspections within the new framework on its website (**www.ofsted.gov.uk**). The common inspection schedule for schools and other post-16 provision evaluates the extent to which *settings, institutions and providers* meet the following outcomes for children and young people:

- being healthy
- staying safe
- enjoying and achieving

- making a positive contribution
- achieving economic well-being.

Comprising four main parts, the evaluation of these outcomes considers the overall effectiveness of the *provision and related services in meeting the full range of learners' needs, the achievements and standards of learners, the quality of provision and the effectiveness of leadership and management in raising achievement and supporting all learners* (Ofsted, 2005, 18–21). A middle leader will have the opportunity to ensure that policy planning is being put into practice and to evaluate the success of that planning.

Ofsted teams are approved by the government. The inspection process should be viewed positively, because it provides the opportunity to recognise and celebrate good practices, and to develop new initiatives.

It is essential that middle leaders ensure that every member of the team is aware of the need to ensure that all necessary documentation is kept up-to-date and is in line with departmental policy. In essence, the inspection process should work for everyone concerned. Inspectors will not wish to see documentation that does not reflect practice.

After the inspection, the outcome must be explained to the SLT and where possible the chair of the governing body. The oral feedback should correspond to the written report ensuring that *judgements* do not come as a *surprise to the school.* Inspectors must ensure that during the post-inspection meetings:

- feedback is effective in explaining the inspection findings and what the school needs to do to improve

- opportunity is provided for the school to understand why judgements have been made
(Ofsted, 2005, 14).

A written report is subsequently *delivered to the appropriate authority for the school and the head teacher* (Ofsted, 2005, 14). In addition, the report is published on the Ofsted website (**www.ofsted.gov.uk/reports**) within three weeks of concluding the inspection process (Ibid.,). Grading categories for all assessments within the school are made on a scale from 1 to 4, where 1 is outstanding and 4 is inadequate.

_____ Effective communication _____

Middle leaders will communicate with colleagues, parents, pupils and other agencies; therefore communication is central to effective school operations. According to the National Policy Board for Educational Administration's (NPBEA) *Principles for our Changing Schools* (1993, 16–4):

communication underlies all organisational and administrative situations, and is essential to decision-making and effective leadership. [. . .] At the heart of communication lies the opportunity to resolve contradictions, quell rumours, provide reassurance, and, ultimately, instil meaning in the complex but engaging task of education.

In schools, teachers and managers use different methods of communication for different purposes; some are more successful than others. Why is it that communication always seems to flow more smoothly in some schools, teams and departments than others? One reason is the current and/or established communication climate. The conditions in which ideas, information and feelings are exchanged directly influence the extent to which communication is a positive or negative force in a school. In practice, middle leaders may make decisions 'on the hoof' without consulting colleagues. While necessary, this may not always be the appropriate means of managing the team.

An open or supportive communication climate promotes co-operative working relationships, leading to effective information-gathering and transfer. Peters and Waterman (2004, 121) highlight the *vast network of informal, open communications which permeate excellent companies.* Supportiveness is communicated most clearly by the following kinds of responses (NPBEA, 1993, 16–4):

- **descriptive** – *statements are informative not evaluative*
- **solution-orientated** – *there is a focus on problem-solving rather than on what cannot be done*
- **open and honest** – *even if criticism is expressed, there are rarely hidden messages; the aim is to help and improve*
- **caring** – *emphasis on empathy and understanding*
- **egalitarian** – *communications value everyone, regardless of their role or status*
- **forgiving** – *error is recognised and minimised*
- **feedback** – *a positive and essential part of maintaining good working relationships and high levels of performance.*

In an open and supportive communication climate, staff feel valued, crises are dealt with and staff are more open themselves. They will feel trusted, secure and confident in their jobs and in the organisation as a whole. Effective teamworking, flexibility and a sense of involvement all contribute to, and benefit from, an open and supportive climate.

A closed communication climate is the antithesis of the above. Where the environment is highly 'political', competition for approval, promotion or resources is high on the hidden agenda. Control is often maintained through the suppression of open forms of communication.

Communication behaviours that are likely to predominate in a closed communication environment include the following (NPBEA, 1993, 16–4):

- **judgmental** – *emphasis on apportioning blame; feedback is negative; people feel inferior*

- **controlling** – *people are expected to conform to certain types of behaviour*

- **deceptive** – *messages are manipulative and hold hidden meaning*

- **non-caring** – *communication is detached, impersonal with little concern for others*

- **superior** – *interaction emphasises differences in status, skills and understanding*

- **dogmatic** – *little discussion, unwillingness to accept other points of view*

- **hostile** – *a predominantly negative approach, placing little importance on the needs of others.*

A closed climate may be a direct outcome of management style. Middle leaders will have an open and positive approach. Some methods of communication may be more effective than others, depending on the situation.

Practical advice

Communication is the exchange of information, which can range from an informal discussion with a colleague to a full report to school governors. Channels of communications in school can be summarised as shown in Table 9.2.

TABLE 9.2 Communication channels

Communication channel	Descriptors
Oral – spoken word	Most preferred – direct and personal
Written	Letters, memos, reports, e-mail; available for future reference
Meetings	Two or more people, formal/informal, planned/unplanned, structured/unstructured
Telephone calls	Immediate, time-consuming, a degree of personal contact

There are advantages and disadvantages to each channel of communication, which are not mutually exclusive. Meetings may fulfil social needs as well as more formal requirements. In addition, schools may have briefings, newsletters (information sheets), noticeboards, prospectuses and informal conversations (chats). Any passing of information between two people will involve communication.

Communication also focuses on seeking information, instructing, motivating, encouraging, supporting and persuading. Middle leaders will need to decide on the purpose of the communication – the message and the most effective means of communicating. An understanding of the communication process will produce effective results (NPBEA, 1993, 16–9). The process involves:

- **message** – *can be intended or unintended, needs to be clear*

- **encoding** – *the ability to put thoughts or words into actions*

- **setting** – *as appropriate: classroom, boardroom, conference room, office*

- **transmission** – *to communicate effectively, messages must be well organised, clear and must make appropriate use of words and body language*

- **decoding** – *the process of interpreting messages*

- **message received** – *this may happen simultaneously to the giving of the message*

- **feedback** – *as a message is decoded the receiver responds to it, listening is critical.*

Some people appear to have an innate ability to communicate; many others acquire skills through study and practice. Potential barriers to communicating, according to the NPBEA (1993, 16–13), are:

- **filtering of information** – *not telling the 'whole story'*

- **organisational structure** – *inappropriate administration*

- **information overload** – *inappropriate timing and content*

- **semantics** – *different words have different meanings*

- **status differences** – *status/roles can interfere with the meaning of the message*

- **over-interpretation** – *reading too much into the message*

- **evaluative tendencies** – *qualitative judgements*

- **stereotypes** – *negative stereotypes based on race, sex, age, role, etc.*

- **cultural and gender differences**

- **arrogance and superiority**.

_____ Verbal and non-verbal communication _____

Person-to-person contact, whether formal or informal, results in verbal and non-verbal communication. Middle leaders will be required to receive and send information. As a consequence of the leader's role and status within the school, non-verbal cues will be important to the team and other colleagues. Non-verbal cues may include:

- **vocal cues** – tone, pitch and general expression
- **body posture** – the way in which you stand or sit
- **body gestures** – what you do with your hands, head and body to explain or support what you are saying
- **eye contact** – how much you look at the other person and for how long
- **body contact** – a gentle touch on hand or arm
- **orientation** – facing the other person or at an angle
- **personal space** – the distance you maintain between yourself and the other person
- **appearance** – the image you create through clothes and grooming.

Listening

The above are also relevant for the receiver of the message. When giving and receiving messages a middle leader has to be an active listener. Being an effective listener is a skill that can be developed and practised in each new situation, whether it be a meeting, a consultation, a telephone conversation or a chance encounter in the corridor. In this context, listening involves not just hearing but also understanding. Knowledge can be gained through active listening. This will lead to appropriate feedback.

The skill of effective listening involves: listening for message content, recognising the barriers, listening for feelings, responding (non-verbal cues), checking to avoid contradictions, encouraging and reflecting. It is essential to concentrate on the general theme and flow of the message as well as the facts, to be positive, seeking points of agreement and attempting to understand the feelings of others. Finally, participants might check understanding with a quick summary at the end of the conversation.

Networking

Networking, the activity of developing personal contacts, is the most acceptable form of politicking as it is endemic to organisations. It is a positive and useful activity for managers to be involved in and, at its most informal, networking is barely distinguishable from friendship. If two colleagues have a chat before a meeting and agree a strategy, this is networking. Clearly networking is a broad term and there are many different types of network.

Networks offer the support and the opportunity to share information. It may be easy to enter networks if you have something that other people want. Networks may exclude as well as include; you should be aware that by identifying with a group there may be negative effects.

Written communication

There will be occasions when both spoken and written communication are needed in order to convey a message. Middle leaders need to be able to communicate clearly in writing. Leaders as role models are in a position to improve communication by their quality of writing as well as by providing an example to teachers and students. Leaders also have an impact on student education, teacher outlook and school image. There is a strong relationship between written skills and job effectiveness.

Identification of audience is important for all forms of communication. Before writing there is a need to consider the audience, to be clear what it is that is being communicated and to feel confident with, and able to convey, the message. The process of writing will also depend on the purpose. A memo to a colleague, for example, will not involve the same amount of detailed preparation as a report for the senior management team or governors.

The following advice is from the NPBEA (1993, 17–13 to 17–14):

1 Memos and letters:

- *know the appropriate audiences for memos and letters*
- *compose letters that include heading, inside address, salutation, body of the letter, complimentary close and signature*
- *write memos that demonstrate the correct form: introduction, body and conclusion*

2 Reports:

- *accurate content*
- *structure – title page and text, table of contents and references*
- *organising headings, sub-headings, the body of the report and graphs*

3 Grants and proposals:

- *sources of grants*
- *basic components for developing a grant proposal: evidence of need, activities/objectives, method of evaluation and project budget*

4 Public announcement:

- *demonstrate basic writing format*
- *plan the layout of a newsletter, effective headlines and captions*
- *developing surveys to gather information from the community*
- *publishing articles in professional journals*

5 Summaries and plans:

- *prepare summaries of articles, disseminations and meetings in as few words as possible*
- *prepare comprehensive plans: objectives, descriptions of current status, strategies, method of evaluation and dissemination of results*
- *correct spelling.*

Meetings

A teacher newly appointed as a middle leader might have to chair meetings. The number of meetings held in a school will reflect the size and culture of the school. Whatever the number, practitioners and managers often have the impression that meetings are a waste of time! Before planning a meeting it is useful to reflect on whether a meeting is necessary.

Advantages

The advantages of meetings are:

- communication
- improve staff skills in communication and decision-making
- sense of involvement and ownership among staff
- democratic – improves job satisfaction
- keep managers and staff in touch.

Disadvantages

The disadvantages are:

- time – meetings take longer to reach decisions and take teachers away from preparation, marking and contact with pupils
- expense – is this the best use of non-contact time?
- limited control – can be dominated by the most senior or the most vocal
- decision-making and communication dependent on the quality of the meeting.

If the quality of school meetings is to improve, it is necessary for all staff to understand the function of each meeting. Everard *et al.* (2004, 58) underline the *critical importance* of meetings in *co-ordinating effort and effecting change*. They further highlight the central role of the manager in ensuring that they are *vehicles for communication and action rather than for confusion and frustration*. Middle leaders are required to plan, lead and participate in meetings which may have one or more of the following functions:

- to communicate information – giving and receiving
- to take decisions
- to influence (and understand) policy
- to monitor and evaluate
- to solve problems
- to plan
- to develop co-operation and commitment
- to motivate.

As stated earlier the size and culture of the school will determine the number of meetings. Similarly the culture and style of each meeting will determine its effectiveness. Understanding the culture and style of meetings will help teachers and managers to:

- make better use of the opportunities
- alter the culture and style, when appropriate.

Meetings develop according to the membership of the team or group, sometimes producing a change in culture and style; this may need to be part of more radical changes in the school as a whole.

There are usually two key roles in formal meetings: chair and secretary (minute taker) (Hedge *et al.*, 1994, 42–62). Middle leaders may be required to chair team meetings and act as secretary to senior management or staff meetings. It is not advisable to chair and take minutes simultaneously. The collective functions of the chair and secretary are:

■ to progress the meeting efficiently

■ to maintain the meeting as a viable working group.

In addition, chairs will decide whether a meeting is to be formal or informal.

Practical advice

Before the meeting:

■ prepare an agenda in advance of the meeting to allow members to consider each point and allow other points to be added to the agenda

■ distribute the necessary papers.

During the meeting:

■ open the meeting

■ state the purpose of the meeting

■ take the meeting through the agenda

■ ensure fair play

■ stay in charge

■ control length and depth of discussions

■ summarise discussion

■ end discussion

■ ensure decisions are taken in the appropriate manner, i.e. conduct a vote, check consensus

■ encourage participation

■ close the meeting.

After the meeting:

■ pursue discussions/actions

■ represent the team at other meetings.

When preparing to chair a meeting, a middle leader should:

- read the necessary papers
- obtain briefing from colleagues, when required
- think through the process (mentally rehearse each item)
- anticipate conflict
- contact speakers/participants to ensure that they are aware of when (and for how long) they are required to speak
- check procedures and rules – know to whom the meeting should report.

Effective chairing of meetings requires effective interpersonal skills. It is the chair's responsibility to ensure that the atmosphere of the meeting is conducive to discussion and that members feel valued. Middle leaders develop skills in managing teams during meetings – take the lead, talk to people, establish acceptable behaviour and set a good example. Haynes (1988, 62–5) suggested that if conflict arises it can be dealt with by:

- clarifying objectives
- striving for understanding
- focusing on the rational
- generating alternatives
- postponing the issue
- using humour.

A chair with a sense of humour may be able to diffuse the situation. Detailed planning may also avoid possible areas/items of conflict. Problems will arise if meetings have unclear objectives and lack leadership. Avoid holding meetings with large groups of people. Have a clear agenda and keep to time.

Middle leaders will also be required to participate in meetings. Aim to become a valued member. The hardest part of managing meetings is arriving at group decisions. This will be discussed later. In sum, a group consensus can be reached if appropriate behaviour is practised in meetings. It is essential for chairs and secretaries to evaluate their practice and to change if required. With good leadership, meetings can be effective.

Information technology

Critical to the effectiveness of management in schools is the ease with which schools can control and monitor relevant administrative procedures.

The use of information technology in schools has developed beyond that of an administrative tool. Management information systems (MIS) are an aid to administration communication. As a consequence, management and staff require training in order to use the system as appropriate. Lancaster (1989, 181) comments:

It is generally accepted that computers can be used either to restrict information by removing the need for information processing and analysis to be delegated, or can be used to facilitate the dissemination and communication of information.

Computer systems

In the context of this chapter ICT is used as an administrative rather than teaching tool. The development of good computer systems will help to control school finance, aid planning and allow monitoring and evaluating of the school's performance. Systems are likely to be required for:

- pupil records and profiling
- staff and personnel records
- examination administration
- admissions
- curriculum management and timetabling
- careers advice
- training needs
- financial administration, covering payroll, expenditure, central purchasing, maintenance of buildings and grounds, income, central accounting and budgeting, local accounting and budgeting and grant claims.

MIDDLE LEADERSHIP QUESTIONS

1 How is ICT used for budgetary work in your school?

2 Can it be improved with better software? Or hardware?

3 Could your school make use of an integrated system?

Hughes (2004) provides specific advice on the technical specification for ICT in Table 9.3 which encompasses more recent developments in learning and teaching and school management. Much of the list on page 196 could be integrated into Table 9.3, thus providing schools with databases that produce greater flexibility in the output of information.

TABLE 9.3 Technical specification for ICT (Hughes, 2004)

	Hardware	Software	Description
Timetabling	PC + printer	Scheduling e.g. Lotus notes MS Outlook MS scheduler Nova-T SIMS	Setting up transparent systems for managing time as a resource and using computing power to solve some of the potential clashes
Communicating	PC + network connection	Communications, e.g. MS Outlook Express Eudora Mail Simeon Mail MSN Messenger MS NetMeeting AOL Instant Messenger Webmail (e.g. Hotmail)	Using computing power to connect with people locally, or farther afield both for learning and teaching purposes or administration
Recording pupils' work	PC + scanner + printer + OMR	Imaging, e.g. Adobe Photoshop	Keeping digital records of pupils' work
Tracking pupils	PDA or laptop or PC	Tracking software, e.g. BromCom	Using computing power to give instant information on the whereabouts of pupils
Budgetary work	PC + printer	Accounting, e.g. Microsoft Excel Microsoft Works Lotus 1-2-3	Generally regarded as number-crunching software especially useful when running a budget

Integrated learning systems	Networked PCs + printer	Virtual classrooms, e.g. SuccessMaker Blackboard	Anytime, anywhere learning for pupils with special learning needs
Creating materials	PC + scanner + printer + digital camera	Desktop publishing, e.g. MS Word MS Publisher MS Works	Using the functionality of computers to make good quality materials
Distributing or publishing materials	PC + network connection	File transfer software, e.g. MS Frontpage FTP Internet Explorer Firefox Opera	Using the interactivity of computers to provide access to materials outside lessons or indeed within them

If the above is to be viable, school and LA computer systems need to be compatible and if appropriate networked. Detailed advice should be available from central government and LAs. Once systems have been implemented, training in their use will be necessary. This is easier if staff have been involved during the system implementation phase. Service level agreements between the LA and the schools will need to be drawn up concerning computer systems. This includes maintaining and running existing systems and developing new systems.

Spreadsheets

It is essential to document the definition, analysis, specification, purpose, programming and testing of spreadsheet models. In practice, however, the need to tackle a problem quickly will often mean that its documentation is postponed until after it has been used, or even postponed indefinitely. If a report is to be produced, then the documentation process is incomplete unless a full report specification is also included. Such a specification must include:

- titles
- descriptive labels

- page numbers and text
- spreadsheet settings
- column widths and formats
- calculations and protection modes.

A directory showing these details should be a feature of the finance manager's specification when commissioning modelling work. It is also helpful to include information that is necessary to customise a spreadsheet, for example any special commands, special equations, input data and anything else required to produce the report. Other relevant information, such as management concepts, is also likely to help prospective users. It is particularly helpful to include a section that explains the inherent logic of the model. Model construction should be part of a continuous process. The model should be reviewed and kept up-to-date, as models that do not reflect actual conditions sufficiently closely can lead to wrong management decisions. Finance managers producing spreadsheets for their own use may not need audit controls, but audit and control issues should be considered if additional staff are involved and as a way of improving systems.

Spreadsheets are also a useful mechanism for preparing charts and graphics for the enhancement of report writing. Different graphics will provide pictorial representations of data. As a consequence, the overall quality and potential impact of the report will be much improved. For staff pay planners and administrators, commercial programs, such as those produced by Kiss Solutions, can be used by schools to reduce the administrative burden of modelling staff costs.

A database will store interrelated data in list form. The selected data can then be extracted to provide the user with information. Schools often hold information on database programs, which are more powerful than spreadsheets. Data can be transferred from these programs to spreadsheets in order to perform calculations.

MIDDLE LEADERSHIP QUESTIONS

1 Have you audited your spreadsheets?

2 Are the spreadsheets standardised across the school?

3 Can the spreadsheets be accessed by all members of staff?

4 Is further training required?

CASE STUDY

Assessment policy

A POLICY FOR ASSESSMENT, RECORDING AND REPORTING IN A SECONDARY SCHOOL

Introduction

Assessment should be concerned with:

- making judgements about what pupils know, can do and understand
- making plans for pupils' progress
- valuing the achievements of pupils
- involving pupils and others in the assessment process
- identifying and helping to improve weaknesses.

The policy sets out to:

- make assessment continuous
- relate assessment to what is taught
- inform parents, colleagues and others (e.g. employers, colleges, etc.)
- strengthen curriculum planning by using assessment information to judge the success of curriculum aims
- measure performance by means of explicit criteria rather than comparing one pupil with another
- make use of assessment information provided by feeder schools
- recognise that pupils' achievement can be wide ranging.

To make this policy effective it is necessary to:

- make clear the learning objectives of a particular course
- develop assessment methods which allow pupils to show what they know, can do and understand
- develop the ability of pupils to review their own progress
- be positive in reporting achievement
- devise methods of recording and reporting which recognise the wide-ranging nature of pupil achievement.

Department marking policy

1 Marking should be done professionally and regularly. It is not necessary to mark every piece of work individually, especially if it is supervised classwork.

2 There should be oral feedback and time for reflection and/or correction or re-drafting by pupils.

3 Marks and grades are not necessary unless the teacher needs to use them to emphasise examination standards, or is marking objectively (e.g. in a 'Unit Test').

4 The awarding of grades is encouraged in years 10–13 in relation to published examination criteria.

5 A comment, preferably positive, should be used wherever possible, which will establish for the pupil their level of achievement and the extent to which they have met the objectives for an assignment.

6 Recording of marks/grades/levels/work seen is important, as is the disciplining of pupils for not doing work set or not handing in work for assessment. The use of assessment files allows rapid access to an individual pupil's achievement record.

7 The use of English should be assessed in geography and so should the use of mathematical/graphical skills. This should either be corrected or a notation used such as 'Sp' for spelling, or 'C' for missing capital letters, and pupils made familiar with their use. Good handwriting should be expected at all times.

8 Pupils should ideally be helped in the process of doing work by a proactive style of teaching. This is at least as important as formal writing. Marking is seen to fulfil a formative as well as summative function.

9 Pupils should learn to write in sentences and in a style which does not require the writing out of questions that they are asked to answer (an exception may be when a question becomes the title).

10 Pupils should be aware of the marking scheme in use and encouraged to discuss the usefulness of marking and how it could better fulfil their learning needs.

———— Summary ————

A middle leader will always keep administration under control and not let it dictate their actions. All documentation should be processed by categorising each paper according to importance.

Middle leaders will need insight into the process of translating the curriculum into the timetable to avoid any possibility of making irreversible decisions which have negative implications (Armstrong et al., 1993a: 56). Middle leaders need to identify the needs of their colleagues and communicate these to senior leadership.

In recent years there have been many debates focusing on assessment and reporting issues in education. Middle leaders will be required to process documentation related to assessment and reporting. At the end of each key stage, a head teacher must comply fully with the arrangements for assessing pupils. While this is the head teacher's responsibility, in practice middle leaders are employed to complete each task.

In the context of administration, the inspection process is perhaps the most demanding of all events in the life of a school. Each school (primary and secondary) is to be inspected every three years by an inspection team which will publish its judgements to a wider audience. The new framework for inspection of schools (Ofsted, 2005), which encompasses the *Every Child Matters* agenda is centred on the school's own self-evaluation.

Communication is central to effective schools. In schools, teachers and managers use different methods of communication for different purposes. An open and supportive communication climate will promote co-operative working relationships – staff will feel valued, trusted, secure and confident.

Communication is the exchange of information, which can range from an informal discussion with a colleague to a full report to school governors. Problems that arise during the communication process are generally caused by the message, encoding, the setting, transmission, decoding or feedback. Some people appear to have an innate ability to communicate; many others acquire skills through study and practice. Verbal and non-verbal communication involve listening and observing. Being an effective listener is a skill that can be developed and practised in each new situation. Networking, the activity of developing personal contacts, is the most acceptable form of politicking in organisations. Networks offer support and a means to share information.

Middle leaders require the ability to communicate clearly in writing. The NPBEA (1993) suggests that the stages in the writing process are pre-writing, drafting, revising, editing and the final product. Information technology makes information easier to access and share, enabling middle leaders to engage in the communication chain in schools. Middle leaders require adequate ICT training in order to access and process information. There is also a responsibility for those designing and contributing to the site network to comply with relevant legislation.

A significant new role for a teacher appointed as a middle leader is the chairing of meetings. Middle leaders are required to plan, lead and participate in meetings. Understanding the culture and style of meetings will help teachers and managers to make better use of the opportunities.

Middle leaders should aim to become valued members of meetings; prepare, think and listen, then speak and encourage others. It is essential to know the audience. With good leadership, meetings can be effective.

Many schools have events when staff and pupils present their work. As schools become increasingly more self-sufficient, creating a positive image is a high priority. Middle leaders have a role related to how the school communicates with the outside world.

REVIEW QUESTIONS

1 It is a requisite that middle leaders know how to prioritise administrative tasks. What measures would you put in place to ensure that documentation is effectively managed?

2 How would you, as a middle leader, develop good assessment practice within your team?

3 Knowledge of the current legal requirements for reporting and assessment is essential. What is the legal framework for current reporting practice?

4 What factors would you take into consideration in the development of an effective school assessment and reporting policy?

5 In the context of remodelling, how should a middle leader prepare for an Ofsted inspection?

6 The conditions in which ideas, information and feelings are exchanged, directly influence the extent to which communication is a positive or negative force within a team. How might you, as a middle leader, develop a positive climate for communication?

7 Before planning a meeting it is useful to reflect if it is necessary. As a middle leader how would you plan, lead and participate in an effective meeting?

chapter ten

Monitoring and evaluation

Context

Monitoring

Evaluation

Summary

Context

This chapter focuses on an element of practice often neglected by leadership teams. Monitoring is an essential stage in strategic and operational planning, requiring detailed consideration by middle leaders. Having implemented a strategy, middle leaders and teams will monitor and evaluate its progress. If plans are not monitored, it is not possible to determine whether the objectives have been achieved. Monitoring will also enable SLTs and department teams (DTs) to obtain the best results from the available resources. The process of monitoring will also enable SLTs and DTs to work towards agreed objectives. Everard *et al.* (2004, 284) underline the need for *yardsticks* by which to recognise when the objectives have been achieved and which can be used to *set a ratchet to prevent backsliding*.

Monitoring

Monitoring is critical to the successful implementation of plans at any level of practice – strategic or operational.

Effective monitoring, which also includes *managing the processes needed to take corrective action in case of a shortfall* (Everard *et al.*, 2004: 285), enables leaders to obtain the best results from the available resources. The process of monitoring will enable middle leaders to lead a team towards agreed objectives. Once objectives have been agreed the department/team can move forward with confidence. From clear objectives comes a sense of purpose. It may be difficult to obtain co-operation and agreement when deciding on departmental objectives. However, it is important to reach agreement within a team if the plan is to work effectively.

Figure 10.1 illustrates the process of monitoring a plan's progress. It is made easier if objectives are clear and practical and agreed by all members of the team (see Chapters 4 and 5).

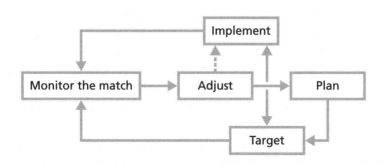

FIG. 10.1 Development planning feedback loop (Hargreaves, 1995)

Monitoring also provides the basis for evaluating practice, so enabling SLTs and DTs to measure and compare performance against agreed criteria and to consider the strengths and weaknesses of continuing with the plan. Everard *et al.* (2004, 285) advocate setting up, *as part of the overall plan for change*, some means of both *gathering reliable information and analysing it… in order to measure if the change has been effective and has become truly assimilated.* They highlight the *'future scenario' description* as a means of ascertaining the appropriate measures to employ. In addition, they suggest that the following techniques can be used as a means of measuring success, where the emphasis is on the *actual outcomes of the change*:

■ *a checklist of procedures*

■ *a questionnaire about role responsibilities*

■ *an analysis of exam results or an attitude survey to be completed by those most likely to know if the change has been successful, e.g. the pupils.*

Most significantly, monitoring will provide a framework in which staff can reflect on their own practice, an outcome of which is enhanced learning.

MIDDLE LEADERSHIP QUESTIONS

1 Who is monitoring what, in which ways and with what effectiveness?

2 Who is responsible for adjusting what, in which ways, when and with what effectiveness?

Source: Hargreaves (1995)

Monitoring is an ongoing activity and is integral to teaching and learning. It should not be left to the end of the year. At the same time, *plans cannot be revised too often or they lose their value as a secure basis for planning* (Fidler, 2002: 20). In the process of planning education, the questions a middle leader needs to ask are as shown in the question box above. The SLT and DT will need to assess the relationship between individual needs (performance targets) and school aims (school improvement plan). Resources will need to be allocated appropriately and plans monitored according to the most beneficial use of internal and external expertise. In practice the SLTs and DTs will also need to monitor development opportunities available from the LA and further government initiative: for example, monitoring any remodelling (see Table 10.1) or a particular subject (see Table 10.2).

TABLE 10.1   Monitoring remodelling

- Performance – targets
- School improvement plan
- Remodelling strategy
- Resources – funding arrangements
- Internal expertise
- External agents
- LA initiatives
- Government initiatives

TABLE 10.2   Geography DIP monitoring activities 2006–07

Area	2006 Autumn term	2007 Spring term	2007 Summer term
Curriculum	New KS3 syllabus introduced, incorporating post-Dearing changes. Timetable blocked with Years 8 and 9 (exception 8.1/2) 5-week blocks, New GCSE course introduced. Heavily revised Year 11 course in operation. A-level course commences in Year 12.	First term of revised KS3 course evaluated. First coursework folio completed by Year 10. First term of KS4 evaluated. Completion of presentation. Year 12 scheme of work.	Full evaluation of KS3 course. Second coursework folio completed by Year 10. Adapt Year 8 programme in the light of changes in sub-programme.
Resources	KS3 – all core texts increased to 30 per set. GCSE – key geography 1 textbook included within scheme of work. A-level core text purchased/library set up. Resource area re-furbished/stock catalogued.	KS3 – final phase of scheme of work initial development. Introduction of further differentiated materials. Inclusion of two units of 'geography-related' material as part of IT training.	Increase number of books in pupil lending library. Increased use of reprographics. New chairs/staff office. Continued production of differentiated materials.

	Premises: refurbishment of geog. res. area/staff office. Improve environment of HU 4/5 and corridors.	Enter bid for screens/new furniture HU 5/carpet for resource area/staff area blackout for HU3/blinds for staff office.	Bid for personal computers for department.
Management	Assessment: introduction of 'title-page recording' of pupil work. New dept marking policy introduced. Centralised recording system introduced. 'Cause for concern' *pro forma* introduced.	Evaluate 'cause for concern' *pro forma*.	Recruit increased numbers for GCSE course 1996–8. Review Year 10 course.
Other	Year 11 Seven Sisters visit. Year 8 farm visits. Head of dept commences MA.	Year 12 Earth Surface Pro. Ctr. Year 8 Manufacturing Industry. Year 9 Environ. visit.	Year 8 Rivers/Year 10. Seven Sisters Year 11/12 res. fieldwork Year 11/12 Channel Tunnel.
Curriculum	Year 11 coursework: folio 3. Year 11 geographical enquiry. Timetable fully blocked (Years 8 and 9).	Evaluate GCSE coursework. Revision sheet for new courses.	First 'decision-making exercise'. First MEG 3 examination. Adapt Year 9 programme in the light of changes to sub-programme.
Resources	Purchase of fieldwork equipment.	Ensure efficiency of filing system – review.	Identify textbook condition and bid for future purchase.
Management	Full computerisation of assessment. Department policy evaluation.	Full knowledge for pupils as to how assessed. Market new 'assessment culture'. Second in	Evaluate KS3 and GCSE course and report.

		dept to take greater role in unit revision and at A level. Senior in dept to lead field trips.	
Other	Year 8 farm visits (inc. dairy). Full fieldwork programme.	Year 12 Earth SPP. Year 8 Man. Industry. Year 9 Geo. Museum.	Fieldwork as 1996. Senior in dept will lead some as part of CPD.

Monitoring will also provide the basis for evaluating practice and learning outcomes. Teams/departments will be able to measure and compare their performance against agreed criteria. Monitoring will assist middle leaders in the planning of staff development by providing an insight into the strengths and weaknesses in their departments/teams.

MIDDLE LEADERSHIP QUESTIONS

1 Who monitors the school in action?

2 How is the monitoring carried out?

3 How are the governors (and parents) kept informed?

4 How is the evaluation carried out?

5 Who prepares the final report?

Most significantly, monitoring will provide a framework in which staff can reflect on their own practice, an outcome of which is the enhancement of quality in the classroom.

Evaluation

Evaluation is a component of development planning and an essential prerequisite to preparing any subsequent plan. The DES (1989, 17) stated that the purpose of evaluating plans is to:

■ *examine the success of the implementation of the plan*

■ *assess the extent to which the school's aims have been furthered*

■ *assess the impact of the plan on pupils' learning and achievement*

■ *decide on how to discriminate between successful new practices throughout the school*

■ *make the process of reporting easier.*

The process of evaluating the effect of a plan on practice is critical to the successful implementation of the plan. In addition, Everard *et al.* (2004, 285) suggest that evaluation will highlight any *unforeseen consequences of the change* which can subsequently be managed or *made the subject of further change.* Evaluation is a collaborative exercise involving (Hall and Oldroyd, 1990d: 34):

■ *asking* **questions**

■ *gathering* **information**

■ *forming* **conclusions**

in order to:

■ *make* **recommendations**.

In contrast to monitoring, evaluation encompasses reviewing the status of a plan's objectives. Through the evaluation process, managers will determine the need to change objectives, priorities and/or practice.

Hargreaves and Hopkins (1991) stress the importance of evaluation in enhancing the professional judgement of teachers. Evaluation can therefore lead to a change in teachers' perception of their practice. For middle leaders the evaluation of department plans can provide the basis for action. Hall and Oldroyd (1990d, 41) offer a checklist for planning and evaluation.

CHECKLIST

Planning and evaluation

1 Purposes, broad guidelines, aims or objectives for the subject under scrutiny which are:

■ clear

■ indicators of desired performance or outcomes.

2 Questions which are:

- unambiguous
- penetrating
- useful.

3 Information which is:

- accessible
- related to questions
- not too voluminous to handle.

4 Conclusions which consider:

- conditions
- effects
- assumptions
- alternatives.

5 Reports which are:

- concise
- focused on audience's need
- likely to inform decision-making.

6 A good evaluation brief:

- specifying much of the above.

Source: Hall and Oldroyd (1990d)

The final stage in the evaluation process is to write the report. A middle leader may have to contribute to the evaluation of a SIP. It will be important to consider the purposes of the report as required. Essentially they need to consider the following aspects of the evaluation process:

- purpose
- content
- process
- context
- outcomes.

Before disseminating the report, a middle leader will need to reflect on each process and ensure that only necessary and relevant information is presented.

———— Summary ————

Monitoring and evaluation are critical to the successful implementation of plans at any level. Having implemented a plan, managers will need to monitor its progress. Monitoring will also enable managers to obtain the best results from the available resources. Most significantly, monitoring will provide a framework in which staff can reflect on their own practice, an outcome of which is enhanced job satisfaction.

Evaluation is a component of development planning and an essential pre-requisite to preparing any subsequent plan. The process of evaluating the impact of a plan on practice is critical to the successful implementation of the plan. In contrast to monitoring, evaluation encompasses reviewing the status of a plan's objectives. For middle managers, the evaluation of department plans can provide the basis for action.

REVIEW QUESTIONS

1 If SIPs are not monitored it is not possible to determine whether objectives have been achieved. What techniques would you employ to measure the success of a SIP?

2 Why is monitoring a DIP an essential aspect of department leadership?

3 How can evaluation of a DIP enhance teaching and/or learning?

RESOURCES

Chapter 11: Financial management

Utilising much of the first edition this chapter will focus on fiscal management and the procurement of funds.

Chapter 12: Workforce reform

This chapter will provide the middle leader with guidance and advice relating to non-teaching professionals in school and college settings.

Chapter 13: Recruitment, selection and induction

Starting from a practical perspective this chapter will guide middle leaders on the recruitment and selection of teaching and non-teaching staff.

Chapter 14: Performance management and professional development

Increasingly important for all practitioners in schools and colleges, middle leaders are responsible for the development of those within their teams. Beginning with appraisal/performance management this chapter provides guidance on professional development.

chapter eleven

Financial management

Government funding

Standards Fund/Schools Development Grant

Value for money

Leadership and management

Local authorities

Budget format and functions

Building and managing a budget

Budget construction

Draft budget

Implementing the budget

Accountability

Summary

Government funding

All middle leaders need to understand the management of fiscal, material, human and time resources as determined by government. This chapter introduces funding policies and processes providing guidance on management and implementation. Further information can be found in the DfES *Financial Management Standard and Toolkit* (see **www.dfes.gov.uk/valueformoney**).

The government funds each local authority (LA) in the form of a Revenue Support Grant which accounts for the LA's need to spend on education based on the Education Formula Spending Share and includes pupil provision for schools through the Schools Funding Spending Share and the local authorities' central provision, i.e. the Formula Spending Share. The Education Act 2002 introduced new regulations regarding the setting of schools' budgets. This was clarified by the Minister of State in letters to head teachers, which outlined the content of a new funding system for LAs. Further changes were introduced in 2005 as illustrated in Figure 11.1.

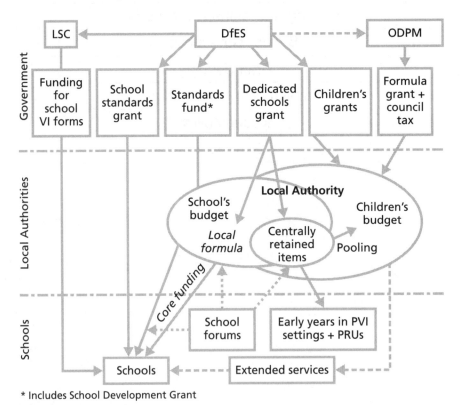

* Includes School Development Grant

FIG. 11.1 Funding responsibilities

Source: Stephen Bishop (DfES, 2005h)

The government is planning to improve funding to schools and other agencies engaged in implementing workforce reform, extended schools and *Every Child Matters*. The aim is to improve efficiency by removing duplication between services and bringing budgets together where appropriate (DfES, 2004c). Additional funds are to be distributed through the Local Change Fund grant and an increase in the Formula Spending Share for children's services. The message to LAs and those who manage children's services is clear (Ibid.):

the increased efficiency of more joined-up working and less duplication gives every incentive to reconfigure baseline budgets in order to support new ways of working.

Further advice is provided at the Secondary Heads Association (SHA) **www.sha.org.uk** and NCSL **www.ncsl.org.uk** websites. The PPA Toolkit (as part of *Time for Standards: Transforming the School Workforce*) is also an extremely useful framework for practice and is available from the NRT website within resource on PPA and financial planning at **www.remodelling.org/downloads/261.pdf**. Further funding can be obtained through bidding.

Standards Fund/Schools Development Grant

The Standards Fund has changed since its origins in the Education Act 1996 as grants for education support and training. Key objectives of the fund are as follows:

- *to maintain an inflation-proof Standards Fund support for schools, as part of the overall package aimed at ensuring stability in school funding. This means that the previously planned reductions in Standards Fund support for schools have been reversed*

- *to contribute to the delivery of the primary and secondary strategies as reflected in local education development plans and individual school targets*

- *to give schools more freedom and flexibility in their use of grant funding to enable them to meet targets in the context of their own needs and priorities.*

(DfES, 2003e)

The School Standards Grant has no restrictions in the use of this grant other than those within the normal delegated budget share. This grant introduced a direct funding route to schools for funds to be used by head teachers.

Value for money

The first principle in the management of resources in schools is value for money. Since the introduction of local funding mechanisms, school resources have been limited. However, early in this process (Arnott *et al.*, 1992), findings from a study for the National Association of Head teachers (NAHT) on the impact of local management in 800 primary and secondary schools, indicated that head teachers welcomed delegation and would not wish to return to full LA control. As remodelling becomes established, this early experience of financial management will provide a good basis for much wider reform. Value-for-money performance is generally expressed in terms of the economy, efficiency and effectiveness with which resources are used as defined by the Funding Agency for Schools' (FAS) three Es; (1999a):

- *Effectiveness* is concerned with the relationship between the intended impact and the actual impact of an activity. How far do the results achieved match those intended? How far do they achieve policy objectives? For remodelling this can be measured by recruitment and retention of staff.

- *Efficiency* is concerned with the relationship between outputs and the resources used to produce them. How far does the activity achieve the maximum output for a given input or use the minimum input for a given output? For remodelling this can be measured by the raising of achievement.

- *Economy* is concerned with minimising the cost of resources used for an activity. For remodelling this can be measured by the involvement of other agencies, parents and voluntary sector.

An integrated approach to value for money recognises that resources used uneconomically and inefficiently in one part of school leadership deprive other areas of resources which might be put to better effect. Initially, remodelling may appear to be uneconomic as some of its benefits will not be immediately apparent. It is clear that value for money concerns much more than the price a school pays for its goods and services or the quality of goods it receives. Improving value for money will involve applying the principles of the three Es across all aspects of remodelling and asking questions about how well the school is doing in relation to those principles. There can be no exhaustive definition of what constitutes or delivers good value for money in schools.

MIDDLE LEADERSHIP QUESTIONS

1 How effective is your school's resource management?

2 How efficient is your school's resource management?

3 Is the school's remodelling policy providing value for money?

4 What are the school's best value practices?

5 How is your school accountable?

6 How are remodelling plans costed and linked to resource management?

7 Have evaluation measures been built into plans and how does the school learn from experience?

8 Do leaders anticipate new demands and opportunities for the school?

9 Are structures and communications within the school organised to support the objectives?

10 Do staff generally understand the school's priorities and how well it is achieving them?

_____ Leadership and management _____

The key to delivering value for money in a school is strong leadership and management. A strong leader inspires, understands and mobilises the school, reading the environment in which the school is operating and building relationships of trust with staff. A sound leadership structure makes sure that the strategic direction is delivered at all levels (FAS, 1999b). Leadership creates a sense of purpose and direction, aligning people and inspiring them to make remodelling a reality as indicated in Figure 11.2.

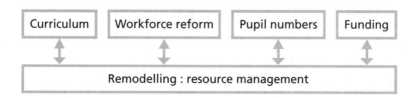

FIG. 11.2 Remodelling: resource management

The reality is the effectiveness of planning, budgeting, monitoring and evaluating outcomes. Resource management is integral to effective school management and therefore should be identified as a role within school leadership equivalent to that of a curriculum or student manager in terms of status and influence.

Local authorities

LAs are responsible for allocation of the overall education budget to schools, although the actual allocation is restricted by government guidelines. Each LA is responsible for determining the exact form of an individual school's delegated budget, based on a formula designed by the LA but set within the guidelines of central government. Interpretation of the legislation will vary according to local factors. LA officers make decisions on staff/pupil ratios, curriculum, advisory support and additional educational needs.

Ultimately, it is the schools in partnership with their LAs through the Schools Forum that ensure spending is targeted to match the available income. Remodelling will involve another stage in the ever-evolving partnership between schools and LAs (children's trusts). In aligning with remodelling, the Schools Forum must continue to ensure that standards and levels of achievement are raised.

MIDDLE LEADERSHIP QUESTIONS

1 How does the LA advise your school on resource management in relation to remodelling?

2 How does the LA monitor school performance against remodelling targets, i.e. workforce reform, *Extended Schools* and *Every Child Matters*?

3 How has the management of your school's finances changed?

4 Do all stakeholders contribute to the management of resources?

5 What factors have the greatest impact on your school's individual budget?

6 What changes are foreseen in the next few years?

7 What is the percentage of your school's budget allocated to staffing? Is this in line with local and national guidelines as stipulated in the *National Agreement*?

8 Does the change management team manage resources in an open, transparent way?

Consistent financial reporting

The use of consistent financial reporting (CFR) is a key element of government strategy in the development and streamlining of financial management in schools. Through the value for money website (**www.dfes.gov.uk/valueformoney**), the DfES states that CFR supports the government's agenda by giving schools the tools to make the best possible use of the resources available to them. CFR is a framework of income and expenditure categories and balances, which are useful for benchmarking. The introduction of one financial reporting framework for all English schools, providing data to populate a national benchmarking website, enables a school to compare its expenditure on any CFR heading with that of similar schools. The framework ensures that there are important distinctions between pay and non-pay expenditure, administration and curriculum costs and if appropriate, PFI.

As of March 2005, there were over 23,000 school records available for comparison on the Schools Financial Benchmarking website released in conjunction with the Audit Commission (**www.schools.audit-commission.gov.uk**) and Ofsted. Guidance on benchmarking has been included to help schools make full use of the website.

Benchmarking enables schools to identify significant differences in spending, consider why those differences might exist and whether they need to think about making different resource-allocation decisions. Thus benchmarking will enable schools to compare their performance, challenge themselves and achieve best value more easily. As CFR develops, schools will be able to map their own performance against expenditure over time. CFR also enables LAs to fulfil their important support and challenge roles (Blandford and Blackburn, 2004).

Schools have developed many strategies to evaluate their effectiveness in recent years, CFR has been set up to provide schools with detailed data and allow greater opportunities to compare and contrast financial decisions of similar schools. CFR will in time reduce the demands on schools to provide data and information to LAs and government as the DfES is to streamline administration in schools by only collecting and issuing essential data. Ofsted will also continue to evaluate the effectiveness of schools in using their resources and CFR will allow clear data presentation and comparison. The Audit Commission processes also help school managers to achieve value for money and promote accountability in spending decisions.

_____ Budget format and functions _____

A budget format should be suited to the organisation's purpose. Finance managers should produce a format which leads budgetholders to describe what is needed and what is wanted. Different information will be required for different stages of the budget process. The main functions that have been suggested for the annual budget include:

1 *determining income and expenditure;*

2 *assisting in policy-making and planning;*

3 *authorising future expenditure;*

4 *providing the basis for controlling income and expenditure;*

5 *setting a standard for evaluating performance;*

6 *motivating managers and employees;*

7 *co-ordinating the activities of multi-purpose organisations.*

(Jones and Pendlebury, 1996, 53)

_____ Building and managing a budget _____

Financial delegation has moved the balance of the allocation and management of finances between government, LAs and schools. If resources are to be managed effectively in schools, school managers need to understand the budgetary process. This is not merely about spending money; budgeting involves management. As shown, the budget is a key document in management and has two aspects, as Jones (1995, 63) explains:

1 *It is a key operational planning document, derived from higher-level considerations such as are expressed in strategy documents and business plans.*

2 *It is a key financial control document, which can be used for keeping spending limits and ensuring that income is planned.*

MIDDLE LEADERSHIP QUESTIONS

1 Can your school plan a long-term budget?

2 Is your school able to review how the budget is constructed?

3 Are there systems to monitor its implementation?

4 What are the pressures on budget management?

Budget construction

Budgets are the means by which a school translates its strategic policies into financial terms providing a statement of intention against which actual results can be measured. Financial projections in the strategic plan should be used as the basis for compiling the annual budget. The budgets are used for the short-term and medium-term management of the school. Budgeting is a key task within the monitoring and review part of the longer-term planning process. It keeps the aims and objectives of the school under constant review.

Schools are required to submit two budgets to the LA. The first is a detailed budget for the current financial year due at the end of April. The second is a summary budget for the following financial year, due by the end of September. Schools may well prefer to prepare both budgets by the earliest possible date driven by the due date for the first budget.

Schools should establish their own planning and budgeting timetable, bearing in mind that some decisions need to be made in advance of the financial year. As part of the planning process, it is important that responsibilities are allocated to appropriate individuals to ensure all relevant financial and non-financial factors are considered.

Before budgets are prepared, information needs to be collated and analysed. It is important to identify those factors which are most likely to affect budget decisions and make sure the information obtained is as reliable and accurate as possible. Information for the budget may be derived from past results and/or may be based on predictions.

The focus of budget construction in schools is teaching and learning. Pupils require space and time to learn; they also require teachers. Teachers need materials to assist the learning process. Traditionally schools have divided pupils' experience into curriculum areas. Finance managers allocate the task of identifying curriculum needs to middle managers, who are responsible for curriculum delivery and pastoral support.

The preparation and implementation of the budget will be carried out within certain constraints. These are a consequence of government legislation, LA policies and/or school policies. Therefore decisions made at the macro or micro level will influence school budgets. Other areas for consideration in budget construction are the relationship between academic and financial years, inflation and income. Finally, finance managers will have to consider:

- monitoring and control:

  operational information

financial information

information on performance

- budgetary control reports:

actual expenditure to date

expected or budgeted expenditure

differences or 'variances' between them

forecasts of likely actual expenditure for the year (specific to each school)

- financial control
- management structure.

Having received their school budget share, finance managers are in a position to draft the school budget.

Building a budget

Finance managers need to follow each of these stages:

- **Budgeting review** Assessment of the current financial position and the causal factors. Key categories are income and expenditure.
- **Budget forecasting** Assess the effect of future financial trends, and what will be required to resource the school.
- **Budget implementation** Place current decisions in the context of the review and future projections. A useful staged implementation process could be:

set out headings and sub-headings of the budget

allocate fixed costs to headings

allocate recurrent costs

bring forward items from the review and forecast; establish priorities

decide between different projects and courses of action

put budget forward for approval by the institution's governors

set check points during the year for possible virement opportunities.

- **Budgetary evaluation** It is important that institutions do not ignore this vital part of the budgetary cycle. Evaluation is the key to the production of an effective budget.

Draft budget

The draft school budget should be presented to several groups from within the school community for discussion. Teaching and support staff should be shown the budget. As the representative of the full governing body, the finance committee is able to change the allocation of funds in the budget if necessary. The full governing body has to approve the budget before it is returned to each LA. Once set under the budget headings, there is scope for the virement of funds.

The process of determining the final budget operates in a time-scale of approximately three months. This process may be complicated by a change in the School Formula Spending Share (SFSS) during this period. It is the duty of the head teacher to inform the finance committee of any changes as they occur. The head teacher is also responsible for adjusting the amounts allocated under each heading within the budget, if the school's allocation is reduced. Once estimates have been established for resources, schools should adjust the estimates to the cash limit. Any reductions to the budget should be realistic.

A school's budget is recorded both centrally and locally. The head teacher is sent a computer printout by the LA; this is coded according to the pre-set headings. This document includes all payments made to the school or by the school. This process will be overseen by the senior leadership team. Should the figures not agree, the head teacher will then contact the LA finance department. All teaching and support staff are paid direct from the LA and these payments are recorded in the document. In addition, the school has a cheque book to be used for local payments.

Implementing the budget

Having planned the budget and received approval from the LA, bursars/finance managers operate the budget. Finance managers must know and understand government legislation and LA policies that govern the assignment and use of resources. Finance managers also need to understand the rationale for building contingency funds, have knowledge of costing concepts, and have the interpersonal skills to involve senior and middle managers and their teams in the decision-making process. Finance managers need to have the skills and ability required to attract new clients, i.e. parents and pupils.

Finance managers should also have the ability to work with senior leaders, managers and governors to match the strengths of teachers with the needs of students. Senior and middle leadership/management teams are involved in the management of specific areas, for example:

■ material resources and systems (e.g. SIMS computing system within the school dealing with income from the LA).

■ buildings and maintenance – the allocation of tasks to the LA, school and contracted specialists for the maintenance and servicing of the school environment

■ Standards Funding Grants.

Finance managers will need to assign materials and equipment according to established criteria, link essential materials to SIP goals and establish a contingency fund. This applies to curricular and extra-curricular programmes. Finance managers will need to develop guidelines and timeframes for grant expenditures and initiate a volunteer programme to help assist them. Finance managers and budget holders need to monitor the implementation of the budget throughout the year as shown in Table 11.1.

TABLE 11.1 Budget activity and action

Budget activity	Activity
Planning	A budget is drawn up for a period of time; this states what ought to happen.
Reality	Events take place in that time period; this is what actually happens.
Comparison	The planned and actual activities are compared: differences may be revealed and measurements of progress and performance made.
Validation	Explanations for the differences sought.
Action	Action is taken where appropriate.

Accountability

The finance manager's responsibilities also include accountability for materials, equipment, and personnel assignments and performance.

Finance managers need to know and understand government and LA regulations governing local management of schools (LMS) accounting. They must be familiar with the LA's accounting system and language and its reporting, auditing, and inventory procedures. This involves maintaining accurate records of the resources purchased, received, expended, stored and wasted during a given time period. Finance managers must also be able to provide written reports to external funding agencies and to account for money received. Periodic accounting is required by law. Finance managers will need to produce accounts to governors, senior managers, staff, parents and the LA.

Effective work schedules and time plans can serve as accountability measures for employing staff. Appraisal documentation provides accountability for staff performance, job descriptions and identification of specific roles in relation to the SIP. The National Policy Board for Educational Administration (NPBEA) describes the responsibilities of finance managers in accounting procedures as specifying records that must be maintained to account for expenditures, in addition to retaining multi-year inventories of materials and equipment (NPBEA, 1993, 13–14). Finance managers should keep files of premises and school meal service schedules and maintain internal accounts for activity funds. They should also maintain daily records of cash received at the site and ensure that there are regular deposits of cash received. It is essential that finance managers submit the required reports to the LA, governors, senior managers, budgetholders and staff. These will include monthly and yearly financial statements for the school involving the examination of reports with appropriate staff or departments.

Within the budgeting process, finance managers need to identify building-level budget codes according to the LA system. It is also important to develop guidelines for grant expenditures in order to meet grant agency submission and reporting deadlines. This process is similar to preparing bids and reports for LAs. All meetings, requests, commendations, warnings and correspondence concerning interagency collaboration efforts should be documented and copied.

Tenders for premise-related expenditure

The premises committee has engaged an architect to advise on work to be carried out on the school's buildings. The budget holder must raise an order for such architectural services. It is the responsibility of the premises committee to ensure compliance with EC regulations.

The budgetholder is responsible for obtaining quotations for minor works, i.e. over £2,500. For higher amounts up to £15,000 to £20,000, firms will be invited to give quotations for the service either by the budgetholder or the school's appointed agent. A minimum of three quotations should be sought unless this is impractical. If this procedure is not adhered to, the reasons for not doing so must be given in writing to the finance manager for reference and audit purposes. Depending on the value of the quotations, budgetholders or finance managers will make a decision as to which quotation is the best value for money. A decision and its reasoning should be recorded in a short report kept by the finance office for audit purposes.

For major works, the procedures will be more detailed. Tender documents will be prepared by the school architect and firms tendering would be sent identical specifications. They would be instructed to place the tender documents and price in a separate sealed 'bid' envelope addressed to the headteacher, clearly marked as enclosing the tender documentation. At least five tenders should be requested. The closing date and time for the receipt of tenders must be adhered to by the headteacher. Tenders are to be logged in by the administrative staff and retained, unopened, until the closing date.

At a pre-arranged time, all tenders will be opened by the headteacher, and typically the finance manager, with the architect on hand, to provide advice and clarification. The premises committee will have some delegated authority from the governing body to accept small tenders, i.e. up to £25,000, but larger tenders will require approval of the full governing body, finance committee and/or responsible officer as appropriate. A tender would not be acceptable if there was any suspicion or accusation made of any collusion, bribery or corruption between any interested parties partaking in the tendering procedure. Acceptance of a tender can only be confirmed by the placing of an official school order.

Question

Having read this case study, what can you do to improve financial management in your school? Use the form shown to structure your ideas.

Focus: premises expenditure

To do	Action
Developing a structure for financial management	
Improving systems for financial management	
Developing principles and practices	
Increasing staff involvement	

MIDDLE LEADERSHIP QUESTIONS

1 Does your school need further development of its premises?

2 How does the school approach its financing of major expenditure of premises?

3 How is maintenance work carried out? Can the procedure be improved?

_____ Summary _____

The principles of resource allocation were determined by the government in the ERA and DES Circular 7/88 (DES, 1988b). The initial effect on the majority of maintained secondary schools in England and Wales was as follows:

- The LA determined the amount of money to be spent, known as the general schools budget (GSB).

- The school was then allocated the aggregated schools budget (ASB) which was determined by a formula.

The government funds each LA in the form of a Revenue Support Grant which accounts for the LA s need to spend on education, based on the Education Formula Spending Share and includes pupil provision for schools through the Schools Funding Spending Share and the local authorities' central provision, i.e. the Formula Spending Share. The Education Act 2002 introduced new regulations regarding the setting of schools' budgets. Further changes were introduced in 2005, the aim being to improve efficiency by removing duplication between services and bringing budgets together where appropriate (DfES, 2004c). Additional funds are to be distributed through the Local Change Fund grant and an increase in the Formula Spending Share for children's services.

In practice, the budgetary process within schools is the responsibility of the head teacher and finance committee, a sub-committee of the governing body.

The LA allocates funds (schools allocation) to the school and the finance committee will then decide on the distribution of funds. The process of distribution is based on previous expenditure under headings prescribed by each LA for the allocation of funds within each school. The draft school budget should then be presented to several groups from within the school community for discussion. Teaching staff should be shown the budget. The head teacher is also responsible for adjusting the amounts allocated under each heading within the budget, should the school's allocation be reduced.

A school's budget is recorded both centrally and locally. Having planned the budget and received approval from the LA, the head teacher then operates the budget.

The allocation of funds to subject departments and teams is determined by middle leaders who prepare a budget on behalf of their teams. Middle leaders will have responsibility for determining and managing their department/team's budget. They will need to know and understand the budgetary processes involved in the school's financial management. Current practice may involve a bidding system, whereby middle leaders will decide on the amount required to fund the running of their department for the next financial year. A useful method of preparing a bid is to compare financial statements from the previous year with similar departments/teams; look for areas where money could be saved (e.g. file paper), and identify the areas which need funding. When completing financial documentation to be forwarded to senior management, ensure that you follow the 'house-style'. A useful method of preparing financial statements is to record materials used throughout the year.

REVIEW QUESTIONS

1 The first principle in the management of resources is value for money. In essence, what does this mean?

2 How can strong leadership contribute to the value-for-money principle?

3 What role do LAs have in the financial management of schools?

4 How might 'benchmarking' help your school in the management of resources?

5 What criteria would you employ in the construction of a school budget?

6 A finance manager's responsibilities also include accountability for materials, equipment and personnel assignments and performance. What procedures should be employed by an effective finance manager to ensure that record-keeping is efficient?

chapter twelve

Workforce reform

Background

Partnership: national structure for remodelling

Leadership implications

Implications for teachers

Leadership responsibility

Workload planning

Summary

Background

Remodelling is not just another initiative; it introduces a new way of managing schools and claims to have the potential to transform the lives of all who work and study in them. As such, any person or organisation involved in the education sector is inevitably involved in remodelling, from the DfES to pupils. The most active participants in implementing the remodelling programme are those shown in the box.

WORKFORCE REFORM KEY PLAYERS

- **Schools** are at the frontline of remodelling. The remodelling process is an opportunity for them to seize the initiative and make a difference to the effectiveness and work–life balance of staff and the way pupils learn.

- **LAs** have at least one nominated remodelling adviser in place; many LAs have a team of remodelling advisers. These advisers support schools through their change process, and champion the remodelling agenda and workforce agreement within the LA. These advisers identify 'early adopter' schools to be fast-tracked through the change management process. These early adopters created the momentum for remodelling across England and served as examples of what remodelling can achieve.

- **The WAMG** (Workforce Agreement Monitoring Group) is a partnership of 11 organisations representing employers, government and unions. It is committed to a better deal for everyone working in schools, including support staff, teachers, head teachers and, most importantly, pupils. The union members represent ATL, GMB, NAHT, NASUWT, NEOST, PAT, SHA, TGWU, and Unison.

- **Governors** have a key role in school remodelling, particularly ensuring that their school is implementing the contractual changes introduced in the *National Agreement* and in making sure that remodelling is central to all their school's future planning.

- **Remodelling consultants** work with LAs to support and advise individual schools as they go through their change processes. Remodelling consultants use their skills to identify the key issues and underlying challenges that schools need to address if remodelling is to be a success.

- **The NRT** (National Remodelling Team) works with LAs, regional centres, WAMG, DfES and other bodies to challenge and support schools
in implementing the *National Agreement*. It also supports forward-
looking ways of remodelling the school workforce in England. The NRT
has been training and co-ordinating **LA remodelling advisers** to help
schools understand the change process and support them in developing their own solutions, and in learning from other schools.

- **The Implementation Review Unit (IRU)** panel of serving head
teachers, teachers and a school bursar scrutinise initiatives from a number of national organisations including DfES, Ofsted, TDA and LAs.
It also has a regional role and will be seeking information directly
from schools to inform its work. The IRU meets regularly with
WAMG and government ministers.

(Source: adapted from NRT website **www.remodelling.org**)

In September 2003 a unique agreement was struck between unions and
government agencies to secure improved working conditions for teachers.
This has led to the remodelling of schools where a teacher's practice focuses
on learning with less emphasis on administrative and support tasks. Set
within the context of the future social, economic, technological and
educational change, teachers will accommodate changes as a matter of
course. Change management will continue to be a normal part of a
professional's life.

The global phenomenon of poor recruitment and retention of skilled
and informed professionals needs to be addressed. Many agencies have
recognised that schools are not static organisations. Set within the context of the 21st century knowledge society, the shared view is that graduates from all disciplines might find teaching a more attractive
profession. A significant factor within the remodelling process is the focus
on supporting teachers, who for many years have worked 'above and
beyond' contracted hours, by reducing the number of administrative
tasks encountered each day.

Schools are central to the government's aim to develop a world-class children's work-
force that is competent and confident and which people aspire to be part of and want
to remain, where they can develop their skills and build satisfying and rewarding careers
so that parents, carers, children and young children trust and respect.

(DfES, 2004b).

Remodelling the workforce underpins the government's drive to improve outcomes for all children and young people so that they are healthy, stay safe, enjoy and achieve, make a positive contribution and achieve economic well-being as detailed in *Every Child Matters* (DfES, 2003b), *Every Child Matters: Next Steps* (DfES, 2004a), *Choice for Parents – the Best Start for Children: A 10 year Strategy for Childcare* (HM Treasury, 2004), *Common Assessment Framework* (DfES, 2005c) and *Common Core of Skills and Knowledge for the Children's Workforce* (DfES, 2005b). Examination of the DfES website (**www.dfes.gov.uk**) shows the importance of workforce reform in current government thinking. Remodelling encompasses three key points of practice:

- *National Agreement* on workload enabling teachers to focus on learning and teaching.

- The *Extended School*, through the engagement of para-professionals and experts in a range of activities, whilst attending to basic needs so that children are able to access a creative and active curriculum.

- *Every Child Matters* to be delivered through increased and enhanced multi-agency and inter-agency collaboration for the benefit of all children.

Remodelling is a process by which a number of previous school initiatives have come together. During the remodelling process, schools are to be self-directed and formulate solutions to their own problems which depend on the involvement and participation of the entire school community. The approach to remodelling is one of continuous change, underpinned by support involving national, regional and local networks. The more creative staff work together to plan, implement and develop effective teams, the greater the impact on practice and attainment in the classroom (Barber *et al.*, 1995). Teachers and support staff need to be guided and supported throughout the process.

The three phases of the agreement are detailed within the DfES website (**www.dfes.gov.uk**). Of the various supplementary documents, the most helpful for schools are those aimed at governors provided at the NRT website (**www.remodelling.org**): *Information Pack for Governors on Workforce Remodelling* (NRT, 2004a) and *Workforce Remodelling – A Guidance for Governors III* (NRT, 2004b). The NRT website also contains a full copy of the National Agreement.

The framework for the workforce reform was based on a seven-point plan aimed at creating time for teachers and head teachers to focus on raising standards in their schools (DfES, 2003a). In brief, these include:

1 a reduction in teachers' overall hours which should be monitored and audited

2 changes to teachers' contracts to ensure that they:

do not have to undertake routine administrative tasks

have a reasonable work–life balance

have reduced the burdens in providing cover for absent colleagues

have guaranteed planning, preparation and assessment (PPA) time to support individual and collaborative teaching

have time allocated for leadership and management activities

3 an attack on paperwork and bureaucratic processes for all staff

4 reform of support staff roles that focuses on helping teachers and supporting pupils

5 the recruitment of new managers with experience from outside education who can contribute to leadership teams

6 additional resources and national 'change management' programmes

7 a commitment to monitor progress.

As the guidance to governors stated (NRT, 2003), the framework, although statutory, would be phased to allow some transition of the *National Agreement*:

Phase one: with effect from 1 September 2003

■ *Monitoring of progress on delivery*

■ *No teacher required routinely to undertake clerical and administrative tasks*

■ *Provision made for teachers and head teachers to enjoy a reasonable work–life balance*

■ *Teachers with management and leadership responsibility entitled to a reasonable allocation of time within school sessions to support the discharge of their responsibilities*

Phase two: with effect from 1 September 2004

■ *Introduce an initial limit on cover for absent teachers with the objective of reaching the point where teachers at a school rarely cover at all*

Phase three with effect from 1 September 2005

■ *Introduce guaranteed professional time for planning, preparation and assessment*

■ *Introduce new invigilation arrangements*

Given that this advice was first published for governors in September 2003, it is quite understandable that school leadership teams are still endeavouring to meet the demands on timetabling and other tasks previously managed and delivered by teachers.

___ Partnership: national structure for remodelling ___

The first priority for schools is to implement the *National Agreement*. In April 2003, the NRT was tasked with co-ordinating the implementation of workforce reform in partnership with the following organisations:

- Workforce Agreement Monitoring Group (WAMG)
- Diocese Directors of Education
- Training and Development Agency (TDA)
- General Teaching Council for England (GTC(E))
- Ofsted
- employers' organisations
- confederations
- other trade unions
- governors.

At a regional level, the regional NRT advisers worked with regional training teams, regional WAMGs and the National College for School Leadership (NCSL) affiliated centres (now NRT Regional Centres); they also utilised internet resources at **www.remodelling.org**. Depending on capacity and funding, both national and regional participants are supported by LA remodelling advisers, remodelling consultants and diocesan schools' advisers. Training has been provided by the NRT through LA remodelling advisers, consultants and training coordinators. There are also NCSL training programme managers and regional training teams to supplement NRT guidance and advice.

Resources are the biggest challenge to expanding the workforce in schools. The government's intention is to recruit an additional 50,000 support staff, but there are considerable doubts as to whether there is sufficient funding for this initiative. Once recruited, training will be needed to prepare those in new roles.

_____ Leadership implications _____

The remodelling process began with consultation with a range of agencies and practitioners, each with expertise, knowledge and experience of working in partnership for the benefit of the school community. Much of workforce reform focuses on teachers, but managers and leaders are also beneficiaries of the changes in legislation that facilitate dedicated leadership time. The core purpose of the head teacher is to provide professional leadership and management for a school. The governors now have a role in monitoring the use of this time in order to enable head teachers to develop the necessary vision and direction to improve the quality of education and to raise standards.

In managing change and to alleviate the burden on head teachers, schools were advised to create CMTs to carry out the change process. Schools have been encouraged to think out of the box, to create new posts in areas previously covered by leadership teams (e.g., example, financial management, ICT support, curriculum support, management of student services and premises); new posts can be funded through the Standards Fund/Grant.

Inevitably, the clearer the plan, the greater the scope for flexibility as staff will be sure of their roles and responsibilities, communication will be effective and planning and decision-making will improve so that the more creative and forward-thinking schools will benefit from workforce reform and the remodelling process. The impetus has remained with the head teacher, whose role has been to ensure that those who have entered into the *National Agreement* with reluctance have gained from the potential opportunities the initiatives offer.

_____ Implications for teachers _____

Within the remodelling agenda, workforce reform has focused attention on the recruitment, management and redeployment of teachers. This is not without controversy as not all trade unions feel comfortable with the changes within the *National Agreement*. Evidence has been gathered from government policies, websites, union publications and interviews with head teachers.

The *National Agreement* aims to raise standards and tackle workload in schools. It is the function of the Workforce Agreement Monitoring Group (WAMG) to monitor the implementation of the *National Agreement*. The WAMG issues guidance notes, which reflect the agreed position of all the signatories, to support schools in implementing the *National Agreement*. Further definitive guidance is presented in the latest statutory *School Teachers' Pay and Conditions Document* (DfES, 2005e) whilst additional advice is given by a number of agencies including:

- NRT
- National Joint Council (NJC) for government initiatives
- governors' associations
- individual trade unions
- LAs.

The NRT has worked with schools to focus teachers' time and energies on teaching and learning, eradicate time-consuming and wasteful activities, bring in new technologies to improve efficiency and effectiveness, assist school leaders to optimise resources and share innovative and effective practices within and between schools, in order to deliver solutions to workload issues appropriate to each school's individual context and circumstances.

In essence, WAMG's guidance explains that support staff will supplement, not supplant, teachers and that every class or group of pupils must have a teacher assigned to teach it. Far from allowing anyone to teach, the new regulations mean that for the first time skilled TAs, nursery nurses and other support staff will work within an agreed framework of direction and supervision by teachers.

MIDDLE LEADERSHIP QUESTIONS

The guide for governors (NRT, 2004b) advises that school leaders and governors should consider:

1 Why and when does the need for cover arise?

2 Can the need for cover be minimised?

3 How will the cover strategy affect the continuity of learning for the pupils?

4 What are the implications for the school's support staff?

5 Has the strategy been incorporated into the budget and long-term financial planning?

6 How easily can a new strategy be implemented in the school?

Consider these questions with regard to your own situation.

Planning, Preparation and Assessment (PPA)

The following is adapted from *Time for Standards: Planning, Preparation and Assessment* (NRT, 2004c). The *National Agreement* states that teachers are doing too much of their PPA in evenings and weekends, and in isolation from each other. While this cannot be changed overnight, the *National Agreement* marks a turning point in carving out some guaranteed PPA time during the school day.

This is the most complicated aspect of workforce reform. Within the *National Agreement* and underpinned by statutory guidance, teachers are allocated time to plan and prepare lessons and to assess pupils' work. The purpose of the guaranteed PPA time is to relieve some of the existing workload pressures on teachers and to raise standards. From 1 September 2005, all teachers (including head teachers) with timetabled teaching commitments, whether employed on permanent, fixed-term, temporary or part-time contracts, have had a contractual entitlement to guaranteed PPA time within the timetabled teaching day.

The amount of guaranteed PPA was set as a minimum of at least 10 per cent of a teacher's timetabled teaching time but not other forms of pupil contact. It is provided as part of a teacher's normal weekly or fortnightly timetable and should take place during the school timetable in blocks of at least 30 minutes. It must be used for PPA and not to cover for absent colleagues. It is for the teacher to determine the particular PPA priorities but does not preclude using time to support collaborative activities. To achieve the minimum allocation of guaranteed PPA time for the majority of teachers has involved one, or a combination, of the following strategies:

- a reduction in teaching time
- changes in the use of existing non-contact time
- redesignation and redistribution of non-contact time from administration of cover, organisation of work experience and the administration of examinations to appropriate support staff.

It should be noted that, in some cases, teaching commitments have increased as a result of remodelling, for example, middle leaders who previously had a reduced teaching load to carry out administrative responsibilities have now returned to teaching as their administrative responsibilities have been taken over by support staff. Some schools have chosen to use higher level teaching assistants (HLTAs) as one of the strategies for releasing teachers for guaranteed PPA time. However, where HLTAs are deployed, the teacher's guaranteed PPA time must not be encroached upon to deal with problems with a class. The HLTA should be employing the school's usual referral system, as a qualified teacher would in case of difficulties or an emergency.

Implementation of a sustainable staffing plan for the provision of guaranteed PPA is a three-step process involving developing strategies, integrating strategies into the school timetable and planning the evolution of strategies over time as an integral part of the SIP. *Time for Standards* (NRT, 2004c) recommended the following stages for the implementation of PPA and the process is shown in Figure 12.1.

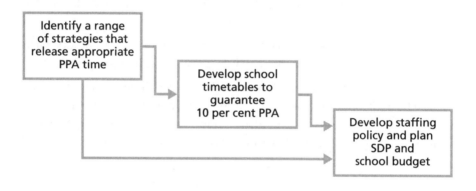

FIG. 12.1 Implementation of PPA (Time for Standards: Planning, Preparation and Assessment (NRT, 2004c))

Stage 1: Maximise the existing teaching resource

Teachers in most secondary schools, and in some primary and special schools, were not timetabled to teach every lesson of every week. Often, they had some timetabled non-contact time which provided an excellent opportunity for schools to provide designated and guaranteed PPA time.

Non-PPA activities carried out during these periods needed to be assessed to evaluate whether they were a good use of teachers' time. Key questions, which still need to be considered, include: Is it necessary? Should we be doing this task? Why are we doing this task? Is the person carrying out the task the most appropriate person to be doing it? Can it be transferred to another person?

Many activities have been reallocated to a more appropriate person, reduced, or even, when appropriate, discarded. It is vital that schools make a thorough assessment of any change to ensure that their quality of care and teaching and learning is maintained or enhanced. Typically, activities that can be reallocated, reduced or discarded include:

■ *Administration* – The transfer of these duties to appropriate support staff. Schools should continually be examining the administration burden of their teachers, to ensure that all their routine administration tasks are redirected to appropriate support staff.

■ *Pastoral care* – Many pastoral duties can be moved outside timetabled teaching time but within school sessions. These duties should also be assessed to evaluate if they could be carried out by an appropriately qualified/trained support staff.

■ *Training and coaching* – Some of these duties do not need to be carried out during timetabled teaching time.

■ *Parent liaison* – Prospective parents are shown around on an ad hoc basis and support staff can be deployed to carry out this duty.

■ *Working with other organisations* – Schools are increasingly working closely with organisations such as the police and social services with the implementation of extended schools and the *Every Child Matters* agenda. Much of this work can be carried out by appropriately trained support staff.

Stage 2: Timetable additional resources

Schools did not have enough non-contact time available to provide all their teachers with the minimum 10 per cent guaranteed PPA, and/or where they wanted to enhance their curriculum, the option to deploy additional unqualified staff to release teachers. These additional appropriately trained and qualified staff have now been brought in from outside the school. By providing appropriate training and support, schools are also able to redeploy existing support staff in roles which build on under-utilised skills, for example, modern foreign language ability or computer expertise.

Key to the deployment of additional staff is that the school curriculum is maintained although schools should look for opportunities to enhance the curriculum by delivering lessons in subject areas that were not previously offered (e.g. contemporary music production). Additional staff should be deployed to carry out specified work, as opposed to supervision. They should have appropriate qualifications and/or experience and have been assigned the appropriate grade. Additional school staff strategies include:

- *Higher level teaching assistants* – HLTAs are expected to make a significant contribution in teaching and learning activities under the direction and supervision of a teacher.

- *Instructors* – A person with 'specialist qualifications or experience or both' can deliver specified work, provided the LA and/or school governing body are satisfied that they have the relevant qualification or experience. Instructors have unqualified teacher status and are employed under the terms of the STPCD. They are contractually entitled to PPA time for the timetabled teaching provided.

- *Specialist staff* – They may already be employed by the school or can be brought in from outside. They may be existing support staff as long as they have qualifications or experience in their speciality, for example, a member of support staff who is a dancer or a native French speaker, sports coaches and local business people. Specialist staff can work with one class or in a 'floating' capacity, working with classes across the school but are not employed under the terms of the STPCD as there is no PPA entitlement for these staff, although schools may chose to provide them with some PPA time.

- *Other teachers* – Teachers can be brought in from outside the school or released internally, through an increase in their non-contact time, perhaps as a result of having fewer cover duties or administrative tasks or by maximising the teaching resource within school sessions. These teachers must be given timetabled commitments, and will be entitled to receive their own guaranteed PPA time. They may be timetabled to teach a number of different classes on a weekly or fortnightly basis. They can be supported by an HLTA or TA accustomed to working with a particular class.

The principles underpinning workforce reform are to be celebrated: advising and supporting teachers to achieve a work–life balance; providing them with 10 per cent PPA time whilst raising standards and extending schools. Is it possible? The wider workforce is the solution: TAs; HLTAs; volunteers and parents.

MIDDLE LEADERSHIP QUESTIONS

The NRT's Guide for governors (NRT, 2004b) has produced a checklist for discussion between governors and head teachers which has been adapted as follows:

1 Have all administrative and clerical tasks been transferred from teachers?

2 Has the school established an action plan?

3 Has time been allocated for all head teachers with leadership and management responsibilities?

4 Is there a sustainable lesson cover policy?

5 Are there plans for invigilating examinations?

Consider these questions with regard to your own situation.

Developing support

There is a strategic role to be played by governors and school middle leaders in developing the role of all support staff, but especially TAs, to support the workforce reform of classroom teachers. In 2003, the DfES guidance was embedded in the *School Teachers' Pay and Conditions Document* which further developed section 133 of the Regulations that gave circumstances where a TA can do work normally undertaken by qualified teachers. This has been agreed in part to provide resources needed to implement PPA through workforce reform, but that does not mean substituting qualified teachers with support staff.

Time for Standards (DfES, 2003a) provided guidance to accompany Section 133 of the Regulations and was intended to safeguard standards in the classroom and preserve the role, status and overall responsibility of qualified teachers in schools. It also addresses the uncertainty over the duties and activities that support staff may undertake to support PPA. It states that support staff:

■ *who may undertake the 'specified work' subject to a number of conditions...;*

■ *must carry out the 'specified work' in order to assist or support the work of a qualified teacher in the school;*

■ *must be subject to the direction and supervision of a qualified teacher in accordance with arrangements made by the head teacher of the school; and*

■ *have the skills, expertise and experience required to carry out the 'specified work'.*

(DfES, 2003a)

The TA's role is further divided into classroom-based activity: supporting and delivering learning and behaviour guidance and support. As indicated, changes will require local decisions and training. The National Joint

Council (NJC) profiles are a structural approach to job and career development, including four levels of progression written in conjunction with section 133 of the Regulations and guidance agreed by WAMG relating to supervision. The four levels are:

- Level 1 – staff will be working under direction/instruction and not left alone with a class.

- Level 2 – experienced staff will be working under instruction/guidance as they develop new skills or gain qualifications.

- Level 3 – staff will work under guidance according to the level of specified work undertaken.

- Level 4 – staff will work under an agreed system of supervision/management. WAMG advises that experienced support staff with appropriate training and qualifications may be given greater autonomy within the framework set by the teacher.

Supervision

Support staff in higher level roles should be working within the school's system of management and supervision which should reflect good practice set out in existing guidance such as WAMG guidance notes. They may be working under the direction and supervision of more than one teacher. Supervision arrangements should include time for teachers and support staff to discuss planning and pupil progress within the contracted hours of the support staff and teachers involved.

Line management

Line management is distinct from the direction and supervision provided by a teacher for activities relating to teaching and learning. Line management covers the more day-to-day matters relating to the management of support staff. Support staff should have only one line manager, usually a senior member of the school's support staff. As indicated in the NJC for local government services job profiles (NJC, 2003), HLTAs may be responsible for the management of other support staff.

The line managers who co-ordinate the work of the HLTA and provide support should undertake appraisal. The teachers who direct and supervise the HLTA should provide feedback to the line manager on progress to inform the appraisal process. Regular reviews allow an assessment of training and development needs so the staff concerned can develop professionally and improve the level of support they can offer.

Specified work can only be carried out by teachers with qualified teacher status (QTS) or someone who satisfies other requirements, for example, support staff may undertake specified work in order to assist or support the work of a qualified teacher. Support staff are subject to the direction and supervision of a qualified teacher in accordance with arrangements made by the head teacher; and the head teacher must be satisfied that the support staff member has the skills, expertise and experience to carry out the specified work.

Leadership responsibility

Appropriate leadership and management is needed if support staff are to be recruited and retained. Head teachers are responsible for ensuring that new or redeployed staff meet the requirements of the support role as determined by a job description for both employed and voluntary staff. Criminal Record Bureau (CRB) checks (see **www.crb.gov.uk**) are also necessary as well as training in behaviour management, first aid and the safe use of equipment within the school. Support staff who assist teachers can expect supervision of activities relating to teaching and learning and line management. This will involve time to discuss planning and pupil progress and the use of the pupil referral system. Line management will be responsible for guidance relating to the role.

Time for Standards (NRT, 2004c) suggests that schools audit the skills and experience of all of its staff and members of the school community including voluntary support. This would assist in the planning of curriculum and enrichment activities.

Workload planning

The workload is designed to be built up to the maximum allocated hours. The emphasis is on departments and the school achieving strategic objectives. Workloads are to be negotiated through middle leaders and approved by the head teacher. All aspects of an academic member of staff's work should be included. This includes building upon an allocated baseline incorporating:

■ teaching

■ management and administration.

Equity is not about all members of staff doing the same thing. Staff will have some control over their workload on the understanding that they are obliged to fulfil core duties, as indicated in Table 12.1.

Aims

Teaching staff will be able to negotiate their workload profile in a way that will encourage staff and career development. Teaching staff will be enabled to engage in work outside their own departmental area. Workload planning will take into account the posts held by individual academic staff. Workload planning will provide the school with a flexibility, and capacity for response to short-term demands. Table 12.1 provides a framework for allocation of workload hours and reflects generic job descriptions. The total commitment must be agreed by those of the School Teachers' Review Body (STRB) or agreed by negotiation with the head teacher.

TABLE 12.1 Allocation of workload hours

	Teaching (%)	Management (%)	Administration (%)	Staff development (%)
Head teacher				
SLT				
Heads of department				
Key stage co-ordinators				
Classroom teachers				

The categories of work are explained as follows:

- *Teaching* – All staff are required to engage in teaching which includes preparation and marking. Teaching also carries an unspecified measure of pastoral responsibility for pupils. The minimum amount of teaching for all staff is recommended to be 10 per cent of the complete workload.

- *Management* – All staff are required to engage in management of the school and departmental activity. This involves attendance at meetings, existing course development and the production of documentation.

- *Administration* – All staff are required to play an active role in registration procedures. The maintenance of and making available student records, and a contribution to evaluation and quality assurance and enhancement procedures, are included within this category. The baseline allocation should reflect this responsibility.

- *Staff development* – All staff will be required to engage in a school or personal development activity.

Process

Personal workload planning (PWP) is closely linked to performance management. Each member of academic staff will take part in a PWP meeting with their line manager before the end of the summer term in preparation for the forthcoming academic year. A second, mid-year (February) meeting will take place in order to make necessary adjustments. Members of staff should use the outcomes of appraisals in order to inform the negotiations for PWP. Records of individuals' workloads should be maintained by the head teacher's office in a format that is accessible to others, in order that availability of staff is readily accessible. This is in line with the principle of transparency.

MIDDLE LEADERSHIP QUESTIONS

Tabulate the workload of the department using Table 12.1.

1 Does it provide an effective workforce management for all members of staff?

2 Are there staff who are over/under-utilised?

3 Will personal workload planning help to develop and improve the school?

4 What are your plans to remodel the workforce in your school?

5 Is further training required?

The introduction of the remodelled workforce will require additional support for leaders, teachers and the newly appointed workforce. HLTAs and middle leaders could be responsible for a range of staff including:

- study supervisors – with responsibility for display
- learning support assistants
- non-teaching examinations officers
- reprographics support staff
- non-teaching cover administrator

- work experience supervisor
- pastoral support assistants
- learning and inclusions officer.

The development opportunities provided for the remodelled workforce should create greater flexibility for teachers. The focus is to enhance the work–life balance for individuals whilst encouraging schools to work collaboratively in sharing ideas on how to work effectively. Fundamental to successful workforce reform is the need for all staff to feel valued.

There will be challenges for each school as they develop an appropriate model of workforce reform. The uncertainty of funding is often cited by school leaders as the reason for failed initiatives; workforce reform arrives at a time of considerable unrest and disagreement. In order to address some uncertainty, a priority for school leaders will be the generation of roles and expectations for all staff.

Training will assist in this process; each member of staff should participate in discussions that determine the nature of the roles of support staff. Teachers will need to know how to manage other adults in the classroom. The opportunities for creative approaches to learning and teaching are endless, but teachers will need to adapt to working with different class and group sizes. Flexibility and training will be central to successful reform.

A possible approach to developing the remodelled workforce could be the introduction of a ten-day timetable where nine days focus on core and foundation subjects and the tenth day is utilised for enrichment activities. Lunch-time supervisors could be employed for break times and given responsibility for low-level administrative tasks in the interim. Support staff could also be used for registration and classroom supervision to allow release for academic mentoring.

The more that creative staff are working together as a team to plan, implement and develop an effective team, the greater the impact on practice and attainment in the classroom. Teachers and support staff will need to be guided and supported throughout the process.

The government has reported on a change management programme developed by the National College for School Leadership (NCSL) that will help schools achieve the necessary reforms. For further information visit the NCSL website **(www.ncsl.org.uk)**.

CHECKLIST ————————————————————————

Developing a remodelled workforce

- The range of activities for the remodelled workforce should be determined by all staff.

- The remodelled workforce should be engaged according to school needs and priorities.

- Consider the training and resources essential to effective change.

———

———— Summary ————

This chapter examined policy and practice in schools as determined by government legislation within the context of workforce reform, *Extended Schools* and *Every Child Matters*. Workforce reform embraces the wider culture change in education and the professions that relate to children, young people and learners whilst addressing teacher workload. Many of the reforms have been developed out of good practice, which includes the child in determining the most appropriate support to improve their development. Key points to consider are leadership, management and planning, resourcing and development.

In 2000, the government, trade unions and supporting agencies met to agree a strategy that would facilitate change in schools. As with previous policies, the purpose of the change was to raise standards in schools. Whilst the approach was to set further targets and create new policies, there was also an emphasis on providing schools with the opportunity and resources to lighten the workload of teachers.

The principles that underpin the strategy for reform require further translation into practice. For every school, remodelling raises strategic and operational challenges. The leadership and management of the remodelling process and workforce reform are critical to a school's success. Development opportunities provided by the remodelling and workforce reform are intended to create greater flexibility for teachers. The focus is to enhance a work–life balance for individuals whilst encouraging schools to work collaboratively in sharing ideas on how to work effectively.

Remodelling provides the opportunity for schools to professionalise all staff. The more that creative staff work together as a team to plan, implement and develop an effective team, the greater the impact on practice and attainment in the classroom.

REVIEW QUESTIONS

1 How can workforce reform enable school leaders to:

(a) focus on teaching and learning

(b) reduce staff workload

(c) raise the attainment of all pupils

(d) enhance the professionalism and status of teachers

(e) provide solutions that extend beyond the traditional boundaries of one school

(f) improve recruitment and retention

(g) improve work–life balance

(h) facilitate change and encourage creativity and risk-taking?

Recruitment, selection and induction

Employment
Recruitment
Selection
Work–life balance
Induction
Mentoring
Summary

—————————— Employment ——————————

This chapter focuses on issues associated with the recruitment, selection and induction of the school workforce. Given the extent to which governors and leadership teams are to engage in the employment and deployment of the wider workforce, further training in recruitment, selection and employment law is recommended. Employment law is notoriously complex and it is advisable for those engaged in any aspect of recruitment and selection to remain up-to-date, be aware of the pitfalls and to seek legal advice.

In the spirit of partnership, the government advises that local authorities (LAs), schools and other agencies share their understanding of the availability of suitable labour and the competing demands from other employers of professional, para-professional and support workers. The following is recommended (DfES, 2005a):

Supporting recruitment ... what works?

- *'Grow your own' approaches – for example, training existing staff (social work assistants and care workers or teaching assistants) to become qualified social workers or teachers, or recruiting local people to train as social workers, either full-time via bursaries and sponsorship, or part-time in employment via college or distance learning routes*

- *offering golden hellos, and/or recruitment bonuses/incentives*

- *enabling participation in starter home/key worker initiatives*

- *offering tasters to provide experience of the work with the employer locally*

- *promoting a positive local media message and improving the image of the council – or other agency – as an employer of choice*

- *exploring targeted or co-ordinated recruitment from overseas.*

—————————— Recruitment ——————————

It is important to ensure that every stage of the recruitment and selection process is fair and non-discriminatory. Prior to any recruitment process the details of the vacant post will need to be clearly defined in the context of the remodelling process (Billsberry *et al.*, 1994). The need to appoint a member of teaching or non-teaching staff will be the result of:

Change
- remodelling
- workforce reform, extended schools and *Every Child Matters*

- SIP and curriculum change
- transfer of role, increased/reduced pupil numbers

or

Maintenance ■ internal/external promotion
- role change/transfer
- maternity leave
- resignation
- retirement.

Job descriptions

Job descriptions are at the heart of any selection process; it is critical that they are an accurate reflection of what is required. If the need to appoint is due to a colleague vacating the post, it would be useful to ask them to analyse what the job entails. The problem with job descriptions is that they often give little indication of what is involved in practice and may need to be revisited at a later date. Each role will be interpreted according to the expectations of the post-holder, colleagues and managers. Clearly, if a role is to be maintained it should be understood by the post-holder.

Having analysed the purpose of the recruitment process, either change or maintenance, the specifications for the post and person will need to be determined. The following checklist provides some guidelines.

CHECKLIST

Job analysis

1 Key questions:

- what is done?
- when is it done?   include teaching, supervisory
- why is it done?   and managerial details
- where is it done?
- how is it done?

2 Responsibilities:

- for others – pupils and teachers
- for resources
- for budgets

3 Working relationships:

- with superiors

- with colleagues

- with other departments and agencies

- with pupils

- with parents

- with team members

4 Job requirements:

- skills and experience

- education and training

- health

- motivation and social skills

- personal qualities

5 Working conditions:

- the school

- the department/team

- social conditions

- funding and pay

6 Check up:

- check with the job holder

- check with line manager

From the job analysis, a job description and person specification can be written. The job description should describe the job, what the job holder is responsible for and what they will be required to do. However, Everard *et al.* (2004, 75) highlight the need to keep the job description *open to revision after appointment as a candidate may emerge with unforeseen talents* which can be effectively employed within the school. The next stage is to write a specification of the kind of person required to fill the job described. It is useful to be as precise as possible about the skills, knowledge, qualifications, experience and attributes which are required for the job.

Job description template

Job Title:

Grade:

Responsible to:

A. Summary of main responsibilities and activities:

- Subject area
- Examination/pastoral
- Age range
- Ability range
- Special needs
- Budgets
- Inspection

B. Specific Responsibilities:

- Staff
- Materials
- Resources

C. Working conditions

- School/LA
- Room
- Work–life balance
- PPA/cover

Person specification

Characteristics	Minimum	Desirable
Education		
Experience		

Training

Communication skills

Special circumstances

Personal attributes

Many posts within the context of remodelling and workforce reform will be recruited in-house but it will still be necessary to follow recruitment and selection procedures. A schedule of dates might need to include advertisement, return of applications, short-listing, references and checking, and interviews before making an appointment. The timescale for each stage of the process should be realistic, especially obtaining references.

Once the documentation has been completed the post will need to be advertised, internally and/or externally. It is important to recognise that the cost of replacing someone in a job can be considerable and the cost of advertising can constitute a high proportion of this expenditure. The content of the advertisement and job description should encourage suitable people to apply. The information contained in the advertisement should be taken from the job analysis and description. Once the planning and checking has been completed, check that the advertisement presents the best possible image of the school. A means of communicating more information is by offering to send further documents. The focus is important: school, training opportunities and full details of the job.

Use the standard school/LA application form or ask applicants to write a letter of application accompanied by a *curriculum vitae* (CV). Candidates will have to show in their applications how they measure up to the detailed job description/specification. Application forms facilitate the retrieval of information; a CV will also offer this information.

Selection

Applicants will be intensely interested in the selection process, which should be efficiently administered. Failure to do so can create an unfavourable impression, so these key points should be considered throughout the selection process:

- candidates will be anxious to know what is happening, so brief the school secretary and administration staff so they can respond to general queries

- application forms and further particulars should be ready to go out immediately; records should be kept of people to whom they are sent
- returned application forms should also be recorded and acknowledged by return of post
- candidates selected for interview should be given as much notice as possible with contact details, a map, timetable for the day, information about any selection processes, details of expenses
- send a courteous letter to those who have not been selected
- if references are required, letters should be sent at the earliest opportunity to ensure they arrive before the date of the interview
- detailed records of all correspondence should be kept at every stage.

The number of applicants short-listed will be determined by the time available for interviewing. The selection team will ensure that the most suitable candidates are selected. A short-listing procedure should be drawn up and several people should be involved. There may already be an established procedure for this process. Those participating in the short-listing process should approach the task systematically, placing the applicants in rank order. It would be helpful to focus on the key requirements from the job and person specifications.

References

Following short-listing, references should be requested. References can sometimes have limitations, as the referees will in most cases want to write a good reference or disguise the candidate's weaknesses. It is helpful for referees to be sent details of the requirements for the job and/or the job specification. If time is short, a telephone reference may be used, followed by a written reference. However, the telephone is considered by some to be an inappropriate and informal referencing method as conversations can be too open and do not allow for carefully considered comments.

The selection interview

The aim of the selection interview is to determine whether the candidate is interested in the job and is competent to do it. Candidates may be compared against each other but more importantly they should be compared to the job specification. A selection interview will involve the following:

- a description of the school and the positive aspects of being a member of staff

- a description of the job in a realistic manner, including any induction processes

- ascertainment of the suitability of the candidate and their personal qualities

- setting out the expectations of the post-holder for the candidate and management team

- enabling the candidate to assess whether they want the job.

The drawing together of all information and decision-making are difficult processes. The evidence will be quite jumbled and will require processing in a logical manner. The panel notes will be vital at this stage. Interviewers can make errors of judgement such as:

- stereotyping based on race, gender, class

- unsubstantiated judgement whereby a candidate is assumed to possess certain skills

- underrating or overrating all candidates.

Any rating of candidates should be preceded by a detailed discussion. Selection is an important public relations exercise and the ground rules should be established at the start. Attitude and profile questionnaires, traditionally employed by companies to assess potential candidates, are now being used more frequently by schools (Everard *et al.*, 2004). They can provide greater insight into the suitability of a potential candidate for the post. However, a rating form (see Table 13.1) prepared in advance of the interview will also assist:

TABLE 13.1 Selection rating form

Specification	Candidates						
	A	B	C	D	E	F	G
Qualifications							
Education							
Experience							
Personal qualities							

The person appointed will be elated whilst the other candidates will feel deflated. The interview panel should provide all candidates with the opportunity to discuss the interview process and to evaluate strengths and weaknesses. These should be well considered and based on the evidence collated during the interview process. Sensitivity should be demonstrated at all times especially with remodelling where candidates are more likely to be current members of staff. The new appointee will require further documentation in support of their role. This should be prepared in advance of the interview to enable the appointee to take away relevant information. Site recruitment practices are important for all posts and further guidance is available at the DfES website **www.dfes.gov.uk**. Careful records should be kept in case unsuccessful candidates claim that the selection process has been unfair or discriminatory.

Finally, CRB checks are completed on the successful applicant after appointment.

Work–life balance

Workforce reform intends to promote a work-life balance for the school workforce. Use the following as a checklist to ensure that support and technical staff are fully integrated into the professional community within your school.

CHECKLIST

Schools and LAs need to: **Completed date**

- ensure that there are job specifications for the school workforce
- establish guidance and training for those involved in interviewing and appointing staff to new posts and for those assuming new responsibilities
- ensure that all staff can demonstrate their proficiency in the role for which they have been trained
- set up induction programmes which make differentiated provision, based on an analysis of individual need, to support new staff who come from a wide variety of backgrounds and experience
- determine their respective responsibilities for the induction training each is expected to provide and its timing

- set up monitoring and evaluation procedures which can identify good practice and make possible its dissemination

Furthermore, schools and LAs will need to: **Completed date**

- pay particular attention to the impact of remodelling, workforce reform, *Extended Schools* and *Every Child Matters*, so that there are no gaps in the responsibilities for the appointment and induction of staff

- maintain monitoring and reporting procedures which ensure that schools and LAs are aware of and are able adequately to support the school workforce

Induction

Effective induction ensures that anyone new to a role or new to the school feels supported and confident, ready to join an effective team, and willing to contribute to their own and the school's development. Specifically for teachers, the requirements for satisfactory completion of the induction period ensure that schools must support NQTs as they build on their previous achievements. This also applies to the wider workforce.

New appointments

When a new member of staff joins the school, identify what they will need to know using the following list:

- job description
- their position in the team/school
- school's aims (SIP) and policies
- relevant documentation, including staff handbook
- reporting and assessment procedures
- members of team – introduce colleagues
- identities of vulnerable pupils.

The new appointee will also require further documentation:

■ contract (including start date and time)
■ staff handbook
■ health and safety details
■ timetable
■ staff lists
■ room lists
■ class lists
■ reports/assessments
■ schemes of work/lesson plans.

The first days and weeks in a new post are stressful for any employee. Many choices will have been considered by all involved and it is inevitable that judgements as to the suitability of the post and post-holder will be determined by their early performance. Induction can assist in this process. The following sections provide some practical guidance on the induction of the school workforce.

Working in schools can be both challenging and stimulating, and induction for newly appointed staff is vital if they are to fulfil their roles in a remodelled school. In any profession, the transition from training to the workplace or into a new role generates certain tensions; employees need to know that the contributions they make are valued and employers need to ensure that staff have the appropriate training.

Figure 13.1 illustrates the range of potential induction activities available to a new appointee. Senior leadership and professional development co–ordinators should ensure that new staff have access to all support mechanisms and relevant information.

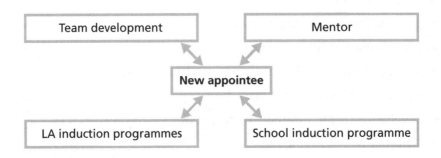

FIG. 13.1 Areas of support for newly appointed staff

The professional development co-ordinator has an important role to play in the induction of the school workforce. Any CPD needs must be identified and the appropriate induction process planned. Release time for staff involved and the money for any supply cover should be available. The professional development co-ordinator can work within this to encourage staff to become involved in the induction programme, actively promoting the development of individuals. They can also ensure the participation of members of staff who have identified such areas for development through the process of appraisal and in development interviews (Rawlings, 1998).

CHECKLIST

What is needed for effective induction?

Effective induction needs to be planned but flexible. The following actions should be taken:

- appoint a mentor
- identify the training, development and personal needs of the new appointees
- negotiate with your new colleague the most appropriate personal and professional support.
- develop a climate of mutual support
- create an environment which is open; respect the needs of others
- promote job-shadowing and observation, laying the foundation for reflective practice
- ensure that the newly appointed member of staff can identify with their team
- ensure that the new appointee will know their role, managers and team
- if necessary, consider external factors such as accommodation, transport and social needs to assist with work–life balance
- ensure that support and professional guidance are relevant
- plan a central induction programme to enable newcomers to meet and discuss their strengths and weaknesses; this programme may begin in the term before the member of staff takes up their post
- provide access to external support networks; subject organisations; support groups; LA advisers.

_____ Mentoring _____

Mentoring is a term which continues to be used in several different contexts in education (Ormston and Shaw, 1993b). It generally means the positive support offered by staff with some experience to staff with less experience of the school. This experience can extend over a wide range of activities, or be specific to one activity. The school workforce may engage in a number of mentoring relationships:

- mentoring of new staff joining their teams
- mentoring of colleagues to support them in their new role
- as a mentee, either of a team leader or senior leader, in preparation for a current or future post.

Mentoring will differ according to need and includes enhancing the mentee's skills and professional development, helping to develop a set of educational values, consulting to help the mentee to clarify goals and ways of implementing them, helping to establish a set of personal and professional standards, and networking and sponsoring by providing opportunities for the mentee to meet other professionals.

Mentors are likely to have a number of roles within the school and they need to decide whom to mentor in the context of their other tasks and responsibilities. Mentoring is time-consuming. Mentees should select their mentor based on professional needs, present and/or future. It is important to understand that mentoring is a continuous staff development activity which, once the system is established, takes place during normal school life. Mentors need to know and understand the essential elements of a mentoring relationship.

Mentoring is a positive mechanism for developing management skills for both the mentor and mentee. As a process, mentoring should move through the stages shown in Figure 13.2. The stages of mentoring will involve a period of induction for the mentor and mentee. During this stage, the mentor and mentee need to ensure that they are the most appropriate people for the role. Interpersonal skills and a good professional relationship are essential for effective mentoring as most mentors are working with experienced staff.

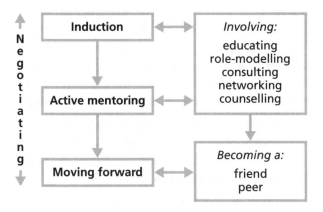

FIG. 13.2 Stages of mentoring

CHECKLIST

What are the essentials of mentoring?

- a recognised procedure, formal or informal
- a clear understanding of the procedure and the roles of mentor and mentee
- trust and a rapport between both parties
- the credibility and genuineness of the mentor as perceived by the mentee
- confidentiality and discretion
- a relationship based on the mentee's perception of their own needs
- a suitable range of skills used by the mentor: counselling, listening, sensitive questioning, analysis and handing back responsibilities
- an appropriate attitude by both parties, for example the ability of the mentor to challenge the mentee, and the self-motivation of the mentee to take action when necessary

In addition, teachers should be aware of equal opportunity issues that need to be addressed in the selection and training of mentors.

_____ Summary _____

Schools have increased responsibility for the recruitment and selection of staff, teaching and non-teaching. As a middle leader it is highly likely that you will be involved in staff recruitment and selection. When appointed to the post, a middle leader will inherit a team. Selection skills are only required when a vacancy occurs. Prior to any selection process the details of the vacant post will need to be clearly defined. As a middle manager, it will be highly inadvisable to embark on any major change without discussing this with others, i.e. your team and senior leadership.

Middle leaders should, in practice, know and understand their role in the school as an organisation. A middle leader should also know and understand the roles of their team. A middle leader should, therefore, be aware of the requirements and expectations for each post.

From the job analysis, a job description can be written. The third stage in the process is to write a specification of the kind of person required to fill the job that you have just described.

Middle leaders should clarify their responsibilities and authority in the recruitment and selection process. Schools should have a recruitment policy that complies with government and (where relevant) LA policies and legislation.

Once the documentation – job analysis, description and specification – has been completed, the post will need to be advertised, internally and/or externally. The LA and/or school may have a specific policy for advertising. The content of the job description should encourage suitable people to apply for the job. The selection process should be efficient; failure to do so can create an unfavourable impression. The involvement of a middle manager at the short-listing stage is useful as they will have an added insight into what type of individual will be most suitable.

Middle leaders should be involved in the reference reading/checking process. It is essential that the recruitment and selection process is approached in a sensitive and professional manner. Interviewing is complex; as a middle manager you will need to prepare for the interview, conduct the interview and be involved in the decision-making process. Preparation is all important; candidates will have taken time to apply and will have a lot at stake, and you will want to select the most suitable applicant.

The drawing together of all information and decision-making are difficult processes. Any rating of candidates should be preceded by a detailed discussion. Offering the job is a delicate process. The person appointed will be elated, the other candidates will feel deflated. The interview panel should provide all candidates with the opportunity to discuss the interview process and to evaluate strengths and weaknesses. These should be well considered and based on the evidence collated during the interview process. Sensitivity should be demonstrated at all times.

REVIEW QUESTIONS

1 What criteria would you employ when preparing a job description?

2 The aim of a selection interview is to determine whether the candidate is interested in the job and competent to do it. What procedures would you employ to assist you in selecting the 'right' candidate?

3 What are the requirements of an effective induction programme?

4 A middle leader will have mentoring responsibilities. What would you do to enhance your performance as an effective mentor?

chapter fourteen

Performance management and professional development

Professional development

Performance, management and review

Leaders' role in professional development

Teacher Training Agency/Training and Development Agency

The General Teaching Council for England

National College for School Leadership

Sector Skills Council

Accreditation

Summary

_____ Professional development _____

Learning and development are central to the process of schooling. Whilst schools provide learning and development opportunities for pupils, they should also provide a learning environment for all their staff. The expertise and experience of its workforce is a school's most valuable resource. School governors and leaders need to take responsibility for the training and development of the staff in their community. Professional development and performance management are critical factors in the effective leadership of the school workforce and can occur in a variety of forms. The following sections focus on defining professional development and performance management through policy and practice.

There has been a crucial shift by the DfES, GTC(E) and the NCSL to provide for professional learning communities. Within the framework of workforce reform, self-development and staff development are prerequisites for effective and improving teaching and schools. Equally, a precondition and an outcome of effective CPD policies is a culture that encourages learning through reflection and development. Ofsted's (2002a, 17) document, *Leadership and management: managing the school workforce*, stated that:

the schools that planned CPD most effectively had a clear and open process by which professional development priorities were determined. They tempered school and departmental priorities against the career aspirations and development needs of individuals.

The characteristics of 'effective professional learning communities' include:

- *innovative and effective practice in managing human and financial resources to create time and opportunity for professional learning and development to optimise its impact*

- *generating models which serve as credible exemplars of 'professional learning communities'*

- *informing leadership programmes about creating and sustaining 'professional communities'.*

(McCall and Lawlor, 2002)

____ Performance, management and review ____

Performance management is an essential element in the development of the school workforce. Its purpose is to provide an opportunity for performance enhancement that motivates and develops individuals.

Performance management and review should improve the quality of education for pupils by assisting the school workforce to realise their potential and to carry out their duties more effectively.

CHECKLIST

What is the purpose of performance review?

- To raise standards through setting targets that enhance performance and to improve provision for pupils and the school workforce
- to link the review cycle to:

  LA education development plans

  school management procedures

  Ofsted – action plan

  annual reviews and development plans

  individual development plans

  induction and assessment
- to plan the professional development of the school workforce within the local LA and national frameworks.

A working definition of performance review is: one professional holding him/herself accountable to him/herself in the presence of another professional. The review may improve the management of teaching and learning within the classroom by helping the school workforce identify ways of enhancing their skills and performance and supporting them in the identification of achievable targets. Performance review should assist in planning professional development individually and collectively within the framework set by the school improvement plan. This will enhance the overall management of the school and provide an opportunity to consider the effective management of change. Performance review should also support the promotion of equal opportunities.

To this end, a school workforce performance review scheme should be a process that is open and based on the mutual understanding by all staff of its context, purpose, procedures, criteria and outcomes. The process and procedures adopted should be fair and equitable and should be seen to be so, both in general and by respecting equal opportunities, particularly

in relation to gender and ethnicity. The process and procedures supporting performance review should also be acceptable to all staff, head teachers, governors and LA personnel. The school workforce should benefit from
participation in the scheme. There should be the opportunity for objective judgements to be made concerning the management of the institution. The review process is summarised in Figure 14.1.

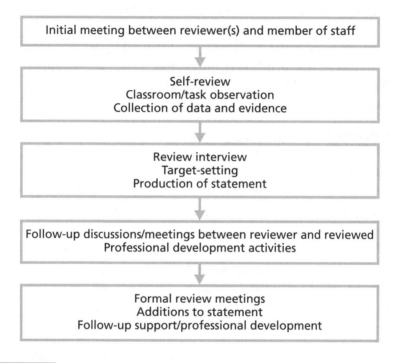

FIG. 14.1   The review process

At all times the scheme should aim to avoid unnecessary bureaucracy and
time-consuming administration by the maximisation of available
resources and the use of data from a range of sources. It should be integral to the school's development strategy and attempt to balance the
demands of professional development and public accountability. A rigorous system of review is one that raises standards, key elements of which
are trust, training, resourcing, time, support and commitment. For performance management to have any meaning it should be seen to inform
the school development process. To this end, schools should aim to have
in place a co-ordinated procedure for ensuring that:

- mechanisms exist for collating professional development needs identified through individual reviews
- there is co-ordination of training needs and related development opportunities
- there are contingency plans for coping with those whose performance is perceived as poor for a variety of reasons (e.g. stress, lack of skills).

As performance review is an annual process, there is an opportunity to agree targets with staff in the light of targets set by the school in the development plan, which will itself be influenced by key points for action in Ofsted reports and benchmark information from national data collected by Ofsted and the LA's educational development plans (EDPs). An overview of target setting is provided in Table 14.1.

TABLE 14.1 Setting targets

Targets linked to	Training	
	Planned by	Delivered through
Whole school	SLT	INSET days
	CPD co-ordinator	Staff meetings
		Conferences
Subject or department	Subject leader or	Department meetings
	line manager	Conferences
Area of responsibility	CPD co-ordinator	Range of activities
Personal professional development	CPD co-ordinator	Range of activities

CHECKLIST

Performance review – what is required?

The management of performance review requires:

- an implementation plan for the performance review scheme
- a statement of aims, the documentation and the organisation of the scheme
- a timetable/duration of cycle/frequency
- a personnel, resources and equal opportunities policy
- a school improvement plan
- a process/cycle
- availability/accessibility

- a job description
- a staff development policy
- professional development record
- co-ordination and resources.

___ Leaders' role in professional development ___

Earley and Fletcher-Campbell (1989, 105) deduced from their research that, *desire for development was seen as one of the hallmarks of a successful department.* They also identified the increasing importance for middle leaders to attend to this area. *Development* is a term encompassing any experience or process which helps to bring out an individual's full potential. Middle leaders should aim to improve the quality of their staff. Responsiblity for achieving targets will lead a middle leader to offer the team training and development.

The GTC (2004, 2) underlines the importance of staff development:

Professional learning and development is an entitlement and responsibility for all teachers. It is an important way of supporting and recognising teachers' expertise. Learning runs through a teaching career, taking place formally and informally through a wide range of learning experiences, deepening and revitalising teachers' skills, abilities and values and knowledge. It is a process of enquiry, supporting teachers to:

- *develop the learning of other pupils*
- *develop a common language for understanding the processes of teaching and learning*
- *engage in improvement of teaching and learning.*

Middle leaders have a responsibility to see that individuals develop new skills. Staff development should not mean an additional activity; often development activities will happen as a matter of course. Staff development includes personal development, team development and school development. It also encourages:

- the promotion of shared values
- the implemention of change
- the promotion of equal opportunities.

The responsibility for developing staff is shared. The school as a whole has a responsibility to develop policies and provide resources for staff development but middle leaders play a major role in staff development. A middle leader will know their staff's work, experience and aspirations.

As a player manager, a middle leader is uniquely placed to assist a colleague's development.

The individual also has a stake in their own development and should take some responsibility for it. Development cannot be imposed; individuals must own the development process or it will not happen. A middle leader can assist staff in their development in several ways:

- role model – staff will adopt your practices and attitudes
- specific guidance/training
- encourage reflection
- sensitive delegation
- promote development opportunities
- act as 'gate-keeper' for information and various opportunities as they arise.

Middle leaders need to identify the development needs of their teams and aim to achieve each, collectively and individually. Recognising development needs is a process involving formal (appraisal) and informal (observation) approaches. A detailed job description will provide a framework for identifying individual needs, equally applicable to current and future posts.

Professional development opportunities are many and varied. McCall and Lawlor (2002) indicate the key factors in a learning organisation:

- *staff see openness to learning as important for them as well as students*
- *they see school development as a cyclical process of organisational learning*
- *they protect, as far as possible, professional development work being interrupted by other issues/events*
- *they examine the effectiveness of the school as a learning organisation, including review of preferred/alternative learning styles*
- *they ensure the free flow of information from courses, inspection, research and self-evaluation.*

The school workforce requires guidance on what is available to assist them in the development of their professional practice. By underlining the following effective CPD programme implemented by a number of schools, Ofsted (2002a, 18) highlights the need for careful planning for effective CPD:

Professional development was often built into the day-to-day life of the schools. Senior managers and teachers appreciated, for example, how opportunities to work with other colleagues in a variety of ways, from planning and teaching lessons to collaborating on projects, were often very influential in improving the teachers' professional knowledge and skills.

The professional development co-ordinator has a responsibility for the management of both internal and external opportunities. Effective communication is essential if all staff are to benefit. Professional development needs to be clear and useful. Ask the question: what does it bring, in the best instances, to professional practice? Professional development experiences perform four major functions; all of which are related to the remodelling process. The four functions are to:

- enhance the personal and professional lives of teachers and staff
- provide a remedy for ineffective learning and teaching
- set the groundwork for implementing school aims
- introduce changes.

In practice, development is a term encompassing any experience or process that helps to bring out an individual's full potential. Development embraces both individual and school improvement. The General Teaching Council for England (GTC(E)) considers the purposes of CPD for teachers to:

- *develop a shared understanding in the profession about what professional development and learning should include*
- *influence national policy and funding*
- *raise teachers' expectations both on entry to the profession and to professional learning communities*
- *enable teachers to reflect on how they can and do contribute to the professional, collective knowledge about teaching and learning*
- *provide the basis for widening opportunities for accreditation and recruitment*
- *provide support for school leaders in making time and support available.*

(GTC(E), 2002)

In a learning community, staff development will include personal, team and school development. Leaders have a shared responsibility to see that individuals develop new skills. Staff development has a wider importance in promoting shared views, implementing change and promoting equal opportunities. It is critical to note that staff development including qualifications should not mean an additional activity; it should be integral to school development.

Professional development encompasses practitioner development, education, training, and support activities experienced by teachers, team leaders and the senior leadership team (Bolam, 1993) – see the box below.

Practitioner development

School-based development; self-development, induction, mentoring, observation, job-shadowing and team-teaching.

Professional education

Award-bearing courses managed and taught at HEIs, focusing on the relationship between educational theory and practice, and leading to higher education accreditation and professional qualifications.

Professional training

Conferences, courses and workshops that emphasise practical information and skills, managed and delivered by LAs, school external consultants or trainers from HEIs; such courses may lead to accreditation towards national standards or academic awards.

Professional support

The responsibility of colleagues in school, through the process of fulfilling contractual conditions of service, e.g. recruitment and selection procedures encompassing job descriptions, promotion, career development, performance management, mentoring, team-building, redeployment and equal opportunities.

_____ Teacher Training Agency/Training and _____ Development Agency

The TTA was established in 1994 by the government to review and develop the training of teachers. Central to its work was the issue of school effectiveness set within the context of the government's school improvement programme. In September 2005, the TTA became the Training and Development Agency for Schools (TDA). The Education Act 2005 gave the TDA greater responsibility for the training and development of the school workforce. To this end the restructured TDA focuses on the three areas of initial teacher training (ITT), the training and development of school support staff and continuing professional development of teachers. In its Corporate Plan (2005–08) the TDA outlined its aims within the context of apposite operational objectives:

Ensure schools have an adequate supply of good-quality newly qualified teachers (NQTs)
Key operational objectives:

- *To recruit sufficient good new teachers to the profession*
- *To allocate and fund ITT places, having regard to demand from schools for newly qualified teachers*
- *To improve the quality of ITT*
- *To update standards for QTS and accompanying guidance*

Enable schools to develop the effectiveness of their support staff
Key operational objectives:

- *To increase support staff participation in training and development*
- *To improve the supply of training and development for support staff*
- *To strengthen the quality of training and development for school support staff*

Enable schools to develop the effectiveness of their teachers and keep their knowledge and skills-up-to-date.
Key operational objectives:

- *To promote the demand for, and access to, appropriate training and development opportunities for teachers*
- *To contribute to the supply of relevant, high-quality training and development opportunities for teachers*
- *To strengthen the quality of the training and development opportunities for teachers.*

Support schools to be effective in the management of the training, development and remodelling of their workforce
Key operational objectives:

- *To provide schools and their staff with good information and guidance on training and development*
- *To support school managers in improving the training and development of their staff*
- *To support schools in remodelling their workforce.*

(TTA, 2005)

TDA standards

Professional standards for classroom teachers should provide clarity about the expectations of teachers at each career stage; provide a reference point for teachers as they review and plan their training and development; and enable schools to make valid, reliable and consistent decisions with regard to the professional development and pay progression of teachers.

The standards in three inter-related sections that are broadly based on the structure of the current qualified teacher status standards are:

- **Professional characteristics/qualities and responsibilities:** *this section sets out the personal qualities that teachers should possess in order to meet their responsibilities;*

- **Professional knowledge and understanding:** *this section indicates the areas about which teachers should be well informed;*

- **Teaching, learning and assessing:** *this section states what teachers should be able to do.*

(TDA, 2006)

Figure 14.2 illustrates the TDA's framework for developing standards for teachers.

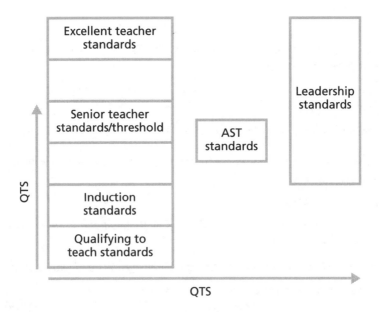

FIG. 14.2 TDA teaching standards

The TDA has enhanced the opportunities of CPD for teachers through the proposed framework of national standards (see Figure 14.2). At each stage of development, implementation and evaluation, new initiatives should involve practitioners. Teachers need to have confidence in the process. Middle leaders need to develop the knowledge and understanding, skills and abilities to manage CPD in their schools.

_____ The General Teaching Council for England _____

The General Teaching Council for England agreed the Statement of Professional Values and Practice for Teachers in 2002.

The Statement is intended to help make sure that the professional work of teachers helps their pupils to develop themselves fully and reach their highest potential in life. It is intended to be an evolving document that will contribute to the definition of teacher professionalism and help in raising standards of achievement by pupils.

The following provides a summary of the main points:

General introduction: the high standards of the teaching profession

- *Teachers inspire and lead young people, helping them achieve their potential as fulfilled individuals and productive members of society.*

- *First and foremost teachers are competent classroom practitioners. The role of teachers is to achieve success for their pupils through a complex network of relationships. They need high levels of commitment, energy and enthusiasm.*

- *To ensure the positive development of individual pupils, teachers work within a framework of equal opportunities and other relevant legislation, statutory guidance and school policies.*

Professionalism in practice

Young people as pupils

- *Teachers use professional judgement to meet the learning needs of young people and choose the best ways of motivating pupils to achieve success. They use assessment to inform and guide their work.*

- *Teachers have high expectations of all pupils. They work to make sure that pupils develop intellectually and personally, and to safeguard pupils' general health, safety and well-being. Teachers demonstrate the characteristics they are trying to inspire in pupils, including a spirit of intellectual enquiry, tolerance, honesty, fairness, patience, a genuine concern for other people and an appreciation of different backgrounds.*

Teacher colleagues

■ *Teachers support their colleagues in achieving the highest professional standards. They are fully committed to sharing their own expertise and insights in the interests of the people they teach and are always open to learning from the effective practice of their colleagues. They respect confidentiality where appropriate.*

Other professionals, governors and interested people

■ *Teachers recognise that the well-being and development of pupils often depend on working in partnership with different professionals, the school governing body, support staff and other interested people within and beyond the school. They respect the skills, expertise and contributions of these colleagues and partners in the interests of the pupils.*

Parents and carers

■ *Teachers endeavour to communicate effectively and promote co-operation between the home and the school for the benefit of young people.*

The school in context

■ *Teachers recognise that professionalism involves using judgement over appropriate standards of personal behaviour.*

Learning and development

■ *Teachers understand that maintaining and developing their skills, knowledge and expertise is vital to achieving success. They take responsibility for their own continuing professional development to ensure that pupils receive the best and most relevant education. Teachers continually reflect on their own practice, improve their skills and deepen their knowledge. They want to adapt their teaching appropriately to take account of new findings, ideas and technologies.*

(GTC(E), 2002)

——— National College for School Leadership ———

The NCSL controls leadership training programmes for aspiring, new and practising head teachers, and middle leaders (subject leaders), and administers funding for networked learning communities, enabling and encouraging schools and teachers to work collaboratively on issues of mutual concern and interests.

——————— Sector Skills Council ———————

In *Every Child Matters: Next Steps* (DfES, 2004a), the government also set out its intention to establish new Sector Skills Council arrangements. In consultation with employers, user groups and employees, the DfES has developed a *Common Core of Skills and Knowledge* which sets out the basic knowledge and skills for effective engagement with the children's workforce as focused in six areas of expertise (DfES, 2005b):

- *effective communication and engagement;*
- *child and young person development;*
- *safeguarding and promoting the welfare of the child;*
- *supporting transitions;*
- *multi-agency working;*
- *sharing information.*

A prospectus details each of the above areas of expertise. The intention is for those who manage the workforce to use the common core (Ibid.):

- *in the design of induction and in-service and inter-agency training, building on existing practice. This will not only support strategies for enhancing front-line practice but will also help establish a greater shared language and understanding across different parts of the workforce;*
- *as a tool for training needs; focusing on supporting individual development;*
- *as a tool for workforce planning.*

The government has asked those organisations in the Children's Workforce networks to review their National Occupational Standards for work with children, young people and families. This is to be done collaboratively and to ensure that the *Common Core of Skills and Knowledge* are built into all revised standards. In support of these developments, the government has implemented:

- a Children's Workforce Development Council (CWDC)
- a *Common Assessment Framework*, multi-agency working toolkits, lead professional guidance and the framework for inspection of children's services
- specific propositions for the early years that can be taken forward with the transformation fund
- to ensure a working group's review of social work and ensure that the local government leadership centre has started its work on management and supervision in statutory social services.

Accreditation

New CPD initiatives should relate to existing good practice and be introduced through school improvement plans. A strategic approach to the implementation of CPD is required if it is to be valued by professional teachers.

Traditionally teachers have continued their professional development through award-bearing courses. Career advancement has been associated with further scholastic and practitioner activity in an HEI set within the context of professional expertise. The majority of HEIs in England and Wales providing teacher education within schools of education offer full-time or part-time master's courses for practising teachers and the wider workforce which develop students' knowledge and understanding of education theory and research, and thus inform practice. Some courses focus on education management while others focus on specialist subject areas.

Having successfully completed a master's course, teachers can continue with an academic education to doctorate level. There are currently two distinct approaches for educationalists: the traditional PhD (Doctor of Philosophy) and the EdD (Doctor of Education). The former requires independent study towards the completion of a thesis which makes an original contribution to the knowledge of the field studied. The EdD is a modularised taught course offered by approximately 40 universities to senior education, health and social professionals.

Accountability is of the essence if the profession is to be valued by all involved. All teachers should have access to CPD within the context of the national standards. Any practical outcome of the consultation process, i.e. implementation of CPD in schools, should be cost-effective, in terms of time and resources.

The pivotal role of middle leaders needs to be identified for the successful implementation of CPD and the national standards for teachers and the wider workforce. CPD should be experienced from qualifying to teach to advanced skills standards.

Summary

In general, middle leaders have a responsibility to see that individuals develop new skills. Staff development should not mean an additional activity; often development activities will happen as a matter of course. Staff development includes personal development, team development and school development. You will need to be aware that staff development has a wider importance as it:

- promotes shared values
- implements change
- promotes equal opportunities.

The responsibility for developing staff is shared. The individual also has a stake in their own development and should take some responsibility for it. Staff development, whilst important and desirable, is just one of many demands placed on a middle leader.

A middle leader will participate in the development of an operational plan for staff development. Good operational plans set clear and specific objectives for each development activity and assign responsibility for those involved. Once targets have been set there must be adequate time, resources and follow-up support for development. Staff development will only be successful with effective training, monitoring and evaluation procedures.

Performance management has been a contentious issue in schools. The purpose of performance review is to motivate and develop individuals. As a middle leader you will be involved in identifying a colleague's strengths and weaknesses, and the setting of targets which are attainable. Performance review is not judgemental, but an audit or an evaluation leading to performance-related rewards or sanctions. A working definition of performance review is 'one professional holding him/herself accountable to him/herself in the presence of another professional'.

Central to an effective scheme of performance review is the preparation of job descriptions. The kind of information required largely determines the type of question selected in the process. Another key component in the process is classroom observation. Setting targets is a critical part of the process.

As a middle leader you will need to be aware of the tensions that exist between personal professional development and institutional development.

REVIEW QUESTIONS

1 How is performance management linked to professional development?

2 As a middle leader how would you plan, implement and follow up a performance review of a member of your team?

3 In your opinion what factors contribute to effective CPD?

4 To what extent should external agencies and whole-school in-service training days be employed in the development of an effective CPD programme?

CODA

The management and development of self is central to effective leadership. This chapter focuses on the needs of middle leaders and the support offered by organisations such as the National College for School Leadership.

chapter fifteen

Self-development: where next?

Self-evaluation

Self-management

Stress

National Professional Qualification for Head teachers

Promotion

Summary

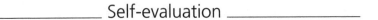

Self-evaluation

All professions are composites of knowledge and understanding, skills and abilities. This chapter focuses on both practical and evaluative issues, and considers the increasing importance of self-development. The case for leaders to work on their own development was made in a 1987 study by Constable and McCormack in Isaac (1995, 128). The report suggested that leaders should:

■ *own their own career, and positively seek out continuous training and development*

■ *acquire the learning habit early in their career*

■ *recognise when new knowledge and skills are required and seek them out.*

This is supported by the more recent research of Earley and Evans (2003, 26) which addressed the current state of school leadership in England. Their findings showed that the majority of head teachers recognised the *importance of self-assessment* of their *own leadership roles.* Self-development involves learning and understanding, a sense of place in relation to job and career. Middle leaders should, as stated, have a clear view of what the job is about; the relationship between teaching and management, SIP and so on. Middle leaders also need to have an understanding of their position in relation to those they manage. As Isaac (1995, 133) commented:

Developing yourself as a manager depends on the extent to which you recognise issues from your reflection, and learn to change your behaviour.

As a manager, the process of learning is difficult. Leaders face many demands including:

■ government demands: deliver the curriculum, register pupils, parents' evenings

■ senior management demands: implementation – action of school policy

■ colleague demands: requests for assistance, information or help from others at a similar level or within your team

■ pupil demands: to inform and liaise

■ externally-imposed demands: social services, police, agencies which work for and with young people

■ system-imposed demands: LMS, LA, budgets, meetings, social functions which cannot be ignored.

Self-development is systematic; we never stop learning and developing. The art of self-evaluation is to be continually learning. Senge (1990) makes it clear:

People with a high level of personal mastery live in a continual learning mode. They never 'arrive'. People with a high level of personal mastery are acutely aware of their ignorance, their incompetence, their growth areas. And they are deeply self-confident. Paradoxical? Only for those who do not see that the journey is the reward.

The culture of the teaching profession and the role of the support staff in schools is changing, reflecting the changing society in which we live, with its proliferation of cultures, beliefs and values. Effective teaching and learning in schools is based on shared beliefs and values. The school community works towards a common goal, reaching for and achieving targets. In practice, staff need to relate their actions to their beliefs and values. If the two do not equate, staff should consider their position in the school in relation to pupils' needs. Schools should be places in which success is celebrated, the 'blame culture' prevalent in the 1980s replaced by the 'caring culture' of the 1990s and beyond. How does this happen? Do staff willingly participate in the change process or are they passive in their response to the dominant ideology of the day? Whilst these are matters of sociological debate, self-evaluation and effective self-development should influence practice in a positive way. A starting point for this process could inform practitioners about their individual aspirations in terms of their career.

A fundamental issue will be the individual's ability to recognise where they are in relation to where they would like to be. As Senge indicated, the most successful among us will never reach their destiny.

Self-evaluation of professional competence is more than an assessment of traditional conformity or technical accountability. It is assessed in terms of moral and prudent answerability for practical judgements actually made within the context of existing educational institutions

(Carr and Kemmis, 1986)

Theory and knowledge can transform staff's beliefs and values. In the process of self-reflection, interaction with educational theory may not dictate practice, but it may transform the outlook of the practitioner. Providing individuals with new concepts is a means not merely of offering them a new way of thinking, but also of offering them the possibility of becoming more aware of their thoughts and actions. The full task of self-reflection and evaluation requires staff to collaborate in decision-making that will transform their situation. The process of self-evaluation encompasses the interaction of staff with the school; staff should consider whether they are in the right school for them.

CHECKLIST

Self-evaluation

Leadership and practitioner questions:

- What do I value?

- What is my present situation?

- Where would I like my career to lead?

- How might I get there?

- What help is available?

Personal qualities needed:

- ability to self-manage

- clear personal values

- clear personal objectives

- an emphasis on continuing personal growth

- effective problem-solving skills

- the capacity to be creative and innovative.

A means of developing the skills required for self-evaluation is to consider the range of knowledge that exists regarding educational practice. The following is adapted from Carr and Kemmis (1986, 3i).

- commonsense knowledge about practice that is simply assumption or opinion; for example, the view that students need discipline

- folk-wisdom of staff, such as the view that pupils get restless on windy days

- skill knowledge used by staff: how to line pupils up or how to prevent pupils speaking while instructions about a task are being given

- contextual knowledge: the background knowledge about this class, this community or pupil, against which aspirations are measured

- professional knowledge about teaching and learning strategies and curriculum

- educational theory: ideas about the development of individuals or about the role of education in society

- social and moral theories and general philosophical outlooks: about how people can and should interact, the uses of knowledge in society, or about truth and justice.

As a process, self-evaluation should inform practice day to day. An effective professional practitioner will be effective in their evaluation of themselves. In practice, self-evaluation will involve making sense of ourselves in situations.

A practice-based approach to self-evaluation is shown in Figure 15.1. Look at the figure and ask: Where am I in this process? In this example questions relate to the practitioner making sense of themselves in a range of situations.

Team work:

- listening
- attitude
- flexibility

Knowledge of:

- current publications
- equal opportunity issues
- learning styles

Relationships with:

- parents
- colleagues
- pupils

Preparation of:

- lessons
- monitoring procedures
- assessment

CHECKLIST

Self-development

Consider the following key issues:

- relationship with self (self-evaluation)
- ability to develop
- level of empowerment – status, value
- choices available
- opportunity for individualistic activities.

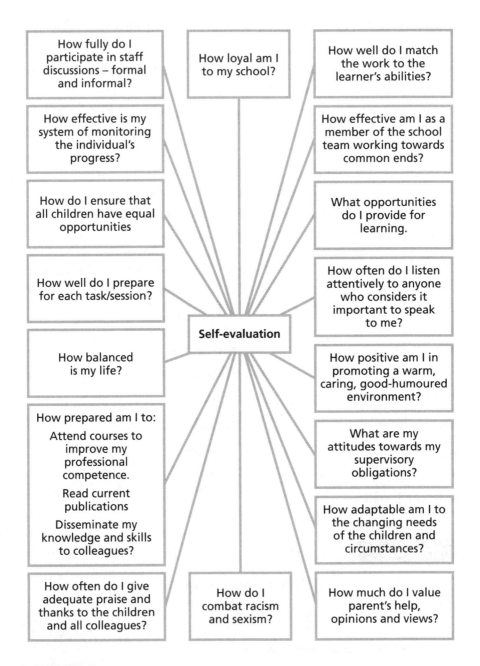

How fully do I participate in staff discussions – formal and informal?

How loyal am I to my school?

How well do I match the work to the learner's abilities?

How effective is my system of monitoring the individual's progress?

How effective am I as a member of the school team working towards common ends?

How do I ensure that all children have equal opportunities

What opportunities do I provide for learning.

How well do I prepare for each task/session?

How often do I listen attentively to anyone who considers it important to speak to me?

Self-evaluation

How balanced is my life?

How positive am I in promoting a warm, caring, good-humoured environment?

How prepared am I to:

Attend courses to improve my professional competence.

Read current publications

Disseminate my knowledge and skills to colleagues?

What are my attitudes towards my supervisory obligations?

How adaptable am I to the changing needs of the children and circumstances?

How often do I give adequate praise and thanks to the children and all colleagues?

How do I combat racism and sexism?

How much do I value parent's help, opinions and views?

FIG. 15.1   A model of self-evaluation (Adapted from Manchester LEA, 1986)

Self-development involves learning and understanding where you are within your job and career. Staff should, as stated, have a clear view of what their job is about: the relationship between teaching, leadership and management, SIP and so on. Staff should also have an understanding of their position in relation to those they manage. For each member of staff, self-development can be difficult. All staff face many demands, including:

- government demands: to deliver the curriculum, to register pupils, parents' evenings
- senior leadership and management demands: implementation – action of school policy
- colleagues' demands: requests for assistance, information or help from others at a similar level or within your team
- pupils' demands: to inform and liaise
- parents' and governors' demands
- externally imposed demands: social services, police, agencies that work for and with young people
- system-imposed demands: LMS, LA, budgets, meetings and social functions, which cannot be ignored.

In addition, there will be other demands such as family, friends, hobbies and social commitments. It is important to understand that teachers and support staff need a balance between their professional and personal lives.

Self-management

Self-evaluation informs self-management. Being a middle leader is a job in its own right, and a very demanding one. A middle leader therefore needs to have a clear view on how to manage their time and organise the workload (Shaw *et al.*, 1992). Middle leaders will find that while responsibility can be appealing, in reality there are parts of the job that include vast amounts of daily administrative tasks. In order to manage time effectively a middle leader will need to identify how to use time and determine goals.

Middle leaders need to adopt systems to aid personal and developmental organisation. The majority of middle leaders have a full teaching commitment, consequently their organisation's systems need to involve:

- day-to-day planning, keeping a diary
- 'in tray', dealing with post and decision-making
- retrieval of information and filing

- organisation of the workspace
- department administration
- management of stock
- management of pupils' work
- classification and storing of lesson materials
- stress management.

Middle leaders should also identify how time is wasted, for example, through:

- procrastination
- delegating inefficiently
- mismanaging paperwork
- holding unnecessary meetings
- failing to set priorities.

Personal planning

A player manager will have many things to fit into a day's work. The middle leader will need to recognise which part of the day or night is the most productive, the time when they may have their most creative ideas, or can concentrate best. For the majority of people, this time is early in the day, when they are freshest, and before the events of the day start to crowd in and push away ideas. A minority of people do their best work late at night.

It has been suggested that about 20 per cent of personal time is prime time, and that, used correctly, it should produce about 80 per cent of the most creative and productive work. The rest of the time is likely to be of lower quality and is nowhere near as productive.

Creative thinking, and the most difficult jobs, deserve high-quality time. If you try to do them at times when there are likely to be many interruptions or you need to catch up, this will lead to frustration. In this low-quality time, it is better to do things which are easy to pick up after interruptions or jobs which have a positive outcome. Apart from the advantage to the individual in using prime time effectively, there are wider implications – for example, the timing of meetings. Important decisions need some of the team's prime time, not the traditional slot of low quality at the end of the teaching day. It is advisable for schools and colleges to timetable team meetings earlier in the day, when vital and creative thinking is needed.

Middle leaders who realise the importance of incubation time for ideas ensure that their team members have had advance warning of issues to be discussed at meetings, so that they come able to participate fully and creatively. In sum:

- your prime time is when you do your best work
- seek to understand how **you** work, and then …
- plan your day accordingly as far as you are free to do so
- hold meetings, as far as possible, at the most effective times
- allow incubation time for the subconscious to work on problems, both for you and for your team.

Setting goals and priorities

One way in which time management can be improved is to review the way in which goals or tasks are identified. This will include both routine matters to attend to and/or some longer-term issues. Whatever they are, it is best to divide them into workable units of activity by once again using the acronym SMART. The task needs to be *specific*, clearly defined. It needs to be *measurable*, so that it is easy to see when it has been completed. It should also be *attainable*. Unrealistic targets are depressing. They also need to be *relevant*, or appropriate, to current and future needs. And finally, tasks should be *time-limited* with defined deadlines. Open-ended tasks have a habit of not getting done.

Once a SMART list of things that need to be done has been drawn up, the next task is to prioritise them. If this is not done, it is easy to feel helpless and stressed in the face of so many things that need to be done simultaneously.

Organising tasks into some sort of order not only makes it easier to finish one thing before going onto the next, but it also legitimises the fact that some of the things have to be put off until later.

Dilemmas arise when the urgent, but unimportant, regularly pushes out the important but less urgent. Schedules need to be readjusted to fit in new and urgent items. This may entail being firm about the time planned for important tasks. To add to the dilemma, individual perceptions of what is important may differ from individual to individual. In sum:

- make a list of daily tasks
- prioritise the tasks according to their urgency and importance
- be ruthless with the order in which tasks are tackled
- examine why tasks are not getting done, and do something about it!

An example of good practice is the teacher's planner. Middle leaders should use this to plan teaching and management time. Plan ahead, anticipate problems.

Handling interruptions

Interruptions are commonly given as reasons for schedules being upset and things not getting done. But in a job like teaching, constantly dealing with people, interruptions are a necessary part of work.

A normal day in the life of a middle leader is full of interruptions. There are ways of handling interruptions that will give the leader more control over their time. The list shown in the box has been collated from many people. Some or all of the points may be useful.

Keep interruptions as short as possible:

- keep to the point – do not get side-tracked into small-talk

- explain your new resolution to manage time better

- arrange to meet at a specified time later: after school may be too open-ended, unless a lot of time is needed, 10 minutes before a lesson-bell limits the time and focuses the discussion

- remain standing – do not settle down comfortably

- when summoned to consult, meet in neutral territory, or in the other person's – it is then easier for you to leave

- use non-verbal signals to give hints: stand up, shift towards door, glance at watch.

Consider the interrupter's needs:

- give them your undivided attention

- do not interrupt, but get them to the point

- do not let your mind wander, it wastes time

- demonstrate that you have understood what is being said by para-phrasing the essence

- ensure, within reason, that they go away satisfied, perhaps with the promise of looking into it later, meeting again later, suggesting alter-native support, even 'put it in writing' if necessary, but . . .

- be assertive in saying 'no' if they are asking too much.

Get back on track at once:

- do not use interruptions as an excuse to procrastinate.

If some of these sound harsh, remember a middle leader has the choice of how to handle interruptions. There will be occasions when they may want to relax and indulge in small-talk, and when being time-conscious is less important than socialising.

Stress

Leaders are exposed to many stresses in their working life. Middle leaders are constantly challenged within the workplace. However, challenges are also opportunities which result in responses placed on a continuum from excitement to excessive tiredness (see Figure 15.2). Everard *et al.* (2004, 125) highlight the need for some stress in all jobs. They suggest that it *provides challenge and motivation, helps to raise performance and is an ingredient of job satisfaction.*

Individuals should know their energy levels. If a challenge cannot be met and creates energy loss, inevitably stress will occur. The consequences of stress can be debilitating. Stress can be exhibited in many ways (e.g. irri-tability, tiredness, excessive drinking, depression). Leaders should be aware of stress in the workplace; it is important to acknowledge personal stress levels and identify and support those who find work stressful.

Stress can be overcome if the imbalances that exist are redressed (e.g. raise low energy levels). Leaders need to look after their own welfare and remain in control. Control may also mean evaluating the use of time, ensur-ing that no one activity makes excessive demands. More specifically, a model of stress will serve to illustrate the effect of stress in a middle leader's working life (see Figure 15.3).

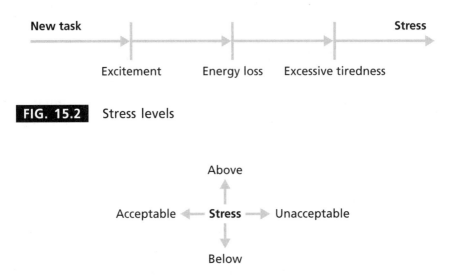

FIG. 15.2   Stress levels

FIG. 15.3   A model of stress levels

The following levels are described by Lifeskills Associates (1995).

Optimum level

When middle leaders and teachers are at their optimum level they are likely to be alert and self-confident. In practice, they will think and respond quickly, perform well, feel well and be enthusiastic, interested and involved in the task which they will carry out in an energetic, easy manner.

Overstressed

Alternatively, when middle leaders and teachers are overstressed they are likely to have feelings of anxiety and mental confusion. In this condition they will not think effectively or solve problems clearly or objectively. They will forget instructions and be inclined to panic. Physically, there will be symptoms such as increased heart rate and blood pressure, excessive perspiration, churning stomach and indigestion. In addition, co-ordination will be impaired and reflexes slowed.

Understressed

If middle leaders and teachers are understressed they are likely to experience a lack of interest or enthusiasm for the task. They can have feelings of futility or depression and believe that nothing matters any more – even a simple job can seem a huge task. They will be bored and lacking in energy. To them the world will look drab and grey and it will be hard to summon up energy to start new jobs or create fresh interests.

Causes of stress

In her *Times Educational Supplement* review of 'What Really Stresses Teachers', Burstall highlighted the following causes of stress in teachers (Burstall, 1996):

Work
- Lack of time to do the job
- Lack of parental support
- Lack of resources
- National curriculum/irrelevant paperwork
- Rate of change
- Lack of LA support
- Poor status of profession
- Staff relationships
- Government interference
- Pressure of meetings

Home
- Worries about own children
- Worries about elderly parents
- Lack of time with family
- Untidiness of others
- Family illnesses
- Housework
- Guilt over not meeting all family's demand
- In-laws
- Having to take work home
- Lack of private space

Managing stress

Having identified the causes, a middle leader should then attempt to manage stress. Brown and Ralph (1995, 95–105) offer the following advice.

1 *Examining beliefs and expectations* – are these realistic and achievable? Is there a need to set more attainable goals?

2 *Time management* – can time be used more effectively? Techniques such as prioritisation, delegation, objective-setting can be considered.

3 *Assertion* – learning how to communicate more confidently at all levels and to deal positively with conflict.

4 *Communication* – looking at patterns of interpersonal communication and self-presentation skills.

5 *Relaxation techniques* of all kinds, such as physical exercise, meditation, yoga, aromatherapy and collection of bio-data.

6 *Support networks* – it is important to build and maintain support networks of family, friends and colleagues, both within and outside schools.

Brown and Ralph (Ibid.) also indicate the importance of how the school as an organisation can help teachers to address the problem of stress. They suggest a variety of ways in which middle and senior leaders can approach this issue:

- Helping to *de-stigmatise* the idea of stress by putting it on the agenda for discussion.

- Encouraging the establishment of *self-help groups* to explore group-problem-solving of school stress factors and to develop appropriate solutions where possible.

- Developing an *empathetic ethos* and offering support for self-help management techniques.

- Identifying and liaising with *people who can help* within the local authority and other relevant organisations.

- Drawing up a *school action plan* after school-wide staff consultation. Factors to consider might include workloads, resources, discipline, relationships, environment, career progression, future staff development and training needs, parental and community pressure.

- Providing *appropriate staff development*, either within the school or at an outside venue.

- Making available information about *counselling services* and encouraging staff to use them where necessary.

In sum, Brown and Ralph (1992, 1994, 1995) found that teachers are unable to destigmatise stress and that organisational needs must be met before personal needs. Change issues also emerge as a significant factor in contributing to stress levels in schools.

Brown and Ralph (1995, 105) conclude that teachers need to recognise, and analyse openly for themselves, signs of stress at work. They emphasise the need for an organisational approach to the management of stress. In particular, teachers need to be reassured that they will not lose professional esteem or promotional opportunities by admitting to stress. This should also apply to middle leaders in practice.

National Professional Qualification for Head teachers (NPQH)

Middle leaders who wish to progress to headship should consider the NPQH. Since the 1980s there has been a strong movement to develop a more focused national framework of competency for head teachers. This led to the provision by the TDA of various programmes. The most significant of these is the National Professional Qualification for Head teachers (NPQH), responsibility for which was assumed by the National College for School Leadership in 2002. In April 2004, the NPQH became mandatory for all head teachers taking up a first appointment to a related post in the state sector. Allowance, however, has been made for a transitional phase until 31 March 2009, when those who have a place on the programme may take up a first headship

Key elements

The NPHQ, underpinned by the National Standards for head teachers, has been developed to cover all aspects of school leadership. Structured to take between six and 15 months to complete, depending on individual requirements, the programme is open to those who have experience of leadership and are aspiring to headship within the foreseeable future. The programme is made available by a number of providers throughout the country.

Access

Candidates embarking on the qualification will have very different experiences and expertise. Assessment centres have a critical role in the initial needs assessment of all candidates, helping them to judge their strengths, weaknesses and development needs in relation to the standards so that they can plan a coherent programme towards gaining the qualification.

Recent research carried out by Earley and Evans (2003, 24) and funded by the DfES addressed various aspects of school leadership in England. By comparing independent and state school leaders, they considered how prepared head teachers were for leadership and examined the general provision made for leadership development. Although the majority of head teachers in both sectors had participated in some form of professional development directly related to leadership, only the minority in both sectors had participated in the NPQH (state: 25 per cent; independent: 6 per cent). At the same time head teachers in both sectors acknowledged the need for training priorities based on the National Standards for head teachers. Although Earley and Evans (2003, 28) suggest that providers of leadership development and management training could employ the National Standards for head teachers to underpin and inform their own CPD provision, this is already in place for the NPQH.

Content of NPQH

The National Standards for head teachers (DfES, 2004f) set out six areas in which expertise is required:

- shaping the future
- leading learning and teaching
- developing self and working with others
- managing the organisation
- securing accountability
- strengthening community.

Each candidate will be required to develop the knowledge and understanding, skills and abilities needed for effective leadership and management in schools. For middle leaders who aspire to become head teachers, the route to headship will be through the NPQH.

Promotion

Middle leaders may consider promotion, and will therefore need to be aware of the process of job hunting. In addition, many internal promotion opportunities will be treated as normal vacancies. You will require skills in completing a CV and/or application form and attending an interview. To be successful requires time and considerable effort. Before embarking on this journey reflect on the advantages and disadvantages of the new post, for example, promotion prospects, curriculum area, travelling time and salary.

As a profession, teaching has a limited amount of literature related to career development. Yet institutions and professions require occasional renewal to avoid stagnation. For the majority of teachers, applying for promotion can be a traumatic and lonely process. There are many factors involved. In brief:

- reflecting on current position
- deciding to move on
- identifying a suitable position
- completing an application
- the interview
- deciding to accept the job
- starting in a new school.

Preparing a CV

The purpose of a CV is to filter applicants and, in practice, this may not be handled very well (Billsberry *et al.*, 1994: 87–98). You must make sure that your CV will not be rejected: do not use coloured paper, list unusual hobbies or produce a book length document! A word-processed CV will allow you to adapt each application to match the job specification. In essence, there are no rules that dictate the content or structure of a CV. To begin with, create a database of your work experience and achievements (e.g. Table 15.1).

TABLE 15.1   Personal audit

	Job 1	Job 2	Job 3
Job title			
Employer			
School/authority			
Date joined			
Date left			
Education			
Qualifications			
Responsibility			
Achievements			
Positions of responsibility outside education			
Extra-curricular interests			

After completing a personal audit, the next stage is to analyse what is wanted by the institution you intend applying to:

- What knowledge, skills and experience must the applicant possess?
- What additional training is required?
- What qualifications should they hold?
- What is the culture of the school/college?
- What personal qualities are required?

You are now in a position to match your CV to the post. Try to identify the key points you want to highlight and the content of your CV will follow. Market yourself: your aim is to make the person reading your CV want to know more about you.

The length of the CV will be determined by the requirements of the post and the job specification. The CV and covering letter must communicate key facts about you, quickly, efficiently and professionally.

Presentation of the CV is critical to your success; use double linespacing and consistent type face and alignments. Use the same style in the letter, CV and envelope.

Application forms

All application forms are different, in that each is for a specific post. As such, completing an application form is extremely time-consuming. Therefore you must be clear why you are applying.

Make several copies of the application form and answer each question in rough. Get someone to read through your responses, leave the rough copy and come back to it fresh. Fill out the form in black ink or type. Once completed, check the application form for spelling mistakes and inconsistencies.

The covering letter is your opportunity to highlight the main qualities of your application. Express yourself in a straightforward style and include any relevant information such as a reference number. Ensure that you include your contact number and address.

The interview

Interviews are stressful and tiring. You will require high energy levels to complete an interview successfully. Interviewers will find reasons to reject rather than reasons to accept. Candidates should prepare in advance the key points which they would like to communicate to the interview panel. Questions and answers must be selective and of quality.

Preparation is essential; find out as much as you can about the school and job. Try to talk to someone from the department before the interview; your research should give you some indication of how successful you will be.

Most interviewers will reach a decision very quickly; therefore the opening minutes of the interview are critical. First impressions do count! Wear a suit and appropriate accessories. Make eye contact with everyone, shake hands firmly, speak clearly and slowly, and smile. Interviewers will not remember the details of every candidate's response, so try to say something memorable. Do not say anything you had not intended to say; occasionally interview panels will remain silent in order to entice you into 'filling the gap'. Remain silent. You will not have to agree with the panel at all times; be professional in your response. You may wish to expand your replies where you have sufficient depth of knowledge and experience. Try to give specific examples of your skills. Try not to be too anecdotal or sound too defensive. If you cannot answer a question say so.

Consider in advance how you will deal with any form of discrimination which may manifest itself during the course of the interview. Be professional and do not ignore prejudice.

Tests

Increasingly, schools are introducing personality profiling and management tests to the selection process. These may also involve in-tray exercises, role play and discussion group exercises. It is unclear how relevant these are and whether they produce a valuable diagnosis. However, as a candidate you will need to approach such tests in a professional manner.

Read each question or direction carefully, manage your time and do not spend too much time on a particular part of the test. There are many different types of personality tests; the most common are questionnaires with multiple-choice responses. There are no right or wrong answers; the test is designed to reveal your personality. A number of questions will be aimed at each personality trait and some questions will check whether the subject is being consistent. You are best advised to answer truthfully.

Accepting the job

When you are waiting for the panel to reach a decision, examine the strengths, weaknesses, opportunities and threats of the job, team and school. You will only have a limited amount of information and should be as objective as possible. Most interview panels will ask candidates whether they would accept the job if offered. The majority of candidates will instinctively answer this positively; however, this may not be the most appropriate job for you. Consider where you have come from, i.e. your current post, and where you intend going to, i.e. your next job. When you have considered all relevant factors, make your decision. Prepare your response.

If you are offered the job and would like to accept, plan what happens next: contracts, timetable, team meeting, etc. You will also need to consider your letter of resignation and remaining weeks in your current post.

Rejection – debrief

At the point of rejection you will experience a mixture of feelings depending on the desirability of the post. Make use of the process, take with you as much advice as possible. Write down the key points to enable you to reflect on your positive and negative attributes. You may of course dismiss these comments. Use the process positively in order to plan for your next application.

Summary

As a profession, teaching has a limited amount of literature related to career development. Yet institutions and professions require occasional renewal to avoid stagnation. Self-development involves learning and understanding of where you are within your job and career. Research supports the case for leaders working on their own development.

Self-development is systematic; we never stop learning and developing. The art of self-evaluation is to be continually learning. Self-evaluation, however, also informs self-management. To manage time effectively, a middle leader needs to identify how to use time and determine goals. In addition, middle leaders should recognise and analyse for themselves the signs of stress at work. Middle leaders, having been established as expert leaders', will be trained for headship. For middle leaders who aspire to become head teachers, the route to headship will be through the National Professional Qualification for Head teachers (NPQH).

Candidates will be required to complete a central compulsory module concerned with strategic direction and development, and covering the implementation, monitoring and reviewing of policies and practices. The qualification may be gained within a year, particularly in the early stages of the scheme, to allow experienced deputies who are close to headship to qualify.

Middle leaders may consider promotion and will therefore need to be aware of the process of job-hunting. In addition, many internal promotion opportunities will be treated as normal vacancies. You will require skills in completing a CV and/or application form and attending an interview. To be successful requires time and considerable effort. Before embarking on this journey reflect on the advantages and disadvantages of the new post, e.g. promotion prospects, curriculum area, travelling time and salary.

All application forms are different in that each is for a specific post. As such, completing an application form is extremely time-consuming. Therefore you must know why you are applying.

Preparation is essential; find out as much as you can about the school and position.

REVIEW QUESTIONS

1 What criteria would you employ to manage your time effectively?

2 As a middle leader aware of daily work demands and commitments, how would you deal with interruptions?

3 What criteria would you employ for a self-evaluation?

4 How would you prepare for an interview for a senior leadership position?

Useful contacts

There are hundreds of sites that relate to school leadership and management of which the following are the most relevant:

www.dfes.gov.uk/   Overall DfES guidance and information

www.dfes.gov.uk/fairfunding/   DfES guidance on fair funding

www.dfes.gov.uk/consultations/govreg   DfES guidance on governor regulations

www.dfes.gov.uk/valueformoney/   DfES's Value for Money Unit

www.teachernet.gov.uk/management/   DfES site for teachers

www.governornet.co.uk/   DfES site for school governors

www.nao.gov.uk/   UK National Audit Office

www.legislation.hmso.gov.uk/   HMSO legislation

www.schools.audit-commission.gov.uk/   School website from Audit Commission

www.parliament.uk/parliamentary_committees/education_and_s kills_committee.cfm The House of Commons Education and Skills Select Committee

www.ngc.org.uk   National Governors' Council

www.architecture.com/go/Architecture/   A Guide for School

Debate/Forums_2046.html   Governors: Developing School Buildings

www.school-works.org   School Works Tool Kit

www.cipfa.org.uk   The Chartered Institute of Public Finance and Accountancy

www.remodelling.org   National Remodelling Team

www.ncsl.org.uk   National College for School Leadership

www.everychildmatters.gov.uk   Every Child Matters

www.lga.gov.uk/OurWork.asp?l   Local Government

Section=59&ccat=374   Association (LGA) Education Finance

www.hse.gov.uk   Health and Safety Executive

www.hse.gov.uk/pubns/indg163.pdf   HSE Five Steps to Risk Assessment

www.dfes.gov.uk/governor/info.cfm   A Guide to the Law for School Governors

www.dfes.gov.uk/schoolsecurity   DfES School Security

www.dfes.gov.uk/h_s_ev/index.shtml   DfES Health and Safety of Pupils on Educational Visits

www.dfes.gov.uk/lea   DfES Code of Practice on LEA – School Relations

www.actionenergy.org.uk/   DfES Building Bulletin 87

ActionEnergy/Products/Product+Detail.htm?cs_id=GPG173&cs_catalog=publications   (2003)

www.constructingexcellence.org.uk/resourcecentre/kpizone KPIzone

www.cabe.org.uk/   Commission for Architecture and the Built Environment

www.riba.org/go/RIBA/Home.html   A Sustainable School RIBA ideas competition (2001)

www.books-raise-standards.co.uk   Book Check Assessor

References and further reading

Adair, J. (1988) *Effective Leadership*, London: Pan Books.

Alexander, R. (1984) *Primary Teaching*, Eastbourne: Holt, Rinehart and Winston.

Armstrong, L., Evans, B. and Page, C. (1993a) *A Guide for Middle Managers in Secondary Schools, Vol 1: Organisations*, Lancaster: Framework Press Educational.

Armstrong, L., Evans, B. and Page, C. (1993b) *A Guide for Middle Managers in Secondary Schools, Vol 2: Relationships*, Lancaster: Framework Press Educational.

Arnold, J. and Hope, T. (1983) *Accounting for Management Decisions*, Hemel Hempstead: Prentice Hall.

Arnott, M.A., Bullock, A.D. and Thomas, H.R. (1992) The Impact of Local Management on Schools: A Source Book. *The First Report of the Impact Project*, University of Birmingham: School of Education.

Assessment Reform Group (2002) Assessment for learning: research-based principles to guide classroom practice, London: ARG.

Ball, S.J. and Bowe, R. (1992) 'Subject departments and the "implementation" of National Curriculum policy: an overview of the issues', *Journal of Curriculum Studies*, 24(2), 97–115.

Barber, M., Evans, A. and Johnston, M. (1995) *An Evaluation of the National Scheme of School Teacher Appraisal*, London: HMSO.

Bell, L. (1992) *Managing Teams in Secondary Schools*, London: Routledge.

Bell, J. and Harrison, B.T. (Ed.) (1995) *Vision and Values in Managing Education*, London: David Fulton.

Ben-Ari, R. and Shafir, D. (1988) *Social Integration in Elementary Schools*, Ramat-Gan, Israel: Institute for the Advancement of Social Integration in Schools, Bar-Ilan University.

Bennett, N. (1995) *Managing Professional Teachers: Middle Management in Primary and Secondary Schools*, London: Paul Chapman Publishing.

Bennis, W. (1959) *Leadership Theory Administrative Behaviour: The Problem of Authority*, Administrative Science Centre, April 22–23 1959, University of Pittsburgh.

Bennis, W. and Nanus, B. (1985) *Leaders: The Strategies for Taking Charge*, New York: Harper and Row.

Best, R., Lang, P., Lodge, C. and Watkins, C. (eds.) (1994) *Pastoral Care and Personal – Social Education: Entitlement and Provision*, London: Cassell.

Billsberry, J., Clark, T. and Swingler, J. (1994) *Job Design and Staff Recruitment*, B600 The Capable Manager, Open Business School: Open University Press.

Black, P. and Wiliam, D. (1998) *Inside the black box: raising standards through classroom assessment*, London: King's College.

Black, P., Harrison, C., Lee, C., Marshall, B. and Wiliam, D. (2002) *Working inside the black box: assessment for learning in the classroom*, London: King's College.

Blandford, S. (1997) *Middle Management in Schools*, London: Pitman

Blandford, S. and Duarte, S.J. (2004), 'Inclusion in the Community: a study of community music centres in England and Portugal, focusing on the development of musical and social skills within each centre', *Westminster Studies in Education*, 27(1), Abingdon: Taylor and Francis.

Blandford, S. and Blackburn, N. (2004) *School Financial Management Handbook*, London: Optimus Publishing.

Blandford, S. and Gibson, S. (2005) *Special Educational Needs Management in Schools*, London: Sage.

Blandford, S. and Graham- Matheson, L. (2005) Remodelling Fieldwork January–June 2005 unpublished.

Bolam, R. (1993) *Recent Developments and Emerging Issues in the Continuing Professional Development of Teachers*, London: General Teaching Council of England and Wales.

Bradley, J., Chesson, R. and Silverleaf, J. (1983) *Inside Staff Development*, Windsor: NFER/Nelson.

Brighouse, T. (1991) *What makes a good school ?* Stafford: Network Educational Press

Brown, M. and Ralph, S. (1992) *Towards the identification of stress in teachers*, Research in Education, 48, 103–10.

Brown, M. and Ralph, S. (1994) *Managing Stress in Schools,* Plymouth: Northcote House.

Brown, M. and Ralph, S. (1995) *The Identification and Management of Teacher Stress* in Bell, J. and Harrison, B.T. (Ed.) (1995) *Vision and Values in Managing Education,* London: David Fulton.

Brown, M. and Rutherford, D. (1996) *Heads of Department – Secondary Schools*, Cambridge: British Education Management and Administration Society (BEMAS) Partners in Change Conference (Cambridge), March 22–27, 1996.

Building futures (2004) *21st Century Schools: Learning environments of the future*, London: Building futures.

Burstall, E. (1996) 'What Really Stresses Teachers', *TES*, 16 February 1996, 4.

Bush, T. and West-Burnham, J. (eds.) (1994) *The Principles of Educational Management,* Harlow: Longman.

Busher, H. (1988) 'Reducing Role Overload for a Head of Department: a rationale for fostering staff development', *School Organisation*, 8(1), 99–104.

Busher, H. (2000a) 'Developing Professional Networks: Working with Parents and Communities to Enhance Students' Learning in Busher, H. and Harris, A. with Wise, C. (2000) *Subject Leadership and School Improvement*, London, Paul Chapman: 89–102.

Busher, H. (2000b) 'Leading and Co-ordinating Diffuse Subject Areas', in Busher, H. and Harris, A. with Wise, C. (2000) *Subject Leadership and School Improvement*, London, Paul Chapman: 43–55.

Busher, H. (2000c) 'The Subject Leader as a Middle Manager', in Busher, H. and Harris, A. with Wise, C. (2000) *Subject Leadership and School Improvement*, London, Paul Chapman: 105–9.

Busher, H. and Harris, A. with Wise, C. (2000) *Subject Leadership and School Improvement*, London: Paul Chapman.

Caldwell, B.J. and Spinks, J.M. (1988) *The Self-Managing School,* Lewes: Falmer Press.

Callaghan, J. (1976) Ruskin College Speech, Oxford.

Calvert, M. and Henderson, J. (1994) 'Newly-qualified teachers: Do we prepare them for their pastoral role?' *Pastoral Care in Education*, 12(2), 7–12.

Calvert, M. and Henderson, J. (1995) 'Leading the Team: Managing Pastoral Care in a Secondary Setting' in Bell, J. and Harrison, B.T. (eds.) *Vision and Values in Managing Education,* London: David Fulton.

Carr, W. and Kemmis, S. (1986) Becoming Critical: Education, Knowledge and Action Research, Lewes: Falmer Press.

Castelikns, J. (1996), 'Responsive Instruction for Young Children: A study of how teachers can help easily distracted children become more attentive', *Emotional and Behavioural Difficulties*, 1(1), Spring.

Centre for Studies on Inclusive Education (CSIE) (2004) *Index for Inclusion: developing learning, participation and play in early years and childcare*, Bristol: CSIE.

Chaplin, B. (1995) 'Improvement through Inspection' in Bell, J. and Harrison, B.T. (eds.) *Vision and Values in Managing Education,* London: David Fulton.

Chapman, J. (ed.) (1990) *School-based Decision-making and Management,* Basingstoke: Falmer Press.

Chartered Management Institute (2004) *Delegating*. Available at: **www.managers.org.uk/content** (Accessed: 1 December 2005).

Chatwin, R. (2004) 'Subject Leaders and School Strategy: Exercising upward influence?', *Management in Education,* 18(1).

Cheminais, R. (2004) *Inclusive schools and classrooms*, SENCO Update, May, 6–7, London: Optimus.

Cline, T. (1992) 'Assessment of special educational needs: meeting reasonable expectation?' in Cline, T. (ed.) *The Assessment of Special Educational Needs*, London: Paul Chapman Publishing.

Cline, T. (ed.) *The Assessment of Special Educational Needs*, London: Paul Chapman Publishing.

Coleman, M. and Bush, T. (1994) 'Managing with teams' in Bush, T. and West-Burnham, J. (eds.) *The Principles of Educational Management*, Harlow: Longman.

Constable, J. and McCormack, R. (1987) *The making of British managers*, London: BIME, CBI.

Coopers and Lybrand (1988) *Local Management of Schools*, London: HMSO.

Cornwall, J. and Tod, J. (1998) *IEPS: Emotional and Behavioural difficulties*, London: David Fulton.

Davies, B. (1994) *Managing Resources* in Bush, T. and West-Burnham, J. (eds.) *The Principles of Educational Management*, Harlow: Longman.

Davies, B. and Ellison, L. (1990) *Managing the Primary School*, Northcote House: Budget.

Davies, B. and Ellison, L. (1997) *Strategic Marketing for Schools: How to Integrate Marketing and Strategic Development for an Effective School*, London: Financial Times/ Pitman Publishing.

Davies, B. and West-Burnham, J. (1990) 'School governors – an effective management force or another bureaucratic layer of school management?' *School Organisation*, 10, 2–3.

Duignan, P.A. and MacPherson, R.J.S. (eds.) (1992) *Effective Leadership. A practical theory for new administrators and managers*, London: Falmer Press.

Department for Education (1992) *Reports on Individual Pupils' Achievements. The Education (Individual Pupils' Achievements) (Information) Regulations 1992 – Circular 14/92*, London: HMSO.

Department for Education (1993) *Reporting on Individual Pupils' Achievements, Circular 16/93*, London: HMSO.

Department for Education (1994) *Code of Practice on the Identification and Assessment of Special Educational Needs*, London: HMSO.

Department for Education and Skills (DfES) (2001a) The *Code of Practice for Special Educational Needs*, London: HMSO.

Department for Education and Skills (DfES) (2001b) *School Action Plus*, London: HMSO.

Department for Education and Skills (DfES) (2002) *Extended Schools*, Nottingham: DfES Publications

Department for Education and Skills (DfES) (2003a) *Time for Standards: Guidance accompanying the Section 133 Regulations issued under the Education Act 2002*, Nottingham: DfES Publications Ref: DfES/0538/2003.

Department for Education and Skills (DfES) (2003b) *Every Child Matters: Summary*, Nottingham: DfES Publications Ref: DfES/0672/2003.

Department for Education and Skills (DfES) (2003c) *Looking for a Bursar*, London: HMSO Ref: DfES/0136/2003.

Department for Education and Skills (DfES) (2003d) *Key stage Strategy*, London: HMSO.

Department for Education and Skills (DfES) (2003e) School Funding System 2004–2006: Statement by Charles Clarke, House of Commons, 17 July 2003, London: HMSO.

Department for Education and Skills (DfES) (2004a) *Every Child Matters: Next Steps*, Nottingham: DfES Publications Ref: DfES/0240/2004.

Department for Education and Skills(DfES) (2004b) *Putting the World into World-Class Education*, Nottingham: DfES Publications Ref: DfES/1077/2004.

Department for Education and Skills (DfES) (2004c) *Every Child Matters: Change for Children in Schools*, Nottingham: DfES Publications Ref: DfES/1089/2004.

Department for Education and Skills (DfES) (2004d) *Five Year Strategy for Children and Learners*, Norwich: TSO.

Department for Education and Skills (DfES) (2004e) *Every Child Matters: Change for Children*, Nottingham: DfES Publications Ref: DfES/1110/2004.

Department for Education and Skills (DfES) (2004f) *National Standards for Headteachers*, Nottingham: DfES Publications Ref: Dfes/0083/2004.

Department for Education and Skills (DfES) (2005a) *Every Child Matters: Children's Workforce Strategy*, Nottingham: DfES Publications Ref: DfES/1117/2005.

Department for Education and Skills (DfES) (2005b) *Common Core of Skills and Knowledge for the Children's Workforce*, Nottingham: DfES Publications Ref: DfES/1189/2005.

Department for Education and Skills (DfES) (2005c) *Common Assessment Framework* **www.dfes.gov.uk**.

Department for Education and Skills (DfES) (2005d) *League Tables*, **www.dfes.gov.uk**.

Department for Education and Skills (DfES) (2005e) *School Teachers Pay and Conditions*, Document 2004 (updated online May 2005) **www.teachernet.gov.uk**

Department for Education and Skills (DfES) (2005f) *Extended Schools: Access to Opportunities and Services for All: A Prospectus*, Nottingham: DfES Publications Ref: DfES/1196/2005.

Department for Education and Skills (DfES) (2005g) *14–19 Education and skills: Implementation Plan*: DfES Publications.

Department for Education and Skills (DfES) (2005h) *School and LEA Funding* presentation by Stephen Bishop, Local Implementation Divison, DfES **www.teachernet.gov.uk**

Department of Education and Science (DES) (1988a) *Education Reform Act,* London: HMSO.

Department of Education and Science (DES) (1988b) *Education Reform Act: Local Management of Schools, Circular 7/88,* London: HMSO.

Department of Education and Science (DES) (1989) *Planning for School Development: Advice for Governors, Headteachers and Teachers,* London: HMSO.

Department of Education and Science (DES) (1991) *Development Planning: A Practical Guide,* London: HMSO.

Donnelly, C. (2000) 'In Pursuit of School Ethos', *British Journal of Educational Studies,* 48(2): 134–54

Drucker, P.F. (1980) *Managing in Turbulent Times,* London: Heinemann.

Earley, P. and Evans, J. (2003) 'Leading and Managing Schools: a comparison between independent and state school leaders', *Management in Education,* 17(1): 24–8.

Earley, P. and Fletcher-Campbell, F. (1989) *The Time to Manage? Department and Faculty Heads at Work,* Windsor: NFER-Nelson.

Etzioni, A. (1964) *Modern Organisations,* Englewood Cliffs, NJ: Prentice Hall.

Evans, A. (1995) *Targets for Tonight,* TES, 15 September, 1995, 27.

Everard, K.B. (1986) *Developing Management in Schools,* Oxford: Blackwell.

Everard, K.B. and Morris, G. (1985) *Effective School Management,* London: Harper and Row.

Everard, K.B. and Morris, G. (1990) *Effective School Management,* London: Paul Chapman Publishing.

Everard, K.B., Morris, G. and Wilson, I. (2004) *Effective School Management,* 4th Ed., London: Paul Chapman Publishing.

Fidler, B., Bowles, G. and Hart, J. (1991) *Planning Your School's Strategy: ELMS Workbook,* Harlow: Longman.

Fidler, B. and Cooper, R. (eds.) (1992) *Staff Appraisal and Staff Management in Schools and Colleges: A Guide to Implementation,* Harlow: Longman.

Fidler, B. (1994) 'Staff Appraisal', *State of the Art Review,* 61–70.

Fidler, B. (2002) *Strategic Management for School Development*, London: Paul Chapman Publishing.

Forde, C., Reeves, J. and Casteel, V. (1996) *Supporting Management Development in Schools. A Partnership Approach,* British Education Management and Administration Society (BEMAS) Partners in Change Conference (Cambridge), March 22–27, 1996.

Foy, N. (1981) 'To strengthen the mixture, first understand the chemistry', *The Guardian*, 2 September 1981.

Friedman, Y. (1986), School, Home and Community in Israel, Alienation and Openness in the Educational Space, Jerusalem: Henrietta Szold Institute (in Hebrew).

Fullan, M. and Hargreaves, A. (1992) *What's worth fighting for in your school?* Buckingham: Open University Press.

Fullerton, H. and Price, C. (1991) 'Culture in the NHS', Personnel Management, 23(3), 50–3.

Funding Agency for Schools (FAS) (1999a) *Value for Money in School Management.*

Funding Agency for Schools (FAS) (1999b) *School Management.*

General Teaching Council for England and Wales Trust (1993) *The Continuing Professional Development of Teachers,* London: GTC.

General Teaching Council for England (GTC(E)) (2002) Summary of the CPD consultation sessions: GTC regional road shows **www.gtce.org.uk.**

General Teaching Council for England (GTC(E)) (2004) Teachers' Professional Learning Framework, **www.gtce.org.uk** (accessed 14 March 2006).

Grace, G. (1998) 'Realising the mission: Catholic approaches to school effectiveness' in Slee, R., Tomlinson, S. and Weiner, G., *School Effectiveness for Whom? Challenges to the school effectiveness and school improvement movements,* London: Falmer Press.

Greenfield, T. and Ribbins, P. (1993) *Greenfield on educational administration: Towards a humane science,* London: Routledge.

Guardian (2005), *Remodelling Supplement* 26 April 2005.

Guaspari, R. (1999), *Music Of The Hear,* New York: Hyperion.

Gunter, H. (1995) *Appraisal and the School as a Learning Organisation,* Keele: Keele University In-service Education and Management Unit, School of Education.

Hackman, R. and Walton, R. (1986) 'Heading groups in organizations', in Goodman, P. (ed.), *Designing effective workgroups,* San Francisco: Jossey-Bass.

Hall, V. and Oldroyd, D. (1990a) *Management Self-development for Staff in Secondary Schools, Unit 1: Self-development for effective management,* Bristol: NDCEMP.

Hall, V. and Oldroyd, D. (1990b) *Management Self-development for Staff in Secondary Schools, Unit 2: Policy, Planning and Change* Bristol: NDCEMP.

Hall, V. and Oldroyd, D. (1990c) *Management Self-development for Staff in Secondary Schools, Unit 3: Team development for effective schools,* Bristol: NDCEMP.

Hall, V. and Oldroyd, D. (1990d) *Management Self-development for Staff in Secondary Schools, Unit 4: Implementing and evaluating,* Bristol: NDCEMP.

Hamblin, D. (1989) *Staff Development for Pastoral Care,* Oxford: Blackwell.

Handy, C. (1993) *Understanding Organisations* (4th Ed), Harmondsworth: Penguin.

Handy, C. and Aitken, R. (1986) *Understanding Schools as Organisations,* Harmondsworth: Penguin.

Hargreaves, A. (1994) *Changing Teachers, Changing Times,* London: Cassell.

Hargreaves, D.H. (1995) 'Self-managing schools and development planning – chaos or control?' *School Organisation,* 15(3), 215–17.

Hargreaves, D.H. (1996) *TTA Annual Lecture 1996 – Teaching as a Research-based Profession: Possibilities and Prospects,* London: TTA..

Hargreaves, D.H. and Hopkins, D. (1991) 'School effectiveness, school improvement and development', planning in Preedy, M. *Managing the effective school,* London: Paul Chapman Publishing.

Harris, A. (2000) 'Subject Leadership and School Improvement', in Busher, H. and Harris, A. with Wise, C., *Subject Leadership and School Improvement,* London, Paul Chapman: 183–96.

Harris, A. and Lambert, L. (2003) *Building Leadership Capacity for School Improvement,* Maidenhead: Open University Press.

Harris, A. and Muijs, D. (2005) *Improving Schools Through Teacher Leadership,* Maidenhead: Open University Press.

Harrison, B.T. (1995) 'Revalving leadership and service in educational management', in Bell, J. and Harrison, B.T. (ed.) *Vision and Values in Managing Education,* London: David Fulton.

Hartley, H.J. (1979) 'Zero-based budgeting for secondary schools', *NASSP Bulletin,* 63(431), 22–28 Virginia: NASSP.

Harvey-Jones (2003) *Making it Happen: Reflections on Leadership,* London: Profile Books.

Haynes, M.E. (1988) *Effective Meeting Skills,* London: Kogan Page.

Hedge, N., Mole, R., LaGrave, J. and Cartwright, B. (1994) *Personal Communications at Work,* B600 The Capable Manager, Open Business School: Open University Press.

Hertz-Lazarowitz, R. and Miller, N. (1992) Interaction in Cooperative Groups, New York: Cambridge University Press.

Hewitt, M. (1996a) *Director's Address,* Annual Conference (Oxford Brookes University), National Education Assessment Centre (NEAC), 26 March, 1996.

Hewitt, M. (1996b) *Quality Assurance How and What?* Annual Conference (Oxford Brookes University), National Education Assessment Centre (NEAC), 26 March, 1996.

Hituv, M. (1989) 'The community school – principles, trends and methods of action', *Dapim,* 8, 87–93

HM Government (HMG) (2003) *Every Child Matters (Green Paper)*, Norwich: TSO.

HM Government (HMG) (2004) *Choosing Health*, Norwich: TSO.

HMI (2003) *Leadership and management: managing the school workforce*, London: HMSO.

HMI and Department for Education and Skills (2004) *A New Relationship with Schools*, London: HMSO.

HMI (2005) *14–19 Education and Skills* (White Paper), London: HMSO.

HM Treasury (2004) *Choice for Parents, the Best Start for Children: A 10 Year Strategy for Childcare*, Norwich: HMSO.

Holmes, G. (1993) *Essential School Leadership*, London: Kogan Page.

Holt, M.J. (1980) *Schools and Curriculum Change*, Maidenhead: McGraw Hill.

Holt, M.J. (1981) *Evaluating the Evaluators*, London: Hodder and Stoughton.

House, E.R. (1973) 'The Dominion of Economic Accountability' in House, E.R. (ed.) *School Evaluation: The Politics and Process*, McCutchon Publishing.

Hoy, W.K. and Miskel, C.G. (1991) *Educational Administration: Theory, Research and practice* (4th Ed), New York: McGraw–Hill.

Hoyle, E. (1986) *The Politics of School Management*, London: Hodder and Stoughton.

Hughes, S. (2004) *Subject Leaders: Resource Management*, London: Optimus.

Ingvarson, L. (1990) 'Schools: Places where teachers learn' in Chapman, J. (ed.) *School-based Decision-making and Management*, Basingstoke: Falmer Press.

Irvine, V.B. (1975) 'Budgeting: Functional analysis and behavioural implications' in Rappaport, A. (ed.) *Information for decision-making, quantitative and Behavioural dimensions*, (2nd Ed) New Jersey: Prentice Hall.

Isaac, J. (1995) 'Self-management and development' in Bell, J. and Harrison, B.T. (ed.) *Vision and Values in Managing Education*, London: David Fulton.

Johnson, B., Whitington, V. and Oswald, M. (1994) 'Teachers' views on school discipline: a theoretical framework, *Cambridge Journal of Education*, 24(2) 261–76.

Jones, B.M. (1995) *Local Government Financial Management*, Hemel Hempstead: ICSA.

Jones, R. and Pendlebury, M. (1996) *Public Sector Accounting* (4th Edn), London: Pitman Publishing.

Katz, D. and Kahn, R.L. (1978) *The Social Psychology of Organisations*, New York: John Wiley.

Knutton, S. and Ireson, G. (1995) 'Leading the team – managing staff development in the primary school', in Bell, J. and Harrison, B.T. (Ed.) *Vision and Values in Managing Education*, London: David Fulton.

LaGrave, J., Mole, R. and Swingler, J. (1994) *Planning and Managing Your Work,* B600 The Capable Manager, Open Business School: Open University Press.

Lancaster, D. (1989) 'Aspects of management information systems', in Fidler, B. and Bowles, G. (eds.) *Effective Local Management of Schools: A Strategic Approach,* Harlow: Longman.

Larson, C.E. and LaFasto, F.M.J. (1989), *Teamwork: what must go right, what can go wrong,* Newberry Park, CA: Sage.

Levacic, R. (1989) *Financial Management in Education,* Buckingham: Open University Press.

Levacic, R. and Glover, D. (1995) *Ofsted Assessment of Schools' Efficiency,* Milton Keynes: Open University Press (EPAM Report).

Lifeskills Associates Limited (1995) *Stress Levels,* London: Lifeskills Associates Limited.

Lincoln, (1982) 'Intra- (and Inter-) Organisational Networks', *Research in the Sociology of Organisations,* 1(1): 1–38.

MacGilchrist, B., Mortimore, P., Savage, J. and Beresford, C. (1995) *Planning Matters,* London: Paul Chapman Publishing.

Maclure, S. (1989) *Education Reformed: A Guide to the Education Reform Act.* London: Hodder and Stoughton.

McCall, C. and Lawlor H. (2002) *School Leadership: Leading and Managing Effective Learning. Professional Excellence in Schools,* London: Optimus Publishing.

McGregor, D. (1966) *Leadership and Motivation,* MIT: MIT Press.

McGuiness, J. (1989) *A Whole-School Approach to Pastoral Care,* London: Kogan Page.

Management Standards Centre (2004) *The National Occupational Standards.* Available at: **www.management-standards.org**. (Accessed: 9 January 2006).

Manchester LEA (1986) *Model for Self-evaluation,* Manchester: Manchester LEA.

Marconi, H.R. and Seigal, G., (1989), *Behavioural Accounting.* Ohio: South Western.

Marland, M. (1989) *The Tutor and the Tutor Group,* London: Longman.

Maslow, A.H. (1943) 'A Theory of Human Motivation', *Psychological Review,* 50(4), 370–96.

Maslow, A.H. (1970) *Motivation and Personality,* New York: Harper and Row.

Mayo, E. (1933) *The Human Problems of an Individual Civilisation,* London: MacMillan.

McLaughlin, T. (2005) 'The Educative Importance of Ethos', *British Journal of Educational Studies,* 53(3): 306–25.

Moll, L.C. and Whitmore, K. F. (1998) 'Vygotsky in classroom practice: moving from individual transmission to social transaction', in: Faulkner, D. Littleton, R. and Woodhead, M., *Learning Relationships in the Classroom,* London: Routledge.

Mullins, L.J. (1993) *Management and Organisational Behaviour* (3rd Ed.), London: Pitman Publishing.

Munby, S. (1994) 'Assessment and Pastoral Care: sense, sensitivity and standards', in Best, R., Lang, P., Lodge, C. and Watkins, C. (eds.) *Pastoral Care and Personal – Social Education: Entitlement and Provision*, London: Cassell.

National College for School Leadership (2006) National Professional Qualification for Headship. Available at: www.ncsl.org.uk/programmes/npqh/index.cfm. (Accessed: 12 January 2006).

National Commission on Education (NCE) (1995) *Learning to Succeed,* London: Paul Hamlyn Foundation.

National Commission on Education (NCE) (1996) *Success Against the Odds,* London: Routledge.

National Joint Council (NJC) for Local Government Services (2003) *School Support Staff: The Way Forward*, London: The Employers' Organisation.

National Leadership Network (1991) *Developing leaders for restructuring schools: New habits of mind and heart,* Washington, DC: US Department of Education.

National Policy Board for Educational Administration (NPBEA) (1993) *Principles for our changing schools,* Virginia: NPBEA.

National Remodelling Team (NRT) (2003) *Workforce Remodelling – A Guidance for Governors,* Birmingham: National Governors' Council. Available at: **www.remodelling.org.**

National Remodelling Team (NRT) (2004a) *Information Pack for Governors on Workforce Remodelling,* Birmingham: National Governors' Council Ref: NRT/0015/2004.

National Remodelling Team (NRT) (2004b) *Workforce Remodelling – A Guidance for Governors* III, Birmingham: National Governors' Council Ref: NRT/0039/2004.

National Remodelling Team (NRT) (2004c) *Times for Standards: Planning, Preparation and Assessment Resource Pack*, Birmingham: National Governors' Council Ref: NRT/0025/2004.

National Remodelling Team (NRT) (2005) *Meeting with ITT Providers Presentation*, January 2005, London: NRT.

National Steering Group (1991) *School Teacher Appraisal: A National Framework,* London: HMSO.

Nightingale, D. (1990), *Local Management of Schools at Work in the Primary School,* Basingstoke: Falmer Press.

Northouse, P. (2004) *Leadership: Theory and Practice*, Thousand Oaks, California: Sage Publications.

Noy, B. (1984), *Parent Participation in the Educational Work of the School*, Jerusalem, Emanuel Yaffe College for Senior Teachers (in Hebrew).

Ofsted (1994) *Primary Matters: A discussion on teaching and learning in primary schools*, London: DFEE Publications Centre.

Ofsted (1994) *A Focus on Quality*, London: Coopers Lybrand.

Ofsted (1996) *The Appraisal of Teachers 1991–6, A report from the Office of Her Majesty's Chief Inspector of Schools*, London: DFEE Publications Centre.

Ofsted (2000) *Evaluating Educational Inclusion*, London: HMI.

Ofsted (2002) *The curriculum in successful primary schools*, London, HMI.

Ofsted (2002a), *Leadership and management: managing the school workforce*, London: HMI.

Ofsted (2003) *Good assessment in secondary schools*, London, HMI.

Ofsted/Audit Commission (2000) Getting the Best from your Budget: A guide to the effective management of school resources.

Ofsted (2005) *Every Child Matters: Framework for the inspection of schools in England from September 2005*, Document Reference 2035, London: HMI.

Oldroyd, D. and Hall, V. (1990) *Management Self–Development for Staff in Secondary Schools*, Bristol: NDCEMP.

Ormston, M. (1996) *Leadership and Leadership Qualities*, Oxford Brookes University: School of Education.

Ormston, M. and Shaw, M. (1993a) *Inspection: A Preparation Guide for Schools*, Harlow: Longman.

Ormston, M. and Shaw, M. (1993b) *Mentoring*, Oxford Brookes University: School of Education.

Peters, T. and Waterman, R. (2004) *In Search of Excellence: Lessons from America's Best-run companies*, London: Profile Books.

Phillips, E.M. and Pugh, D.S. (1988) *How to Get a PhD. Managing the peaks and troughs of research*, Milton Keynes: Open University Press.

Poster, C. (1982) *Community Education*, London: Heinemann.

Prawat, R.S. and Nickerson, J. R. (1985) The relationship between teacher thought and action and student affective outcomes, *The Elementary School Journal*, 85: 529–40.

Preedy, M. (1991) *Managing the effective school*, London: Paul Chapman Publishing.

Pugh, D.S. and Hickson, D.J. (1989) *Writers on Organisations* (4th Ed), Harmondsworth: Penguin.

Raywid, M. A. (1984) 'Synthesis of research on schools of choice', *Educational Leadership*, 41(7): 70–78.

Rawlings, J. (1998) *The Role of the Staff Development Coordinator in Schools*, MA Management Paper, Oxford: Brookes University.

Rutter, M., Maughan, B., Mortimor, P. and Ouston, J. (1979) *Fifteen Thousand Hours: Secondary Schools and their effects on children*, London: Open Books.

Sammons, P., Thomas, S. and Mortimore, P. (1996) *Improving School and Department Effectiveness,* British Education Management and Administration Society (BEMAS) Partners in Change Conference (Cambridge), March 22–27, 1996.

Sandwell Department for Education and Lifelong Practice (2005) *Draft Extending Schools: A Code of Practice,* Sandwell: Sandwell Department for Education and Lifelong Practice/Sandwell Education Business Partnership.

Senge, P.M. (1990) *The Fifth Discipline – The art and practice of the learning organisation,* New York: Doubleday.

Sergiovanni, T. (2001) *Leadership: What's in it for schools?* London: Routledge Falmer.

Serow, R.C and Solomon, D. (1979) 'Classroom climates and students' inter group behaviour', *Journal of Educational Psychology,* 71: 669–76.

Shaw, M. (1994) 'Current Issues in Pastoral Management', *Pastoral Care in Education,* 12(4), 37–41.

Shaw, M., Siddell, T. and Turner, M. (1992) *Time management for Teachers,* Oxford Polytechnic: Oxford Centre for Education Management.

Skelton, M., Reeves, G. and Playfoot, D. (1991) *Development Planning for Primary Schools,* Windsor: NFER/Nelson.

Slee, R., Tomlinson, S. and Weiner, G. (1998), *School Effectiveness for Whom? Challenges to the school effectiveness and school improvement movements,* London: Falmer Press.

Solity, J. (1992), *Special Education,* London: Cassell.

Spicer, B. (1990) *Program Budgeting: A way forward in school management* in Chapman, J. (ed.) (1990) *School-based Decision-making and Management,* Basingstoke: Falmer Press.

Spinks, J.M. (1990) *Collaborative decision-making at the school level* in Chapman, J. (Ed.) (1990) *School-based Decision-making and Management,* Basingstoke: Falmer Press.

Stainback, S., Stainback, W., Esat, K. and Sapon-Shevin, M. (1994) 'A commentary on inclusion and the development of a positive self-identity by people with disabilities', *Exceptional Children,* 60: 486–90.

Stenner, A., (1988) 'LFM in a Primary School', in Downes, P. (ed.) (1988) *Local Financial Management in Schools,* Oxford: Basil Blackwell Ltd.

Stoll, L., Fink, D. and Earl, L. (2003) *It's About Learning (and it's About Time): what's in it for schools?* London: Routledge Falmer.

Tannenbaum, R. and Schmidt, W.H. (1973) 'How to choose a leadership pattern', *Harvard Business Review,* 36(2), 95–101.

Taylor, F.W. (1947) *Scientific Management,* London: Harper and Row.

The Industrial Society (1982) *Delegation (Handout 4) Management in schools and colleges,* London: The Industrial Society.

Thomas, H., Kirkpatrick, G. and Nicholson, E. (1989) *Financial Delegation and Local Management of Schools; Preparing for Practice,* London: Cassell.

Torrington, D. and Weightman, J. (1989) *The Reality of School Management,* Oxford: Blackwell Education.

Training and Development Agency (TDA) (2006) Jacqui Nunn *Presentation to Canterbury Christ Church University Faculty of Education 12 January 2006.*

Trethowan, D. (1985) *Teamwork,* The Industrial Society.

Teacher Training Agency (TTA) (1996b) *Teaching as a Research-based Profession: Promoting Excellence in Teaching,* London: TTA.

Teacher Training Agency (TTA) (2005) *Corporate Plan 2005–2008,* London: TTA.

Tuckman, B.W. (1965) 'Development sequence in small groups', *Psychological Bulletin,* 63(6), 384–99.

Vygotsky, L.S. (1962) *Thought and Language,* edited and translated by Hanfmann, E. and Vakar, G., Cambridge, New York: MIT Press.

Wallace, M., Hall, V. and Huckman, L. (1996) *Senior Management Teams in Primary and Secondary Schools,* British Education Management and Administration Society (BEMAS) Partners in Change Conference (Cambridge), March 22–27 1996.

Warwick (1983) *Decision Making,* London: The Industrial Society.

Weber, M. (1918) *The Protestant Ethic and the Spirit of Capitalism,* Heidelberg: University of Hidelberg.

West, N. (1995) *Middle Management in the Primary School,* London: David Fulton.

West, N. (1998) *Middle Management in the Primary School,* 2nd Ed., London: David Fulton.

West-Burnham, J. (1992) *Managing quality in schools,* Harlow: Longman.

West-Burnham, J. (1994a) 'Strategy, Policy and Planning' in Bush, T. and West-Burnham, J. (eds.) *The Principles of Educational Management,* Harlow: Longman.

West-Burnham, J. (1994b) 'Inspection, Evaluation and Quality Assurance' in Bush, T. and West-Burnham, J. (eds.) *The Principles of Educational Management,* Harlow: Longman.

West-Burnham, J. (1995) 'Supporting staff through appraisal' in Bell, J. and Harrison, B.T. (ed.) *Vision and Values in Managing Education,* London: David Fulton.

Westhuizen, P.C. van der (1996) *Resistance to Change in Educational Organisations,* Bristish Education Management and Administration Society (BEMAS) Conference (Cambridge), March 22–27 1996.

West Sussex Advisory and Inspection Service (1994) *Head of Department as a Leader and Manager*, Sussex: West Sussex County Council.

White, R. and Lippitt, R. (1983) 'Leadership behaviour and member reactions in three social climates', in Cartwright, D. and Zander, A. (eds.) *Group Dynamics*, London: Tavistock Publishing.

Williams, M. (1991) *In Service Education and Training*, London; Cassell.

Workforce Agreement Monitoring Group (WAMG) (2003) *Raising Standards and Tackling Workload: A National Agreement*, 15 January 2003.

Workforce Agreement Monitoring Group (WAMG) (2005) *Guidance Note No 11*.

Wragg, E.C., Wikeley, C.M., Wragg, C.M. and Haynes, G.S. (1994) *A National Survey of Teacher Appraisal*, Leverhulme Teacher Appraisal Project, Exeter: University of Exeter, School of Education.

Wragg, E.C. (1994) 'Under the Microscope', TES, 9 September 1991.

Index

accountability 4, 6, 27–8, 140, 226–7
accounting systems 227
accreditation 282
action plans 91–2, 300
  for administration 174
  for innovation 81
active learning 159, 161–2
administration 4, 172–82, 201–2
  action plan 174
  current folders 174
  documentation 172–3, 201
  efficient and effective practice 172–5
  filing 174
  and information technology 195–9,
    202–3
  reallocation of duties 242
  reporting 179–81, 202
  time allocation 173
  to do lists 174
  workload planning 247–8
  see also Ofsted inspections;
    timetabling
advertisements, recruitment 257, 266
aims 60, 75–6, 89, 116–17
  see also goals and targets; objectives
Aitken, R. 8
analysis of change 145–6
appearance 190
application forms 257, 304
appraisals 227
Armstrong, L. 133, 175, 202
Arnott, M.A. 218
assessment 175–9, 202
  Assessment Reform Group
    recommendations 175–6
  attainment targets 177
  benefits of 176–9
  CAF (common assessment
    framework) 167–8, 170
  and head teachers 177
  policy development 181–2, 200–1

attainment targets 177
attitude questionnaires 259, 305
audits 85
autocracy 24

balanced pattern 43–4
Barber, M. 235
barriers to communication 189
behaviour of leaders 25–7
behaviour management 28–34
beliefs and values 5, 18, 82, 129, 289
Ben-Ari, R. 159
benchmarking 221
Bennett, N. 132
Bennis, W. 9–10
Billsberry, J. 253, 303
Black, P. 175, 178
Blackburn, N. 221
blame culture 289
Blandford, S. 40, 53, 165, 221
body gestures 190
body posture 190
Bolam, R. 276
bottom-up change 143–4
Bradley, J. 131
break times 249
Brighouse, T. 172
Brown, M. 299–301
buddy training 154–5
budgets 222–6, 230–1
  computer system specification 197
  constructing a budget 223–4
  current year 223
  draft budgets 225
  evaluation 224
  following year summaries 223
  forecasting 224
  head teachers' responsibilities 225
  implementation 224, 225–6
  information collection 223
  main functions 222

budgets (*continued*)
  reviews 224
  submission to local authorities 223
building with the community 51–2, 55
buildings 42, 63
  expenditure quotations and
      tenders 228
  school design 42
bureaucracy 10
Burstall, E. 299
Bush, T. 4, 124–5, 129–30
Busher, H. 6, 44

CAF (common assessment framework)
    167–8, 170
Caldwell, B.J. 23, 62–3, 108
career advancement 245, 282, 302–7
caring culture 289
Carr, W. 289, 290
Castelikns, J. 159, 162
chairing a meeting 194, 195
change management 140–56
  analysis of change 145–6
  bottom-up change 143–4
  co-option 151
  coercion 151
  deepen stage 152, 153
  deliver stage 152
  develop stage 152
  discover stage 151–2
  evaluation 152
  expert approach 144
  in extended schools 147–8
  forced change 149
  implementation 149–51
  influences on 146
  mobilise stage 151
  and negotiation 150
  resistance to change 147–8
  strategy for change 148–9
  teams 136–7, 144–5, 238
  top-down change 143
  see also remodelling; workforce reform
channels of communication 188–9
Chapman, J. 62
Chartered Management Institute 25
charts and graphics 199
Chatwin, R. 6
Cheminais, R. 160
childcare provision 38
Children's Act (2004) 163

children's trusts 164–6
Choosing Health 54
climate of communication 187–8
Cline, T. 158
closed door pattern 43
co-option 151
coaching 242
code of practice for partnerships 46–8
coercion 151
cognitive development 159
Coleman, M. 124–5, 129–30
collaboration 108 125, 130, 162–3
  framework 62–4, 108
Collarbone, Dame Pat 142
commitment 18
common assessment framework (CAF)
    167–8, 170
*Common Core of Skills and
    Knowledge* 281
communication 130, 186–95, 202, 300
  barriers 189
  channels 188–9
  closed climate 188
  computer system specification 197
  listening skills 19, 190
  meetings 189, 192–5
  networking 6, 191
  non-verbal 190, 202
  open and supportive climate 187
  process 189
  verbal 190, 202
  written 191–2, 202
communities
  building with the community
      51–2, 55
  community schools 49–51
  music centres 52–3
  patterns of connection 43–5
  schools as a community 37–41
  sports centres 53–4
  see also extended schools
computer systems 196–8
confidence 158, 159
conflict 7–8, 19, 195
consensus 24
consent 24
consistent financial reporting 221
Constable, J. 288
consultants 233
consultative management 20, 24, 48

continuing professional development *see* professional development
contracts of employment 236
Cornwall, J. 158
costs of recruitment 257
creative arts development plans 114–19, 116–19
Criminal Record Bureau (CRB) checks 246
culture 15, 34, 52, 55, 64–70, 76, 193
  blame culture 289
  caring culture 289
  and ethos 42
  person culture 69
  power culture 66–7
  role culture 67–8
  sub-cultures 64, 69
  task culture 68
current folders 174
curriculum
  content 112
  development and management 134
  planning 110–19
  see also timetabling
CVs 257, 303–4
cycle of planning 80, 106

databases 199
Davies, B. 72
decision-making 62, 109–10, 119, 127
delegation 24–5, 34, 174
democracy 24
department improvement plan 107–8, 114–19
department size 17
destigmatising stress 300
development policy *see* professional development
diaries 174
difficult colleagues 19
dilemmas and conflict 7–8, 19, 195
discipline 29
disruptive pupils 31
distributed leadership 23–4
division of responsibilities 15
documentation 172–3, 201
  of spreadsheet models 198–9
Donnelly, C. 41
double-loop thinking 70
draft budgets 225

Drucker, P.F. 140
Duarte, S.J. 53

Earley, P. 22, 273, 288, 301–2
economy 218
EdP (Doctor of Education) 282
Education Act (2002) 48, 216–17
Education Act (2005) 276
effectiveness
  of leaders 6, 8, 18, 19, 20–2, 28, 83
  managerial qualities 20–2
  personal qualities 19, 20, 21
  of schools 22, 40, 60
  of teams 22–3, 124–6, 129–30
  and value for money 218
efficiency
  in administration 172–5
  and value for money 218
Ellison, L. 72
employment law 253
empowerment 63
energy levels 297
enrichment activities 49
environment 42
ethos 41, 42, 300
Evaluating Educational Inclusion 101
evaluation 100–1, 209–12
  of budgets 224
  of change 152
  reports 211
  see also monitoring; reviews
Evans, J. 22, 288, 301–2
Everard, K.B. 4, 124, 126, 193, 205, 206, 210, 255, 297
Every Child Matters (DfES) 37–9, 42, 53–4, 167, 182, 235, 280–1
expectations 30
expenditure quotations and tenders 228
expert approach to change 144
extended schools 37–9, 235
  change management 147–8
  code of practice 46–8
  and consultation 48
  definitions 55
  funding 37, 50
  management 48–9
  partnerships and support 51
  range of potential services 50
eye contact 190, 305

faith schools 74
Fidler, B. 9, 60, 70, 79, 80, 85, 86, 110,
    172, 206
filing 174
financial management 216–31
    accountability 226–7
    accounting systems 227
    benchmarking 221
    budgets 222–6, 230–1
    consistent financial reporting 221
    leadership and management 219–20
    quotations and tenders 228
    value for money 218, 221
    see also funding
flat structures 60, 62
Fletcher-Campbell, F. 273
flexibility 14
forced change 149
forecasting 224
Formula Spending Share 216, 217, 230
Foy, N. 64
framework for practice 11–12
Friedman, Y. 43
funding 216–17, 230
    for extended schools 37, 50
    Formula Spending Share 216,
        217, 230
    local authority responsibilities 220
    Local Change Fund 217
    national funding structure 132
    and organisational structure 17
    Revenue Support Grant 216, 230
    Schools Development Grant 217
    Standards Fund 217

GCSEs 111–12
General Teaching Council 94, 95, 275,
    279–80
gestures 190
Gibson, S. 40, 165
goals and targets 40, 60, 79, 97, 272,
    295–6
    of teams 125, 127, 130
    see also aims; objectives
government policy 140–1, 163–4
    recruitment 237, 253
    wraparound childcare 37
    see also funding
governors 233, 235, 238
Grace, G. 71
grant proposals 192

graphics in reports 199
Greenfield, T. 11
Guaspari, R. 53

Hackman, R. 125
Hall, V. 7, 22–3, 109, 146, 210
Handy, C. 8, 64–5, 76, 126
Hargreaves, D.H. 83, 205, 206, 210
Harris, A. 18, 23–4, 63
Harrison, B.T. 11
Harvey-Jones, J. 9
Haynes, M.E. 195
head teachers
    and assessment 177
    budget responsibilities 225
    of effective schools 22
    National Professional Qualification
        301–2
    National Standards 302
    role 4, 238
Hedge, N. 194
Hertz-Lazarowitz, R. 160
Hickson, D.J. 11–12, 26
hierarchies 6, 60, 61
hierarchy of needs 26–7
Hituv, M. 45
HLTAs (Higher Level Teaching
    Assistants) 240–1, 243, 245–6
Holmes, G. 8
Hopkins, D. 83, 210
Hughes, S. 196
human relations approach 10

implementation
    of budgets 224, 225–6
    of change 149–51
    of SIP (school improvement plans)
        91–2
Implementation Review Unit 234
inclusion policy 98–100, 158–62
    Index for Inclusion 101
individual learning plans 161–2
induction 261–3
ineffective leaders
    managerial qualities 21–2
    personal qualities 21
information technology 195–9, 202–3
    computer systems 196–8
    databases 199
    management information systems
        (MIS) 196
    spreadsheet models 198–9

innovation 146, 154
  action plans 81
INSET programmes 150
inspections *see* Ofsted inspections
instructors 243
integrated learning systems 198
integrity 19
interdependencies 6
interlinking model 61
interruption handling 296–7
interviews 258–60, 304–5
involvement 44–5, 110, 150, 159,
  169–70
Ireson, G. 14, 24, 131
IRU (Implementation Review Unit) 234
IRU (Internal Review Unit) 141
Isaac, J. 288

job analysis 254–5
job definition 8
job descriptions 175, 227, 254–6
job offers 259–60, 266, 306
Jones, B.M. 222
Jones, R. 222

Kahn, R.L. 43
Katz, D. 43
Kemmis, S. 289, 290
Kiss Solutions 199
Knutton, S. 14, 24, 131

LaFasto, F.M.J. 125
LaGrave, J. 106
Lambert, L. 63
Lancaster 196
Larson, C.E. 125
Lawlor, H. 269, 274
leadership
  behaviour of leaders 25–7
  definitions 4, 8–11
  dilemmas and conflict 7–8, 19
  distributed leadership 23–4
  effective leaders 6, 8, 18, 19,
    20–2, 28
  in financial management 219–20
  framework for practice 11–12
  for learning 4
  managers compared to leaders 6
  responsibilities 4
  role of middle leaders 12–14

situational leadership 130
  and status 7
  structure of leadership 15–18
  styles of leadership 10–11
  theories and practice 8–10
  whole school context 14–15
learner involvement 159, 169–70
learning behaviours 158, 160
letter writing 191
liaison responsibilities 135
Lincoln, 6
line management 245–6
listening skills 19, 190
local authorities 163–6
  funding responsibilities 220
  remodelling advisers 233
Local Change Fund 217
lunch-time supervisors 249

McCall, C. 269, 274
McCormack, R. 288
McLaughlin, T. 41
management
  accountability 27–8
  behaviour management 28–34
  consultative management 20, 24
  definition 4
  of extended schools 48–9
  line managers 245–6
  managerial qualities 20–2
  managers compared to leaders 6
  player managers 5–8, 34
  styles of management 12, 20
  workload planning 247
management information systems
    (MIS) 196
Maslow, A.H. 26–7
Mayo, E. 26
meetings 189, 192–5
  advantages 192
  chair 194, 195
  conflict during 195
  culture and style 193
  disadvantages 193
  preparations 194, 195
  secretaries 194
memos 191
mentoring 264–5
middle leadership, definition 4–6
Miller, N. 160

mission statements 60, 71–5, 76–7, 82
  and faith schools 74
modelling 131
Moll, L.C. 159, 162
monitoring 100–1, 128, 205–9, 212
  see also evaluation; reviews
motivation 25–7, 34, 130–1, 137
Muijs, D. 23–4
Munby, S. 170
music centres 52–3

National Agreement 234, 235–7, 238–9
National College for School
  Leadership 280
national curriculum see curriculum
national funding structure 132
National Occupational Standards
  80–1, 92
National Professional Qualification for
  Head Teachers (NPHQ) 301–2
National Standards for head
  teachers 302
NCE (National Commission on
  Education) 18, 45–6
negotiation 113, 150
networking 6, 191
Nickerson, J.R. 158–9, 169
nodes 6
non-verbal communication 190, 202
Northouse, P. 19, 125, 126
Noy, B. 44, 45

objectives
  of creative arts development 116–19
  of professional development 277
  setting clear objectives 205
  of SIP (school improvement plan)
    89–90
  SMART objectives 104, 295
  see also aims; goals and targets
Ofsted inspections 182–6, 202
  evidence gathering 184
  handbooks 101
  notice of 182
  performance and assessment 184
  post-inspection meetings 186
  quality of the educational
    experience 185–6
  reports 184, 186
  scope of inspections 183
  self-evaluation forms (SEF) 184

Oldroyd, D. 7, 22–3, 109, 146, 210
open door pattern 43
open and supportive communication 187
operational planning 80–1, 107, 119
optimum stress levels 298
organisational structure 15–18, 60–2
Ormston, M. 182, 264
out of school hours activities 38
overstressed condition 298

parents
  involvement 44–5
  liaison 242
  reporting to 179–80
parking disruptive pupils 31
participation 23–4, 34, 150
partnerships 51, 163–4, 167, 168–9
  code of practice 46–8
pastoral care 135, 242
patterns of connection 43–5
pay grades 133
peer relationships 159–60
Pendlebury, M. 222
performance reviews 269–73
  Ofsted inspection reports 184
persistence 19
person culture 69
person specification 255, 256–7
personal planning 294–5
  workloads 246–9
personal qualities 19, 20, 21
personal space 190
personality tests 259, 305
Peters, T. 10–11, 69, 187
PhD (Doctor of Philosophy) 282
planning
  action plans 81, 91–2, 174, 300
  curriculum planning 110–19
  cycle of planning 80, 106
  and decision-making 109–10,
    119, 127
  department improvement plan
    107–8, 114–19
  individual learning plans 161–2
  operational planning 80–1, 107, 119
  personal planning 294–5
  and policy development 82
  principles 104
  problems and constraints 104–6

process stages 81–3, 105
school improvement plan 76, 83–92, 102, 104
strategic planning 76, 79–80, 101–2, 106, 119
timetables 80, 82
workload planning 246–9
player managers 5–8, 34
policy development
assessments 181–2, 200–1
inclusion policy 98–100, 101, 158–62
and planning 82
professional development 92–7 82, 248, 263, 269, 273–83
reporting 181–2
post-inspection meetings 186
Poster, C. 49
posture 190
power culture 66–7
PPA (planning, preparation and assessment) time 240–3
practitioner development 276
Prawat, R.S. 158–9, 169
premises *see* buildings
Primary National Strategy 101
primary school middle leaders 131–2
prime time 294–5
professional development 92–7 82, 248, 263, 269, 273–83
accreditation 282
career advancement 282, 302–7
definition 273
leaders' role 273–6
National College for School Leadership 280
operational objectives 277
performance reviews 269–73
practitioner development 276
professional education 276
professional support 276
Sector Skills Council 280–1
standards 278–9
Statement of Professional Values and Practice 279–80
training 154–5, 237, 242, 249, 276
Training and Development Agency (TDA) 276–9
see also self-development
professional education 276
professional standards 278–9
professional support 276

profile questionnaires 259, 305
promotion 282, 302–7
public announcements 192
Pugh, D.S. 11–12, 26
pupils
disruptive 31
organisation 112
responsibilities for progress 134
support 165–6
teacher–learner relationship 158–9, 169
tracking 197
PWP (personal workload planning) 246–9

quality of the educational experience 185–6
questionnaires 259, 305
quotations and tenders 228

Ralph, S. 299–301
rating forms 259
rational-economic model 26
Rawlings, J. 263
Raywid, M.A. 44
reading documentation 175
receiving school reports 179, 180
record keeping 134
recording pupils' work 197
recruitment 234, 253–7, 265–6
advertisements 257, 266
application forms 257, 304
costs 257
CVs 257, 303–4
employment law 253
government advice 253
government targets 237
job analysis 254–5
job descriptions 227, 254–6
person specifications 255, 256–7
see also selection
references 258
relationships
between teacher and learner 158–9, 169
networked relationships 6, 191
peer relationships 159–60
relaxation techniques 300
remodelling 45–6, 48–9, 136, 142–3, 153–5

active participants in 233–4
consultants 233
national structure 237
NRT recommended stages 151–2
poor response environment 146
see also change management;
workforce reform
reports 179–81, 191, 202
charts and graphics 199
consistent financial reporting 221
evaluation reports 211
Ofsted inspection reports 184, 186
policy development 181–2
to parents 179–80
resistance to change 147–8
resource allocation 134, 206, 207–8,
219–20, 230
value for money 218
responsibilities
division of responsibilities 15
of leaders 4
of middle leaders 133–5
pastoral care 135
of teachers 4, 158
Revenue Support Grant 216, 230
reviews 100–1
of budgets 224
of performance 269–73
see also evaluation; monitoring
Ribbins, P. 11
roles
ambiguity 8
conflict 8
culture 67–8
of middle leaders 12–14
overload 8
sources of role strain 7–8
switching roles 6
underload 8
room availability 113

safety policies 135
Sandwell 47
Schmidt, W.H. 11
School Action Plus 166
school design 42
school environment 42
school improvement plan *see* SIP (school
improvement plan)
school leaver reports 179, 180–1

schools as a community 37–41
Schools Development Grant 217
scientific management 10
secondary school middle leaders 131–2
secretaries 194
Sector Skills Council 280–1
selection 257–60, 265–6
interviews 258–60, 304–5
job offers 259–60, 266, 306
questionnaires 259, 305
rating forms 259
references 258
rejection 306
short-listing 258
see also recruitment
self-actualising model 26
self-development 288–307
goal setting 295–6
interruption handling 296–7
personal planning 294–5
stress management 297–301
self-esteem 88
self-evaluation 184, 288–93
self-help groups 300
self-management 293–7
self-managing schools 23
self-perception 159
SEN policy *see* inclusion policy
SENCO (special educational needs
co-ordinators) 165
Senge, P.M. 289
Sergiovanni, T. 64
Serow, R.C. 158, 169
Shafir, D. 159
Shaw, M. 182, 264, 293
short-listing candidates 258
SIP (school improvement plan) 76,
83–92, 102, 104
action plans 91–2
aims 89
audits 85
implementation 91–2
objectives 89–90
process 85–91
sub-plans 86
uniqueness 85–6
and vision 88–9
situational leadership 130
size of schools 132
size of teams 124, 137

Skelton, M. 83–4, 85
skills development 126–8, 159
SMART objectives 104, 295
social development 99
social interaction 159–60
social model 26
social network theory 6
Solity, J. 161
Solomon, D. 158, 169
span of control 60, 76
specialist staff 243
Spinks, J.M. 23, 62, 62–3, 108
sports centres 53–4
spreadsheet models 198–9
staff development policy *see* professional
    development
Stainback, S. 158
stakeholders 4
standards 125, 278–9 ,
    National Occupational Standards
        80–1, 92
    National Standards for head
        teachers 302
Standards Fund 217
Statement of Professional Values and
    Practice 279–80
status 7, 132, 189
stereotypes 189
Stern, Isaac 53
Stoll, L. 40, 41, 83, 158
strategic planning 76, 79–80, 101–2,
    106, 119
    see also SIP (school improvement
        plan)
strategic thinking 79
strategy for change 148–9
stress management 297–301
    causes of stress 299
    destigmatising stress 300
    optimum stress levels 298
    overstressed condition 298
    understressed condition 299
structure see organisational structure
styles of leadership 10–11
styles of management 12, 20
sub-cultures 64, 69
sub-plans 86
supervision of support staff 245
support networks 30, 38, 150, 165–7,
    300
support staff 244–6, 249

Criminal Record Bureau (CRB)
    checks 246
duties and activities 244, 245-6
Higher Level Teaching Assistants
    240–1, 243, 245–6
job and career development 245
line management 245–6
supervision 245
systems theory 30, 43

tall structures 6, 60, 61
Tannenbaum, R. 11
targets *see* goals and targets
task culture 68
Taylor, F.W. 10, 26
teacher assistants *see* support staff
teacher availability 112
Teacher Training Agency 276–9
teams 124–38
    accountability 4
    change management teams
        136–7, 144–5, 238
    and collaboration 125, 130
    development stages 129
    effective teamwork 22–3, 124–6,
        129–30
    functions and purposes 126
    goals and objectives 125, 127, 130
    influences on working habits 128–9
    monitoring and evaluation 128
    motivation 130–1, 137
    need for leadership 125
    organisation and briefings 127
    pastoral teams 135
    planning and decision-making 127
    role of middle leaders 5, 6
    size 124, 137
    skills development 126–8
    standards of excellence 125
    status of team members 7
tenders 228
time management 173, 299
    personal planning 294–5
    planning, preparation and
        assessment 240–3
    workload planning 246–9
Time for Standards 244
timetabling 112–19, 175, 202
    computer system specification 197

curriculum content 112
and job descriptions 175
negotiation and compromise 113
pupil organisation 112
room availability 113
teacher availability 112
use of time 112–13
to do lists 174
Todd, J. 158
top-down change 143
trade union agreements 234, 250
training 154–5, 237, 242, 249, 276
see also professional development
Training and Development Agency
(TDA) 276–9
Trethowan, D. 124
Tuckman, B.W. 129
Twigg, Stephen 47

Ultralab project 42
understressed condition 299
union agreements 234, 250
uniqueness 85–6

value for money 218, 221
values and beliefs 5, 18, 82, 129, 289
verbal communication 190, 202
vision statements 20, 60, 70–1, 76–7,
83, 88–9
vocal cues 190
vocational GCSEs 111
Vygostsky, L.S. 159

Walton, R. 125
WAMG (Workforce Agreement
Monitoring Group) 233, 238–9
Warwick, 109
Waterman, R. 10–11, 69, 187
Weber, M. 10
West, N. 126
West-Burnham, J. 4, 81, 84
Westhuizen, P.C. van der 147–8
Whitmore, K.F. 159, 162
Wiliam, D. 175
work organisation 132
work-life balance 249, 250, 260–1
workforce reform 147, 153, 233–51
contracts of employment 236
deployment of unqualified staff
242–3
information packs 235
leadership implications 238
National Agreement 234, 235–7,
238–9
PPA (planning, preparation and
assessment) time 240–3
teacher working hours 234, 236
union agreements 234, 250
workload planning 246–9
see also change management;
remodelling; support staff
working hours 234, 236
workload planning 246–9
wraparound childcare 37
written communication 191–2, 202

yardsticks 205